MISSOURI IN THE FEDERAL SYSTEM

Second Edition

Stephen C.S. Chen, Ph.D.
Professor of Political Science
Lincoln University of Missouri

UNIVERSITY
PRESS OF
AMERICA

LANHAM • NEW YORK • LONDON

Copyright © 1983 by

University Press of America,™ Inc.

4720 Boston Way
Lanham, MD 20706

3 Henrietta Street
London WC2E 8LU England

Library of Congress Cataloging in Publication Data

Chen, Stephen.
   Missouri in the federal system.

   Bibliography: p.
   Includes index.
   1. Missouri–Politics and government. I. Title.
JK5416.C48   1983   320.9778   82–24834
ISBN 0–8191–3037–0 (pbk.)

PREFACE TO THE SECOND EDITION

Since the publication of this book in July 1981, a series of political events has happened in Missouri. Some occurred to fill the urgent needs of the state; others followed in the wake of trends or changes on the national scene. Among these events the most significant were the establishment of the Department of Corrections and Human Resources, the enactment of a string of anti-crime and reform laws, the redrawing of the state's districts, the adoption of a constitutional amendment to offer important technical changes in the districting procedure for the General Assembly, and particularly perhaps the most furious battle ever fought in Missouri history over the elimination of one of the ten congressional districts in 1981.

To keep up with these significant changes, I lost no time in updating this book. I have therefore, after deliberate consultations with the authorities concerned, revised five chapters entirely and large parts of the others with updated material and available sources.

Here I should express my deep gratitude to Dr. Jerold H. Isreal, law professor of the University of Michigan; Dr. Jerald Gunther, law professor of Stanford University; Mr. Robert Van Ark, secretary of the Missouri Public Expenditure Survey; Ms. Virginia Young, reporter of the Missouri Times; and Professor Kate L. Turabian, author of A Manual for Writers, for their friendly help. I should again especially thank Secretary of State James C. Kirkpatrick and his Administrative Assistant Timothy R. Coughlin and Executive Director Juanita Donehue of the Missouri Association of Counties for their continuous enthusiastic assistance.

Stephen C.S. Chen

Jefferson City, Missouri
May 1983

PREFACE TO THE FIRST EDITION

This book extensively discusses the constitutional provisions, political institutions, and judicial process of Missouri with special emphasis upon present facts, recent reforms, and current trends rather than historical legacy.

Since much of Missouri's political system, like that of
other states, is based upon the national pattern, this book
is written with the federal system as background. In addition to the separation of powers doctrine, the system of
checks and balances and what not, we even note that the Missouri governor's two term limit and his "disability review
board" system are essentially modelled upon the 22nd and
25th Amendments to the United States Constitution, which
respectively limit the President's term of office and provide a way to break the "presidential disability" deadlock.
Further, with frequent reference to the political systems
of other states and foreign nations, this volume gives read-
ers not only a thorough understanding of Missouri government
but also brief insights into the governments of other states
and foreign nations, particularly Britain. Additionally,
this book clarifies many vague ideas often confusing students
(e.g., the relationship of the constitution to statutes, judicial review, statutes, judicial decisions, and rules and
regulations). It likewise sheds light on the origins of
terms which usually baffle many inquisitive minds (e.g., the
"Speaker" [why not the "President"] of the House of Representatives, the "three readings" in the legislative procedure, the "executive sessions," etc.). By and large, this
book, written in a lucid style and supported with numerous
graphic charts, structural diagrams, and current illustra-
tions, affords students not only a clear and full grasp of
Missouri government and politics but also some practical
knowledge of political science, particularly American national government.

I would like to express my deep gratitude to those
who have kindly helped me with information, consultation,
or partial editing of the manuscript. Among them are Secretary of State James C. Kirkpatrick and his Administrative
Assistant Timothy R. Coughlin; former Lieutenant Governor
William C. Phelps and his Research Assistant Jeanne M.
Schwinke; Attorney General John Ashcroft and his former Assistant Attorney Larry R. Marshall; State Representative
James R. Strong; Mr. John F. Britton, Missouri's prominent
lobbyist; Mr. Bill Thompson, Missouri Supreme Court Counsel;

Associate Circuit Judge McCormich V. Wilson; Ms. Juanita Donehue, Executive Director of Missouri Association of Counties; Dr. George S. Parthemos, Political Science Professor of Georgia University; Prefessor Robert L. Robinson, Criminal Justice Coordinator of Lincoln University; Mrs. Ann Bestor, former Executive Director of Missouri Democratic Party; Mr. Shannon D. Cave, Executive Vice-Chairman of the Missouri Republican Party; Mr. Gary Markenson, Executive Director of the Missouri Municipal League, and many others.

I should especially like to thank Dr. Rosemary Hearn, English Professor of Lincoln University, and Ms. Sandra Fuhrman, former Research and Information Director of the Missour House of Representatives and presently Research Director for Lieutenant Governor Kenneth J. Rothman, for their editing of the entire manuscript. I should also especially thank Missouri Supreme Court Librarian Mrs. D. A. Divilbiss and her assistants, and Missouri Legislative Librarian Mrs. Anne G. Rottmann for their assistance in research. Additionally, I am deeply grateful to Mrs. Elizabeth Witz, Mrs. Delores L. Shepherd, Administrative Assistant to State Senator Gwen B. Giles, and my many other lovely students working in the State Capitol for typing and timely help.

But my very special thanks go to former Missouri State Treasurer and 1980 Democratic gubernatorial candidate Dr. James I. Spainhower. But for his untiring and invaluable assistance, this book would not have been possible. During his busiest hours on the campaign trail, he carefully and tirelessly reviewed and revised my entire manuscript, mostly in the car driven by his friends on long, hot summer days. Such kindness will never escape my memory.

I shall accept any responsibilities for errors in this book. I would appreciate any comments, suggestions, and/or corrections. These will be taken into account in a second edition.

Stephen C.S. Chen
Jefferson City, MO
March 1981

ACKNOWLEDGEMENTS

The following author and publishers are gratefully ac-
knowledged for granting me to use their copyrighted materials
from:

"Basic Principles of the Administration of Justice with Particular Reference to Missouri Law" by John Scurlock in UMKC
Law Review, winter 1975. Reprinted by permission of Professor Scurlock.

Black's Law Dictionary (1979) and Introduction to the Criminal
Justice System (1979) by Hazel B. Kerper and revised by Jerold
H. Israel. Reprinted by permission of the West Publishing
Company, St. Paul, Minnesota.

Congressional Quarterly Guide to Current American Government,
Fall 1969. Reprinted by permission of Congressional Quarterly,
Inc., Washington, D.C.

Contemporary Political Ideologies by Roy C. Macridis, copyright 1980. Reprinted by permission of Winthrop Publishers,
Inc., Cambridge, Massachusetts.

Ideologies and Modern Politics by Reo M. Christenson et al.,
copyright 1981. Reprinted by permission of Harper and Row
Publishers, Inc., New York, N.Y.

Understanding American Government by Robert Weissberg, copyright 1980. Reprinted by permission of Holt, Rinehart and
Winston, New York, N.Y.

TABLE OF CONTENTS

CHAPTER I MISSOURI IN THE FEDERAL UNION

The United States is a federal union.[1] In contrast with
a unitary system wherein all power to govern is vested in the
central government, a federal system is one in which authority
is somewhat equally divided between the central government and
the governments of territorial subdivisions, called "states" in
the United States.[2] In a unitary system, the central government has omnipotence over all territory and is therefore superior to all the subdivisional governments, the governments of
constituent or component units. In federalism, theoretically,
the central government and the subdivisional governments are on
an equal basis. They are equally supreme and sovereign in their
own spheres, and they have real powers of their own, explicit or
implied in the constitution which creates the system. That is
to say, neither of them receives powers from the other. They
both derive powers from the same source, the constitution. But
in unitarism, the constitution grants all powers to the central
government, which in turn parcels out such powers to its subdivisional governments as it sees fit. Therefore, the central
government can alter subdivisional or local powers arbitrarily
and can even abolish its subdivisions or localities, if it so
desires. In a federal union, a subdivisional government may
sue the central government before court if they disagree over
the extent of governmental authority, but never in a unitary
state. Additionally, in federalism both governments govern
the people, while in unitarism the central government governs
the people through its subdivisional governments. Subdivisional
governments are undoubtedly the agents of the central government
in unitarism, but they may also be the central government's
agents (as in West Germany and Switzerland) or administrative
arms for cooperative programs (as in the United States) in federalism. However, there has been a steady drift toward decentralization and local autonomy in unitary states like England.

While the nation-state relations in the United States

---

[1]There are twenty-one federal states in the world, namely,
Argentina, Brazil, Canada, Mexico, USA, Venezuela (America),
Austria, Czechoslovakia, Switzerland, USSR, W. Germany, Yugos-
lavia (Europe), Burma, India, Malaysia, Pakistan (Asia), Aus-
tralia (Oceania), Cameroun, Libya, Nigeria, and Tanzania
(Africa).

[2]Variously known as "states" in Australia, "provinces"
in Canada, "republics" in USSR, "cantons" in Switzerland,
"lander" in W. Germany, and "departments" in France.

are federal, the state-local relationships are primarily unitary. Theoretically all local governments are creatures of a state and have no constitutional authority of their own. They have no inherent powers;[3] they exercise only such powers as the state grants to them and are subject to its control. So in the beginning, state legislatures had almost unlimited constitutional authority over local governments, but with the advent of the twentieth century, the state-local relationship has been invariably drifting toward federalism and has become what is known as "semi-federalism" or "little federalism." State constitutions and legislative acts frequently grant local governments certain powers of self-government, particularly through "home rule," which imbues state constitutions with some federal principles. Though home rule cities and counties are free of state interference, by no means are they sovereign or independent in any sense comparable to the state in its relationship to the federal government.

A third category of governmental system is confederation. This is a league of sovereign states joined together with a central government exercising limited powers on matters of common concern such as foreign affairs and defense. The central government derives powers from the sovereign states and

Figure 1.1   Three Governmental Systems

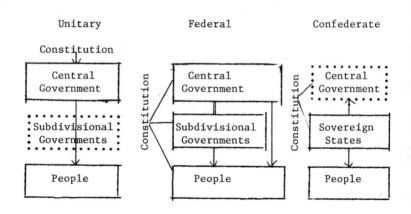

---

[3]Inherent powers of a government have no constitutional basis but grow out of its existence.

2

therefore exists at their mercy. Thereupon, only the sovereign states have powers to govern the people. The United States was a confederate state under the Articles of Confederation, 1781-1789. The Confederate States of America established in the South during the Civil War is another example of a confederacy. There is no such state existing in the world today; only the United Nations approximates this form of government.

VERTICAL FEDERALISM

I. FEDERAL-MISSOURI RELATIONS

A. Distribution of Powers

Figure 1.2 Distribution of Powers between the National Government and States

The U.S. Constitution

National Government

Missouri & Other States

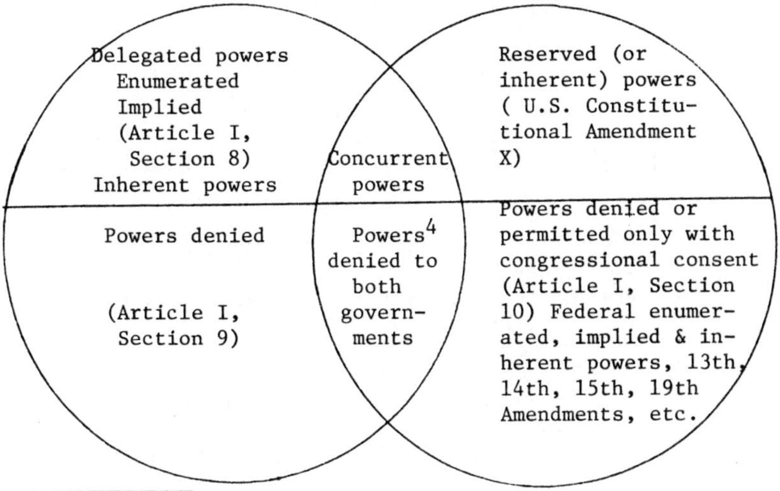

Delegated powers
Enumerated
Implied
(Article I,
Section 8)
Inherent powers

Concurrent powers

Reserved (or inherent) powers (U.S. Constitutional Amendment X)

Powers denied

(Article I, Section 9)

Powers[4] denied to both governments

Powers denied or permitted only with congressional consent (Article I, Section 10) Federal enumerated, implied & inherent powers, 13th, 14th, 15th, 19th Amendments, etc.

----

[4]Powers denied to both governments are: bill of rights, ex post facto law, bill of attainder, powers to tax export, to grant titles of nobility, to reinstitute slavery, to abridge the privileges and immunities of citizens in the United States, to deprive any person of life, liberty, and property without due process of law, etc.

1. The federal powers (denied to Missouri and other states)

   a. Enumerated Powers--the powers explicitly and exclusively delegated to the national government by the United States Constitution and thus implicitly denied to Missouri and other states:

      (1) To regulate federal elections (U.S. Constitution,[5] Art. I, sec. 4);
      (2) To regulate interstate and foreign trade (I, 8);
      (3) To regulate naturalization and bankruptcies (I, 8);
      (4) To coin money (I, 8);
      (5) To fix standards of weights and measures (I, 8);
      (6) To provide for the punishment of counterfeiting (I, 8);
      (7) To establish post offices and post roads (I, 8);
      (8) To grant patents and copyrights (I, 8);
      (9) To establish federal inferior courts (I, 8);
      (10) To define and punish piracies and felonies on the high seas and offenses against international law (I, 8);
      (11) To declare war (I, 8);
      (12) To make rules concerning captures on land and water (I, 8);
      (13) To raise, support, and regulate armies (I, 8);
      (14) To provide, maintain, and regulate a navy (I, 8);
      (15) To organize, arm, and discipline the militia and call it out into national service (I, 8);
      (16) To govern the District of Columbia, etc. (I, 8);
      (17) To decide on the time of choosing presidential electors and the time for electors to cast votes (Art. II, sec. 1:4);
      (18) To provide for succession to the presidency (II, 1:6);
      (19) To designate who may appoint inferior officers (II, 2:2);
      (20) To define the U.S. Supreme Court's appellate jurisdiction (Art. III, sec. 2:2);
      (21) To designate a place for trial of offenses not committed within any state (III, 2:3);
      (22) To determine the punishment for treason (III, 3:3);
      (23) To prescribe how public acts, records and judicial proceedings shall be proved and their effect (Art. IV, sec. 1);

---

[5] Hereafter cited as "U.S. Const. amend."

(24) To admit new states to the Union (IV, 3:1);
(25) To approve the junction of two or more states or parts thereof with the state legislatures concerned (IV, 3:1);
(26) To dispose of and govern the territory and property of the United States (IV, 3:2);
(27) To elect a U.S. President by the House of Representatives and a U.S. Vice President by the Senate (U.S. Constitutional Amendment XII);[6]
(28) To define U.S. citizenship (Amend. XIV);
(29) To levy income taxes without apportionment according to population (Amend. XVI);
(30) To elect a U.S. Vice President by Congress, etc. (Amend. XXV)

b. Implied powers based on the elastic (necessary and proper) clause (Art. I, sec. 8:18)

c. Inherent powers

(1) To acquire territory;
(2) To conduct foreign affairs, etc.

2. The powers of Missouri and other states

a. Reserved powers (inherent powers of the states)

Powers not delegated to the national government nor denied to the states are reserved to the states respectively or to the people (Amend. X)

b. Powers denied to Missouri and other states by the U.S. Constitution:

(1) Specifically denied in Article I, Section 10:

(a) To enter into any treaty, alliance or confederation;

(b) To grant letters of marque and reprisal;

A letter of marque and reprisal is written authority or a license granted by a government to the owner of a private ship to capture enemy ships and goods on the high seas. Such an authorization was banned by the Declaration of Paris in 1856.

---

[6]Hereafter cited as "U.S. Const. amend."

(c) To coin money, issue paper money, or make anything legal tender except gold and silver coin to pay debts;

(d) To pass a bill of attainder or ex post facto law;

   A bill of attainder is a legislative act which convicts and punishes a person without a judicial trial.

   Ex post facto law is a retroactive criminal law to the disadvantage of the accused. It is a law that makes a crime an action which was legal when taken, or a law that increases the penalty for a crime after it has been committed. The prohibition does not apply to civil law or the criminal laws favorable to an accused person.

(e) To make law impairing the obligation of contracts;

(f) To grant a title of nobility.

(2) Prohibited by the U.S. Constitutional Amendments:

(a) To reinstitute slavery (Amend. XIII);
(b) To abridge the privileges or immunities of U.S. citizens (Amend. XIV, 1);
(c) To deprive any person of life, liberty or property without due process of law (Amend. XIV, 1);
(d) To deny any one the equal protection of the laws (Amend. XIV, 1);
(e) To pay any debt incurred in aid of a rebellion (Amend. XIV, 4);
(f) To deny U.S. citizens the right to vote because of race (Amend. XV);
(g) To deny U.S. citizens the right to vote because of sex (Amend. XIX);
(h) To levy a poll tax in federal elections (Amend. XXIV);
(i) To deny any citizen the right to vote at age eighteen (Amend. XXVI).

c. Powers permitted to Missouri and other states only with congressional consent (Art. I, sec. 10):

(1) To levy duties on imports or exports except absolutely necessary inspection fees to be collected

on exported or imported goods. The net proceeds
therefrom go to the U.S. treasury. Such inspection
laws are subject to congressional revision and
control;

(2) To levy a tax upon a ship according to its tonnage
for entering or leaving their ports;

(3) To keep troops or warships in peacetime;

(4) To enter into agreement or compact with other
states or foreign countries;

(5) To engage in war unless actually invaded or in
imminent danger.

d. Restriction upon Missouri and other states by the
federal Bill of Rights:

Though the first ten amendments to the U.S. Constitution were primarily adopted to restrict the
national government[7] only, since 1925[8] they have
gradually been extended through the "due process of
law" clause or "equal protection of the laws" clause
of the 14th Amendment to restrain the states.

e. Limitation by national law:

The United States Constitution, U.S. laws and
treaties are the supreme law of the land.[9] They
are superior to any state's constitution and laws.

3. Concurrent powers

Not all powers delegated to the national government in Article I, Section 8 of the U.S. Constitution
are exercised by that government alone. It shares
certain powers with the states such as power to tax,
to borrow money, to establish courts, to make and enforce laws, to exercise the power of eminent domain,[10]
to spend money, to charter corporations, etc., because
both the national and state governments directly act
upon the people. The states have power to act in the
fields not preempted or completely regulated by Congress.

---

[7]Barron V. Baltimore, 7 Peters 243 (1833).

[8]Gitlow V. New York, 268 U.S. 652 (1925).

[9]U.S. Const. art. VI, sec. 2.

[10]Government takes away private property for public use
with just compensation (U.S. Const. amend. V.), otherwise it
is confiscation.

B. National-state Obligations

1. National obligations to Missouri and other states (Article IV)

    a. Guarantee of a republican government (Sec. 4);
    b. Protection against invasion, and, at the request of the state legislature or the governor (when the legislature cannot be convened), against domestic violence (Sec. 4);
    c. Respect of the territorial integrity of the states (Sec. 3).

2. Missouri's and other states' obligations to the nation:

    a. Election of federal officials

    The federal government does not hold elections. The elections of U.S. senators,[11] representatives, and presidential electors are conducted by the states. State legislatures are authorized to fix the "times, places, and manner" of electing the members of Congress, but Congress reserves the power to make or alter such regulations.[12] State legislatures are also authorized to fix the manner of selecting presidential electors, but Congress may determine the time of choosing them.[13] It has prescribed the first Tuesday after the first Monday in November of even-numbered years as the day for such elections.

    (1) Election of U.S. representatives (congressmen)[14]

    Every two years Missouri elects a congressman from each congressional district. Because of shifts in population, the number of congressmen in each state may change when the 435 seats in Congress are reapportioned after each decennial census. Election of the House representatives by district is required by the Federal Apportionment Act of 1842.

---

[11]U.S. Const. amend. XVII.

[12]U.S. Const. art. I, sec. 4.

[13]Ibid., art. II, sec. 1:2 & 3.

[14]Though this term means all members of Congress, it customarily refers to the members of the U.S. House of Representatives.

(2) Election of U.S. senators

      Each state has two senators in Congress,
and no state can be deprived of equal representation in the upper house without its consent.[15]
Senate terms are staggered with one-third of the
senators elected every two years. For instance,
Senator Thomas E. Eagleton was re-elected on November 4, 1980 (his term expires on January 2,
1987), while Senator John C. Danforth was re-
elected on November 2, 1982 (his term expires on
January 2, 1989).

(3) Election of presidential electors

      Before each presidential election every
legally recognized political party in Missouri
nominates a partisan slate of electors (equal to
the number of senators and representatives in
Congress from Missouri, but they cannot be presidential electors) by its party convention or committee. The presidential candidate who polls the
most popular votes (plurality, not majority)
statewide in the November general election wins
all electoral votes in Missouri--a rule commonly
known as "winner-takes-all." Presidential electors of the party whose candidate carries Missouri meet in the historical Missouri Capitol in
Jefferson City on the first Monday after the
second Wednesday in December to cast the official
votes for their party candidate. Presidential
electors of other states meet in their capitals
on the same day. The presidential candidate who
receives a majority of electoral votes (at least
270 out of 538)[16] nationwide is elected.

b. Participation in constitutional amending process

    (1) Missouri may request Congress to call a convention
to propose amendments to the U.S. Constitution.

    (2) Missouri may either ratify or reject the amend-

---

[15] U.S. Const. art. V.

[16] In addition to 535 presidential electors equal to the
number of the senators and representatives in Congress, the
District of Columbia has three electors (U.S. Const. amend.
XXIII).

ment proposals to the U.S. Constitution proposed by Congress or by a national convention called by Congress at the request of two-thirds of the state legislatures.[17] In Missouri all federal constitutional amendment proposals affecting the individual liberties of the people or impairing the right of local government should be submitted to conventions of the people for action.[18]

Missouri has ratified all fourteen amendments (13th-26th inclusive) since it entered the Union on August 10, 1821. With the exception of the 21st Amendment repealing the 18th Amendment which prohibited intoxicating liquors, all thirteen Amendments were ratified by the General Assembly. The 21st Amendment was ratified by the constitutional convention in Missouri on August 29, 1933. Missouri did not approve the proposed Equal Rights Amendment in 1982.

c. Maintenance of state militia at national service

With federal aid, Missouri provides and trains militia or National Guard as it is officially called, which may be called into national service by the President at any time to execute federal laws, suppress insurrection, or repel invasion.

C. From Dual to Cooperative Federalism

Federalism, one of America's great political inventions, has undergone vast changes. Though the supremacy of the national government was written into the U.S. Constitution[19] and upheld by court interpretations[20] as the central principle of American federalism, it was challenged by states'-righters with various doctrines[21] and finally defied on the

---

[17]U.S. Const. art. V.

[18]Missouri, Constitution, (1945, revised 1982), art. 1, sec. 4. Hereafter cited as "Mo. Const."

[19]Implied powers (U.S. Const. art. I, sec. 8); the supreme law of the land clause (Ibid., art. VI).

[20]McCulloch v. Maryland, 4 Wheaton 316 (1819); Gibbons v. Ogden, 4 Wheaton 1 (1824).

[21]Interposition, Nullification, and Dual Federalism.

battlefield. Though national supremacy won the war, dual
federalism, that asserted co-equal sovereignties between
two levels of government, survived it and flourished until
the late 1930s.

After the war, however, national powers grew rapidly.
There has been a great centralization of authority in Washington especially in this century, partly due to the constitutional basis[22] but chiefly as a result of the World
Wars, the Depression, and particularly great economic and
social changes in the wake of industrialization and urbanization. Today numerous local problems have become national
and can therefore not be solved without the assistance of
the national government. The national government also re-
lies upon states and localities for the administration and
operation of federally sponsored and financed programs.

The increasing involvement of the national government in
local affairs has not, however, destroyed the American
federal system but changed it from "dual federalism," marked
by a division of functions, supremacy, and independence in
its own sphere, to "cooperative federalism" calling for
mixed functions, shared powers, and joint responsibilities
among all levels of government. As a matter of fact, most
problems have cut across the traditional divisions of authority and blurred the distinction of responsibility between the national and state governments, especially diverse
and intricate economic and social programs such as welfare,
crime control, eduction and health. As a result, competition, rivalry, and conflict are now replaced by coordination, partnership, and harmony in inter-governmental
relationships.

Perhaps nowhere else can cooperative federalism be
better illustrated than in the federal grants-in-aid program.
Cooperative federalism is therefore sometimes known as fiscal
federalism. Though federal aid originated in the Land Ordinance of 1785, whereby the Confederation Congress provided
funds for schools in the Northwest territory, it did not
flourish until the late 1930s nor did it come to full blos-
som until the mid-1960s. Beginning with Lyndon B. Johnson,
most Presidents coined terms to identify their own federal
aid programs. President Johnson used the term "Creative
Federalism," Richard M. Nixon "New Federalism," and Jimmy

---

[22]The war powers, the power to tax and spend, and the power
to regulate interstate and foreign commerce (U.S. Const. art. I,
sec. 8).

Carter "Shared Responsibility Federalism."[23] Cooperative
federalism features intergovernmental partnership to provide present-day services instead of competition and con-
flicts. Creative federalism broadens cooperative federalism to include other public and private groups and individuals in concerted efforts, to loosen the strings on aid,
to initiate the block grant approach, and to consult local
authorities on federal programs in order to promote local
initiative and solution. New federalism establishes the
regular and general revenue-sharing program, a plan to
funnel funds, power, and responsibility back to states,
localities, and the people in order to achieve responsible
decentralization. Shared-responsibility federalism empha-
sizes extensive consultations and direct cooperation among
all levels of government on the formulation and implementation of policies, which are still subject to the federal
approval. President Ronald Reagan, inheriting Nixon's New
Federalism, proposed in 1982 to turn over 43 federal programs to the states from fiscal year 1984 through 1987.

There are three main types of federal grants: categorical, block, and revenue-sharing. Categorical grants
may be classified as "formula" and "project."[24]

Figure 1.3 Federal Grants-in-aid

Types	Characteristics	Requirements
Categorical		Matching funds & strings
Formula –	According to a formula es-tablished by the federal government	
Project –	Upon a prospective grantee's application	
Block	Broad general programs ac-cording to formulas that allow more discretion to the grantees	Matching funds not required in most programs; loose strings
Revenue-sharing	Funds to be used entirely at the grantees' discretion	No matching func no strings

[23]Robert Weissberg, Understanding American Government
(New York: Holt, Rinehart, and Winston, Inc., 1980), p.73.

[24]See Marshall E. Dimock, Gladys O. Dimock and Douglas M.
Fox, Public Administration, 5th ed. (New York: Holt, Rinehart
& Winston, 1983), p.68.

Traditionally federal grants-in-aid has been in the form of categorical (formula) grants. Requiring matching funds in various ratios and attaching tight strings like federal guidelines, regulations and inspection, these grants are made to states, localities or other public and private entities for specific projects. Now about 80 percent of all federal grants, categorical grants may be either formula or project. Formula grants are distributed among all qualifying units according to a formula established by the federal government, while project grants require applications from prospective recipients to secure specific federal approval. In 1966, the block grant approach[25] was initiated to consolidate separate aid categories into a single broad general block such as health, education, law enforcement and the like and to provide funds to the states for these general purposes. With little or no matching requirements and loose strings attached, the states may use these funds largely at their own discretion or allocate them to local units according to federal guidance. As time goes on, block grants appear to be growing. In 1981, President Reagan proposed to combine 84 categorical programs into six block grants in the 1982 budget.

The revenue-sharing approach is to give federal funds to states and local governments separately with neither matching funds required nor strings attached.[26] It was proposed by President Nixon as part of his "New Federilism" and inaugurated under the State and local Fiscal Assistance Act of 1972. The Act authorized $30.2 billion in federal funds to be distributed among some 38,000 governmental units for a five-year period. In 1976, Congress renewed the program and provided $25.5 billion for forty-five months from 1977 through 1980. On December 29, 1980, President Carter signed legislation to extend the federal revenue-sharing program once again. The program provided $2.3 billion annually for state governments for two fiscal years, 1982 and 1983, and $4.6 billion a year for local governments for three years beginning on January 1, 1981. Funds are allocated according to a complex formula based on population, per capita income, and state and local taxing efforts.

---

[25] The block grant approach was first used in the Partnership for Health Act of 1966. The Omnibus Crime Control and Safe Streets Act of 1968 was regarded as the best example of use of the block grant.

[26] Except that the funds are forbidden to be used for a program which discriminates against any person because of race, color, national origin, sex, age, religion, or physical handicaps or any lobbying activity concerning revenue-sharing, etc.

D. National-state controversies

Relations between the national government and states are not always harmonious; they sometimes run afoul of each other. Whenever disputes arise between any agency of the national government and a state, federal courts have exclusive jurisdiction over their cases. For instance, in 1980 Missouri had two lawsuits against the U.S. Army Corps of Engineers for their construction of the dam and hydroelectric power plant at Stockton and of the Harry S. Truman Dam and Reservoir at Warsaw, both in Missouri.

II. NATIONAL-LOCAL RELATIONS

The United States Constitution makes no mention of localities.[27] The power to create and regulate local governmental units is entirely reserved to states by the Tenth Amendment. Before the Great Depression of the 1930's, federal-local relations were loose and insignificant. The Depression, followed by WWII, drastically changed the picture. Amid the unemployment avalanche and under the weight of soaring relief expenditures and dwindling revenues, the cities could not but cry to Washington for help. The states, however, could not run to their rescue, for the states themselves were already in the maelstrom of distress. During the war, the direct federal-local relationships grew rapidly in the areas of emergency defense, housing, and airport construction.

The national emergencies have thrown the nation and localities into formal, direct relationships. But current urban problems, increasing economic woes, and pressing mutual needs, together with the inability and unwillingness of the states to meet local financial and political challenges, have driven the localities much closer to Washington than ever before. Today numerous federal funds flow directly and continuously into local as well as states' treasuries. There are about 450 federal programs aiding cities and other localities directly in the areas of transportation, housing, health, urban renewal, education, social services, city planning activities, law enforcement, anti-poverty programs, and so forth.

HORIZONTAL FEDERALISM

The United States Constitution governs not only federal-state relations but also the relationships among the states

---

[27] Except that it authorizes Congress to govern the District of Columbia (Art. I, sec. 8) and to establish local governments in federal territories (Art. IV, sec. 3).

to achieve horizontal harmony.

MISSOURI'S RELATIONS WITH OTHER STATES

I. Full faith and credit[28]

The United States Constitution requires each state to give "full faith and credit"--to recognize and give effect-- to other states' statutes, public records, and judicial decisions. That is, the civil (not criminal) law of Missouri as well as the rights established under the records, contracts, wills, deeds, mortgages, or other property rights in Missouri must be fully enforced in other states. Missouri must, of course, reciprocate such faith and credit to other states. For instance, a Missouri court rules that White should pay damages to Brown; but without satisfying the judgment, White moves to New York bag and baggage. If Brown files a suit in a New York court to enforce Missouri's ruling, the New York court must comply with his request. After having found the Missouri judgment properly authenticated, it will issue an enforcement order without looking into the merits of the case.

An Exception to the "full faith and credit" doctrine is, however, divorce decrees. A Missourian, for example, and his wife go to Nevada and obtain a divorce in a court after having stayed there just six weeks necessary to establish residence in the state. Such an easy and quick divorce decision may be denied in a Missouri court. The U.S. Supreme Court ruled in <u>William v. North Carolina</u>[29] that a couple must have acquired a bona fide domicile in a state before a court there could have jurisdiction to grant a divorce.

II. Interstate citizenship--privileges and immunities[30]

A state is required to afford the same treatment to the citizens of other states as to its own. The U.S. Constitution prevents its discrimination against out-of-state residents by denying them the equal protection of law, access to courts, trade, travel, property rights, or indiscriminatory tax rates. But a state may deny non-residents certain political rights, such as voting, holding public office or serving on juries, until they have

---

[28]U.S. Const. art. IV, sec. 1.

[29]325 U.S. 226 (1945).

[30]U.S. Const. art. IV, sec. 2; amend. XIV, sec. 1.

fulfilled residence or other requirements. It may also
place some restrictions upon certain professional practices or trades requiring special skills such as law,
medicine, and barbering or on the use of some state's
proprietary facilities such as state colleges or universities, fish, game resources, and so on. Therefore, states
invariably charge out-of-state students higher tuition or
limit enrollment in state institutions of higher education
to their native students, charge higher fees for hunting
and fishing, and license out-of-state lawyers, physicians,
and teachers after they have passed professional examinations.

III. Interstate rendition[31]

The U.S. Constitution obligates states to return fugitives accused or convicted of crimes to the state where the
crimes were perpetrated. For example, a person, after
having robbed a bank in Jefferson City, Missouri, flees to
Illinois. When later he is discovered in Springfield, Illinois, the Missouri governor may request the Illinois governor to place him under arrest until Missouri officers ar-
rive to bring him back to Missouri. Though such a request
is routinely honored, the Illinois governor may reject it
if he feels that circumstances warrant refusal. The fugitive, for example, may have been living in Illinois for
many years as a law-abiding citizen; he may not receive a
fair trial after return to Missouri; the Missouri law may
be unduly harsh; or the alleged offense may not be a crime
in Illinois.

The U.S. Supreme Court, however, has no power to force
compliance. It only construes interstate rendition as
"moral duty" rather than a legal obligation.[32] In 1934,
Congress used its commercial power to make it a federal
crime to flee across a state line to escape prosecution for
robbery, murder, and other specified crimes. When arrested
by federal agents, the fugitives are usually turned over to
the states from which they fled. In 1936, a Uniform Criminal Extradition Act was written. More than forty states
have adopted and agreed to extradite fugitives on the groun

---

[31]U.S. Const. art. IV, sec. 3. The return of fugitives
from justice to the states from which they have fled is often
known as "extradition," but more properly it should be called
"rendition." "Extradition" is used to refer to the international proceeding.

[32]Kentucky v. Dennison, 24 Howard 66 (1861).

of interstate comity or practical administration or for
fear of retaliation.

IV. Interstate cooperation

In order to advance close cooperation with other
states, Missouri has created a 15-member Missouri Commission on Interstate Cooperation. It includes all members
of the Interstate Cooperation Committees in both the Senate
and the House of Representatives as well as the governor's
Interstate Cooperation Committee, with five members from
each committee. The governor, the House speaker, and the
Senate president pro tem are ex officio members of the
commission with the Senate president pro tem as ex officio
chairman. The commission is instrumental in, inter alia,
encouraging and assisting the government officers of
Missouri to foster friendly relations with those of other
states. It proposes (1) interstate compacts, (2) uniform
or reciprocal statutes to be adopted by the National Conference of Commissioners on Uniform State Laws, and (3) uniform
or reciprocal administrative rules and regulations, and
facilitates their adoption.

The interstate cooperation lies largely in the fields
of uniform state laws, crime control, elimination of trade
barriers, combined correction agencies, law enforcement,
flood control, diversion of water, mass transit, construction of bridges over interstate rivers, civil defense, environment, health, etc.

A. Interstate consultation

Numerous forms of interstate cooperation have developed in recent years. One of them is consultation.
Promoted by the Council of State Governments, interstate consultations encourage joint efforts to solve
mutual problems. Organized in 1935, the Council publishes the monthly periodical State Government and the
biennial Book of the States. It offers information
service to states, serves as secretariat for other
interstate organizations such as the Conference of
State Governors (created in 1908), and also lobbies in
Washington for state causes.

B. Uniform state laws

To ease trade across state boundaries, the National
Conference of Commissioners on Uniform State Laws drafts
and recommends to state legislatures "model laws" for

17

enactment, mostly commercial laws. Created in 1892, the Conference is the oldest interstate organization in the United States.

C. Interstate compacts

Interstate compacts are agreements between or among states. Therefore, they may be bilateral, regional, or nationwide and are in a large variety of subject areas. Though the U.S. Constitution requires interstate compacts to be approved by Congress, actually only those which tend to increase state authority or encroach upon national power are subject to congressional consent.[33] So far Missouri has signed fifteen interstate compacts, namely, Southern Interstate Nuclear Compact, Multistate Tax Compact, Bistate Development Compact, Interstate Compact for Education, Interstate Compact on Mental Health, Kansas-Missouri Air Quality Compact, Interstate Compact on Juveniles, Interstate Compact on Child Placement, Tennessee-Missouri Bridge Compact, two Missouri-Illinois Bridge Compacts, Missouri-Illinois-Jefferson-Monroe Bridge Compact, Kansas City Area Transportation Authority Compact, Vehicle Equipment Safety Compact, and Non-resident Violater Compact.

V. Interstate disputes

Disputes among states are heard by the U.S. Supreme Court, the only tribunal having such jurisdiction in this country.

---

[33]Virginia v. Tennessee, 148 U.S. 503 (1893).

CHAPTER II CONSTITUTION AND LAW

CONSTITUTION

Although a constitution is customarily referred to as the written instrument of a body politic, a constitution may roughly be defined as the fundamental law or set of basic principles or rules which govern whatever an organized body may be--a nation, state, city, international organization, civic body, institution, corporation or even a club. The United States has a constitution, as do Missouri and the Democratic and Republican parties. Labor Unions, universities, student bodies, and even Lions Clubs all have constitutions, but names may vary from one organization to another. The first American Constitution was called the Articles of Confederation. The constitution of the League of Nations was called "covenant." The United Nations' constitution is called "charter"; West Germany's, "basic law." Most local constitutions (city or county) are known as "charters."

Written and Unwritten Constitution

A constitution may be classified as "written" or "unwritten." A written constitution is a single written document like the Missouri Constitution and the United States Constitution, the oldest written constitution existing in the world today. An unwritten constitution is made up of the principles and rules of government scattered throughout numerous volumes or in various sources, such as the British Constitution.[1] Therefore, written and unwritten constitutions are also known as "documentary" and "non-documentary." Actually such a distinction has already paled into insignificance. Today there is no constitution which is entirely unwritten and no constitution entirely written. An overwhelming number of statutes have been written by the British Parliament into the constitution, and numerous unwritten traditions are quietly running the American Government as part of the U.S. Constitution, such as the current presidential electoral system.

---

[1] The British Constitution contains four important components: (1) historical documents, such as Magna Carta of 1215, the Petition of Rights of 1628, etc.; (2) statutes of the British Parliament; (3) case law or judicial decisions; and (4) conventions or customs. Today, besides the British Constitution, the constitutions of Israel, Bhutan, and some Middle Eastern sultanates and kingdoms are classified as unwritten constitutions.

The constitution discussed hereafter is, of course, a
written constitution. Since a constitution is the basic law
of a state, it takes precedence over any other form of law--
whether statutes (called ordinances in local governments and
collectively known as statutory law) enacted by legislatures
or case law (court decisions) made by judges. A written
constitution should be short,[2] concise, and ambiguous--brief
in provisions, general in terms, simple in language, and
vague in contents--with the details and classifications left
to statutes. But sometimes even after all this, law is
still too general, too brief, and too vague. Therefore,
rules or regulations prescribed by administrative agencies
or orders issued by executives or administrators are required
to fill in details for enforcement. That is to say, administrative rules or regulations and executive orders are more
specific than law just as laws are more specific than constitutional provisions.

Therefore, law is subordinate to the constitution just as
rules, regulations, and orders are subordinate to law. Should
law run afoul of the constitution, the latter would undoubtedly prevail. If rules, regulations, or executive orders fall
out with law, the former will be definitely null and void
unless those executive orders rest squarely upon the constitution, i.e., have constitutional authorization.[3] The power
to pass on the constitutionality of legislative acts, executive orders, and administrative rules or regulations by a
court is called judicial review.[4]

---

[2]The longest state constitution is the Constitution of
Georgia (about 500,000 words). The shortest one is the
Constitution of Vermont (about 6500 words). The Louisiana
Constitution was the longest for many years (200,000 words)
but was shortened to less than 35,000 words in 1974.

[3]In 1953, the U.S. Supreme Court declared President
Truman's executive order to authorize the seizure of steel
mills and their operations unconstitutional because it not
only lacked constitutional or statutory authorization but
also violated the Taft-Hartley Act of 1947. Youngstown
Sheet & Tube Co v. Sawyer 343 U.S. 597 (1953)

[4]Judicial review may include three kinds of actions: (1)
a higher court reconsiders a lower court decision, (2) a
court reviews the actions of administrative agencies in determining whether any officials have acted ultra vires
(beyond one's power), and (3) courts (not only the Supreme

Executive orders or proclamations are issued by an executive authority of a government such as the United States President or some administrative authority under his direction to interpret, implement or give administrative effect to constitutional provisions, statutes, or treaties. The issuance of executive orders is also one of the long standing powers of governors, since state legislatures often pass general or rather vague statutes, delegating governors or other executive officers authority to make more specific the provisions of statutes. Derived either from the constitution or from statutes, executive orders and administrative rules and regulations have the same force and effect as law. Since they have general applicability as law, they are therefore often referred to as administrative law and are subject to judicial review.

Judicial review is, of course, a power involving courts because courts have the power to interpret law, and the constitution is a law. But not all judicial or court decisions are

Figure 2.1   Relationships among Constitution, Law and Rules

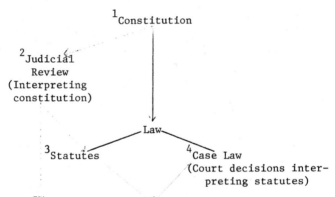

^{1}Constitution

^{2}Judicial
Review
(Interpreting
constitution)

Law

^{3}Statutes

^{4}Case Law
(Court decisions interpreting statutes)

^{5}Executive orders or proclamations
Administrative rules, regulations or orders

Court) determine the validity of statutes or executive actions on constitutional grounds (whether or not they have violated the constitution). It is the third kind of judicial review that Americans customarily think of when the term is used.

judicial review. Judicial review differs from ordinary judicial decisions in that judicial review interprets a constitutional provision, while ordinary judicial decisions interpret law or, more specifically, statutes. Britain, a
country renowned for the rule of law or constitutionalism,
has numerous judicial decisions every year but no judicial
review. In that country, statutes are the most important
component of the Constitution, not subordinate to it as U.S.
law is to the U.S. Constitution. Since judicial decisions
are to interpret and supplement statutes, they are un-
questionably inferior to them.

The chart on the preceeding page shows the constitution,
judicial review, statutes, case law (court decisions), executive orders, and administrative rules or regulations in the
order of precedence.

A modern constitution usually includes at least four
parts: (1) the structure or framework of the government, its
powers and duties; (2) intergovernmental relations; (3) civil
rights; and (4) constitution-amending process. A national
constitution may also lay down fundamental policies, particularly foreign policy, powers and duties of subdivisions, political parties, etc. A state constitution usually contains
a variety of policy statements on such subject matters as
local governments, suffrage and elections, taxation and finances, state property and lands, public education, corporate
enterprises, and the like. State constitutions frequently
intrude into the realm of legislation by taking over many
problems which should be left to statutes, such as the fixing
of salaries, thereby making themselves verbose and cumbersome
and frequently subject to amendments.

Rigid and Flexible Constitutions

Constitutions may also fall into two categories according
to amending procedure: rigid and flexible. A rigid constitution is one requiring a complicated, involved and difficult
procedure for its formal amendment. The United States and the
Missouri Constitutions are two shining examples. A flexible
constitution can be formally amended as easily as ordinary
statutes and without a special procedure. The British Constitution can be changed overnight by an act of Parliament.
Therefore, almost all written constitutions (except New Zealand's) are rigid constitutions.

THE CONSTITUTION OF MISSOURI

Missouri had three constitutions before the existing one was adopted in 1945. The 18th state in size with an area of 69,674 square miles, Missouri was organized as a territory in 1812 and admitted to the Union as the 24th state on August 10, 1821, the year after the Missouri Compromise. Based upon the Congressional Enabling Act of March 6, 1820, the first constitution of Missouri was written and adopted without popular vote by a 41-delegate convention meeting in St. Louis from July 12 through July 19, 1820. The second constitution was adopted on June 6, 1865, two months after the Civil War. Ten years later, the third one was framed on October 30, 1875. It was longer than the first two constitutions. The present one was adopted on February 27, 1945 and is about 42,000 words long.

Capped by a short preamble, which reads "We, the people of Missouri, with profound reverence for the Supreme Ruler of the Universe, and grateful for his Goodness, do establish this Constitution for the better government of the State," the basic law of Missouri includes twelve chapters:

      I. Bill of Rights (31 sections)
     II. The Distribution of Powers (1 section)
    III. Legislative Department (53 sections)
     IV. Executive Department (53 sections)
      V. Judicial Department (27 sections)
     VI. Local Government (33 sections)
    VII. Public Officers (14 sections)
   VIII. Suffrage and Elections (7 sections)
     IX. Education (10 sections)
      X. Taxation (15 sections)
     XI. Corporations, Railroads and Banks (13 sections)
    XII. Amending the Constitution (3 sections)

Constitution-amending Procedure

Proposal	Ratification
(Each proposed amendment contains one amended and revised article of the Constitution, or each new article contains one subject and matters properly connected therewith.)[5]	
1. A joint resolution by the General Assembly at any time if a majority of the elected members in	

------

[5] Mo. Const. art. 12, sec. 2 (b).

each house approves.[6]

2. By popular initiative petitions[7]

    a. Signed by at least 8% of the legal voters (the number who voted for the governor at the last election)[8] in each of at least 2/3 of Missouri's congressional districts;

    b. Filed with the secretary of state at least four weeks before election.

By a simple majority vote cast at the next general election in November or at an earlier special election called by the governor

3. By a constitutional convention

    Since 1962, and every 20 years thereafter, the secretary of state shall, and at any general or special election the General Assembly by law may, submit to the voters of the state the question "Shall there be a convention to revise and amend the Constitution?" If a majority of votes cast thereon is for a convention, the governor shall call an election of delegates within three (3) to six (6) months. There shall be 83 delegates to the convention: two (2) to be elected from each state senatorial district and 15 elected statewide. Each delegate must possess the qualifications of a state senator and not hold any other public office of trust and profit.[9]

At a special election between two (2) and six (6) months after the convention

Results proclaimed by the governor

---

[6] Ibid., sec. 2 (a). Thirteen states require approval by the legislature in two successive sessions.

[7] Ibid., art. 3, sec. 50. Only 14 states use the popular initiative to propose constitutional amendments.

[8] Ibid., sec. 53.

[9] To elect delegates in each senatorial district, each established political party shall nominate one candidate from each district and file the certificate of nomination with the secretary of state at least 30 days before the

The General Assembly and the people may propose individual and isolated constitutional amendments, but they cannot devote themselves to a comprehensive, sweeping revision of the constitution because they are always occupied with routine business. This is why a special constitutional convention is called every twenty years in Missouri if the people so desire. No convention was called in 1962 and 1982. An amendment or a revised constitution shall take effect 30 days after the election if approved by a majority of votes cast thereon.[10] From 1945 through 1982, there were ninety-one (91) amendment proposals to the Constitution: seven (7) by the popular initiative and the remainder by the General Assembly. Fifty-five (55) amendments were adopted, including two (2) proposed by initiative petitions.

---

election. Each candidate shall be voted for on a separate ballot bearing the party designation. Each voter shall vote for one candidate. The two candidates receiving the most votes shall be elected.

Candidates for delegates-at-large shall be nominated by petitions only, which shall be signed by voters equal to 5% of the legal voters in the senatorial district in which the candidate resides. Initiative petitions must be filed with the secretary of state within 30 days before the election. All such candidates shall be voted for on a separate ballot without party designation. The fifteen candidates receiving the most votes shall be elected.

All delegates shall meet in Jefferson City, Missouri, within six months after the election. Officers of the organized militia, school directors, justices of the peace and notaries public are not prohibited from being delegates to the convention. Mo. Const. art. 12, sec. 3 (a) & (b).

A constitutional amendment proposal providing for a convention of 102 delegates with 3 to be elected from each state senatorial district on a nonpartisan ballot and lowering the age requirement from 30 to 24 was defeated in November 2, 1982 election.

[10] Ibid., sec. 2 (b). In every state a constitutional amendment is ratified by the electorate except in Delaware where the legislature votes favorably thereon in two successive sessions without popular vote. In Nevada, ratification of amendments proposed by constitutional initiative requires favorable votes in two consecutive general elections. In five states an amendment must receive a majority vote in election, not only on the amendment.

LAW

Law may briefly be defined as a system of rules and principles of conduct enforceable by sovereign authority. It may be classified according to source or authorship, subject matter, nature of the parties involved, and its nature.

VARIETIES OF LAW

I. Classification according to source or authorship

There are two major sources or authorships of law: statutes and case law (including equity).

A. Statutes or statutory law

A statute is an express law on a specific subject, usually enacted by a legislature. It may also be made by the people through the initiative and referendum. It is also called code law, legislation, or written law.

B. Case law or common law

It is a body of court decisions. It is variously known as judge-made, bench-made, or unwritten law; but most commonly it is synonymous with common law. Common law[11] originated in England in the twelfth century, but its basic legal principles and concepts later found their way across the Atlantic into the charters (constitutions) and laws of the American colonies and finally into the United States Constitution. With the exception of Louisiana, the states which later entered the Union also incorporated the principles of the common law into their legal system.[12]

Statutory law and case law are interrelated. Courts interpret statutory law when it is susceptible to more

---

[11] Before the Norman conquest in 1066, local customs and laws prevailed in the feudal courts throughout England. King Henry II (1154-1189) sent his own royal judges on circuit around the country to adjudicate local disputes and to inquire into local customs and laws. While applying the accepted local laws to cases, the judges gradually fused them into a unified body of rules known as the common law, the law common to the entire realm, in contrast with local feudal laws.

[12] Therefore, common law is also known as Anglo-American law besides English or Anglo-Saxon law.

than one meaning, while legislatures amplify, modify, and write case law into statutory law. To be more specific, case law is supplementary to statutory law. In applying the law to a given case, judges look first into statutes; only when they cannot find any suitable rule to cover the point at issue do they turn to judicial precedents and apply case law. In common law, a precedent once established in the decision of a case must be followed in similar cases unless it is found repugnant to the established principles of justice and overruled by the United States Supreme Court or the highest court of a state. Adhering to previous decisions is called "stare decisis," meaning "let the decision stand."

Traditionally common law has dealt with the relations between individuals over matters of a private nature, while statutory law has been concerned more with the whole community.

C. Equity[13]

Equity is another form of remedial justice which is provided when no adequate remedy can be found in common or statutory law. It actually is a supplement to common law and part of its fabric. In cases "at law," the only remedy is money compensation. In cases "in equity," there are many other remedies than money compensation. There are two kinds of equity decrees: injunction and specific performance. Injunction, the most common equity, prevents damage from occurring to some one. Common law provides remedies with compensation in a civil lawsuit only after persons have suffered injury; sometimes, however, an award cannot compensate for an irreparable

---

[13]Toward the end of the thirteenth century (probably after 1280) in England, the king's courts could not provide adequate justice to certain cases due to the rigid common law. Disappointed litigants turned to the king for justice. The king referred their petitions to the Lord Chancellor, his prime minister, for relief. In the early fourteenth century, the petitions went directly to the Chancellor, who had become known as "keeper of the king's conscience." By the middle of the same century, the Chancery had become a new and distinct court. As time went on, the Chancery developed a system of law alongside the common law, known as "equity." Today, equity is administered by the Chancery, one of the three divisions in the High Court of Justice (equivalent to the U.S. district court) in London.

injury.[14]

Specific performance requires the performance of an obligation created by contract. In other words, it is a court order commanding the party who violated the contract to fulfill it. This extraordinary remedy is applied only when money cannot compensate the injured party for not having the contract performed. Therefore, the subject matter must be unique, such as land in a special location, valuable painting or antique.[15] Disobedience to a court order is contempt of court punishable by fine or imprisonment.

Equity applies only to civil cases. There are no separate federal courts of equity in the United States. The regular U.S. Courts have jurisdiction over all equity matters. Among states, only Arkansas, Delaware, Mississippi, New Jersey, and Tennessee retain entirely separate courts of equity. Under its first constitution (1820), Missouri had separate chancery courts, but soon abolished them. So today in Missouri the same courts have law and equity jurisdictions.

II. Classification by subject matter

Law may be classified as civil law, criminal law, administrative law, constitutional law, and the like.

A. Civil law

Civil law governs the relations between individuals and/or private organizations and defines their legal

---

[14]For instance, John's parents bought him a luxurious car as a college graduation gift, but his jealous cousin, James, threatens to destroy it. If John waits until the car has been destroyed to sue James in a civil suit under common law, James, at most, will compensate him with another car. John, however, could lose his irreparable gift from his parents. In this situation, John may bring action in a court of equity to prevent James from damaging it.

[15]Suppose Olive, an antique dealer, signed a contract with Brown to sell him a Ming vase (a vase made in the Chinese Ming dynasty, 1368-1644) but later backed out of the deal. Brown may sue him in the court of equity, asking for specific performance of the contract. If the request is granted, Olive is forced to sell the vase to Brown.

rights and duties. It therefore concerns such matters as contracts, torts,[16] domestic relations (like divorce) and so on.

B. Criminal law

Criminal law defines each crime and sets forth its punishment. The criminal act is an act conceived to cause harm not only to individuals but also to society as a whole. Crimes are classfied as felonies and misdemeanors.[17] Felonies are serious criminal offenses such as robbery, rape, kidnapping, murder, arson, etc. Misdemeanors are minor crimes such as traffic violations, petty theft, etc. A single act may be both criminal and civil. For instance, if Peter beats David and knocks out his teeth, the court imprisons Peter because he is convicted of a criminal act. In a civil case, David can be compensated with money for the loss of teeth.

On May 26, 1977, the Death Penalty Act[18] was signed by Missouri governor Joseph Teasdale providing for mandatory death in certain specific categories of murder, particularly pre-meditated murder. On July 6 of the same year, Missouri's 142-year old criminal code (enacted in

---

[16]Tort is a private or civil (as contrary to public or criminal) wrong or injury other than breach of contract. It involves injury to a person (resulting from assault, battery, defamation, false imprisonment, negligence, etc.) or to property (resulting from trespass, conversion, fraud, etc.).

[17]In Missouri, a felony is a criminal offense with sentences ranging from more than one year imprisonment to the death penalty. A misdemeanor is a criminal act punishable by a maximum of one-year imprisonment. Felonies are classified into four classes and misdemeanors into three, while infractions are not further divided. Infraction is an offense, but does not constitute a crime, punishable only by fine or fine and forfeiture or other civil penalty. §556.016 & 557. 016, RSMo (Missouri Revised Statutes) 1978.

[18]In 1972, the U.S. Supreme Court ruled, 5-4, that the death penalty was unconstitutional in Furman v. Georgia (408 U.S. 238) because of its discriminatory application, thus striking down capital punishment across the nation (see Chapter III.) However, as of May, 1980, thirty-four states, including Missouri, have reinstated capital punishment.

1835) was revised. The General Assembly repealed many
obsolete statutes, simplified and updated the criminal
acts, and categorized crimes and penalties. It also
liberalized penalty for several sex crimes. However,
several months after the new criminal code went into
effect in January, 1979, a stringent law was made
against rape.

C. Administrative law

Administrative law concerns the powers and procedures of governmental administrative agencies. It regulates relations among different agencies and private
parties to whom the law applies. The sources of administrative law include executive ordinances, statutes, court
decisions, and administrative rules and regulations.

D. Constitutional law

Standing at the pinnacle of the legal hierarchy as
the most public and most political variety of law, constitutional law involves interpretation and application
of the constitution. It defines the nature and limits
of governmental powers along with the rights and duties
of individuals in relation to the state and its governmental organs.

Put simply, constitutional law is a collection of
decisions made by courts, especially the supreme courts,
through judicial review.

III. Classification by the nature of the parties involved

Classified according to the nature of the parties involved, law falls into two categories: public law and private law. Public law relates to public matters of general
concern, such as governmental organization and procedure,
the powers and responsibilities of state officials and the
civil rights of individuals (such as administrative law and
criminal law). Private law governs the relationship between
private individuals or groups (civil law), such as disputes
over property, contracts, negligence, wills, and divorce.
Public law differs from private law in that at least one of
the parties involved is the state.

IV. Classification by nature of law

Law may also be substantive or procedural. Substantive law establishes, defines, and regulates the rights and

duties of and among persons, e.g., criminal law, which defines crimes and prescribes penalties. As opposed to substantive law, procedural law merely prescribes the rules, methods or procedures of exercising and enforcing such rights and duties in a court or obtaining redress for infraction of them, e.g., law of pleading and Rules of Criminal Procedure for the Courts of Missouri.

TWO BASIC LEGAL SYSTEMS IN WESTERN CIVILIZATION[19]

I. Anglo-American common law system

This legal system is based upon common law and is therefore characterized by emphasis upon judicial decisions. In other words, under this system, court decisions are regarded as a major source of law. Belonging to this category are the legal systems of Britain, the United States and all its states except Louisiana, and most English-speaking countries that were formerly British colonies.

II. Continental European civil law system[20]

Characterized by emphasis upon statutes as its major source of law, this legal system was first adopted in continental European countries. Later it spread to Latin America, Asia (Turkey, China and Japan, etc.), some new African nations and those places of Latin heritage, such as Louisiana, because of early Spanish influence. In these civil law system countries, "case law" is relatively less important since the rule of stare decisis is not so widely observed.

Though traditionally the American legal system has been categorized as a common law system, legislation has been playing an increasingly significant role in the United States as well as in Britain ever since the second quarter of the nineteenth century. So today the Anglo-American legal system is actually a blend of common and statutory law.

---

[19] Besides the above two legal systems, there is a third one in the world: the Islamic system. Islamic law is based on the Koran, the Bible of Moslemism.

[20] In this context civil law has nothing to do whatsoever with civil jurisdiction or law involving civil, as distinguished from criminal, action. The civil law system owes its origin to Roman Law, particularly the Justinian Code of A.D. 533 and later the Civil Code or the Code of Napoleon of 1804.

Figure 2.2   Relationships Among All Kinds of Law

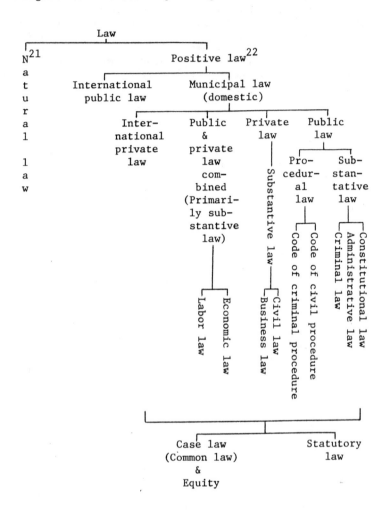

---

[21] Natural law, referred to as the right reason of man, governs human societies in the absence of, or as a supplement to, positive law.

[22] Positive law is the law made and enforced by the political authority of the state.

MISSOURI LAW

Though legally Missouri is within the Anglo-American common law framework, yet every year sees numerous statutes streaming out of the General Assembly. The following volumes contain the statutes, court decisions, Supreme Court rules, and administrative regulations of Missouri, some even dating back to the dawn of the nineteenth century.

I. Statutes

A. Laws of Missouri

Compiled and published by the secretary of state of Missouri according to the date the law was enacted, the Laws of Missouri contains the statutes and resolutions passed by the two houses during the regular and extra sessions of the General Assembly as far back as 1804, when Missouri was still a U.S. territory. It also in- cludes the proposed amendments to the Missouri Consti- tutions, both adopted and rejected, as well as a table of the bills vetoed by the governors. The secretary of state, at the close of each legislative session, pub- blishes the Session Acts, which consists of all the laws passed by the General Assembly during the session.

B. Missouri Revised Statutes Annotated, 1939

Arranged under a classification system pursuant to the laws enacted by the sixtieth General Assembly, the Statutes has completely replaced the former revisions. It contains 32 volumes published by the Vernon Law Book Company, Kansas City, Mo. and the West Publishing Com- pany, St. Paul, Minnesota.

C. Vernon's Annotated Missouri Statutes

Published by the West Publishing Company in 1970, Vernon's Annotated Missouri Statutes includes the exist- ing constitutional provisions, statutes, and numerous additions and changes enacted by the General Assembly together with the latest judicial constructions and in- terpretations of the Constitution and statutes. There are sixty-one volumes of Missouri statutes and four volumes of tables and index.

D. Missouri Revised Statutes, 1949, 1959, 1969, 1978

The state Constitution of 1945 requires revision

and publication of all statutes at least every ten
years beginning in 1949. At the end of every ten
years, in the years ending in "9", the general statute laws are revised, digested, and published by the
Committee on Legislative Research of the General Assembly. The committee also publishes annual supplements of the statutes, including changes in laws
since the last revision. The Revised Statutes of
1949 are in three volumes, 1959 in four, 1969 in five,
and 1978 also in five.

II. Case Law

A. Southwestern Reporter,[23] 1886-1928

Published by the West Publishing Company, the
Reporter covers Missouri court decisions from August
2, 1886 through February 1928 in 300 volumes.

B. Southwestern Reporter, Second Series, 1928 to date

The second series of the Southwestern Reporter
covers the Missouri cases from February 15, 1928 to
date in 632 volumes.

C. Shepard's Southern Reporter Citations

Published by Shepard's Citations, Inc., Colorado
Springs, Colorado, it is a compilation of citations
to all cases in the Southwestern Reporter including
affirmances, reversals and dismissals by the United
States Supreme and higher state courts. There are two
volumes and two supplementary volumes:

Volume I (1950), Supplement (1950-1976)

---

[23]Southwestern Reporter also covers the court dicisions
of Arkansas, Kentucky, Tennessee, and Texas; Atlantic Reporter: Connecticut, Delaware, Maine, New Hampshire, New Jersy,
Maryland, Rhode Island, Pennsylvania, and Vermont; Southern
Reporter: Alabama, Florida, Louisiana, and Mississippi;
Northeastern Reporter: Illinois, New York, Indiana, Massachusetts, and Ohio; Northwestern Reporter: Iowa, Michigan, Nebraska, North Dakota, South Dakota, Minnesota, and Wisconsin;
Southeastern Reporter: Georgia, South Carolina, North Carolina, Virginia, and West Virginia; and Pacific Reporter: A-
laska, Arizona, California, Colorado, Hawaii, Idaho, Kansas,
Montana, Nevada, New Mexico, Utah, Oklahoma, Oregon, Washington, and Wyoming.

Volume II: Part I and II (1976), Supplement (1976–
            1981)

D. Missouri Digest, 1821 to date

    The Missouri Digest, composed of 32 volumes and
several supplementary volumes, covers not only the
Missouri cases, both state and federal, from 1821 to
date, but also every point of law digested therefrom.
Published by the West Publishing Company, 1930–1979,
the Digest provides a modern time-saving key number
system to help busy legal practitioners to find cases
quickly from other jurisdictions. The popular West
key number system, under which court decisions are
arranged, is universally recognized as the standard
classification of American case law.

E. Missouri Reports, 1821–1956

    Published by various publishers in 365 volumes,
this book covers the cases argued and determined in
the Supreme Court of Missouri since 1821.

F. Missouri Appeals Reports, 1876–1954

    Vols. 1–16 (1876–1885) – Cases argued and determined
                            in the St. Louis Court of
                            Appeals.

    Vols. 17–137 (1885–1909) – Cases determined in the
                            St. Louis and the Kansas
                            City Courts of Appeals.

    Vols. 138–241 (1910–1954) – Cases determined by the
                            St. Louis, the Kansas
                            City and the Springfield
                            Court of Appeals.

G. Missouri Case Finder

    Consisting of eight volumes, the Finder was
edited by Charles L. Carr and published by the Lawyers Cooperative Publishing Company and the Bancroft
and Whitney Company, Rochester, N.Y., in 1963. It
is characterized by a thoroughly tested system of
case-point finding, covering Missouri evidence decisions (1941–1962) together with substantive law
points. Supported by three volumes of Cumulative
Supplement (1972) covering cases through 458 SW2nd,
the book provides judges and lawyers with a new

time-saving method for research into all recent court
evidence decisions and points of law.

III. Court Rules

Vernon's Annotated Missouri Rules

Published by the West Publishing Company, 1970-1981,
the seven-volume Missouri Rules covers 102 Supreme Court
Rules governing the Missouri Bar and the Judiciary, juvenile courts, small claims courts, Court of Appeals, civil
and criminal proceedings, municipal and traffic rules,
and interpretations and constructions of the rules.

IV. Administrative Regulations

Code of State Regulations, 1978

The first Administrative Procedure Act was passed
in 1945. Thirty years later, in July 1975, the General
Assembly passed the Code of State Regulations Act and
directed the secretary of state to develop a uniform
system of formalizing, numbering, indexing, and publishing all rules of all state agencies. The six-volume
Code of State Regulations was published at the end of
the same year. The proposed rules by all state administrative agencies must be published in the monthly Missouri Register for public comments for at least 30 days
before they take effect. Normally the rule-making process takes about 90 days.

CHAPTER III   MISSOURI CITIZENSHIP & CIVIL RIGHTS

MISSOURI CITIZENSHIP

State citizenship in the United States, like national citizenship, is succinctly defined in the first section of the Fourteenth Amendment to the United States Constitution, which reads "All persons born or naturalized in the United States, and subject to the jurisdiction thereof,[1] are citizens of the United States and of the state where they reside." So constitutionally any American citizen, whether born (even of alien parents) or naturalized in the United States is automatically the citizen of the state where he is born or naturalized. To be more specific, those who are born or naturalized in Missouri and reside therein are Missouri citizens. But those who are born or naturalized in other states may also become Missouri citizens simply by taking up residence in this state. Therefore, Missouri, like other states, has no control over who holds state citizenship. However, every state may establish residency requirements for eligibility to practice law, medicine, or other professions or for other purposes. In Missouri there is a one-year residency requirement; in other states residency requirements may vary from three months to two years. Besides, persons born outside the United States but of American parents are also natural born citizens[2] according to American laws.

The United States Constitution authorizes Congress to establish uniform rules for naturalization.[3] Naturalization

---

[1]Persons born in the United States but not subject to its jurisdiction at the time of birth are not American citizens, such as those born (1) of foreign diplomats (ambassadors, ministers, but not consular officers), (2) of alien enemies on the occupied American soil, and (3) on foreign public vessels in American territorial waters.

[2]This is called the law of blood or jus sanguinis. The rule whereby one acquires citizenship by the place of birth is called the law of soil or jus soli. While the 14th Amendment to the U.S. Constitution established jus soli in conferring American citizenship, a series of congressional acts and court decisions grant American nationality according to jus sanguinis. Among the acts are the Nationality Act of 1940, the Immigration and Naturalization Act of 1952, the Immigration Act of 1965, etc.

[3]U.S. Const. art. 1, sec. 8.

is the legal process through which an alien becomes a citizen of one country. Naturalization may be collective or individual. The inhabitants of a territory or designated groups of people may be collectively naturalized by treaty, congressional act or joint resolution.[4] To be individually naturalized, an alien must be at least eighteen years of age, have entered the United States legally, have never belonged to any subversive party, particularly the Communist party, have good moral character, be able to read, write, and speak English, and have a basic understanding of American history and government. He must also have been lawfully admitted for permanent residence and have resided in the United States for at least five years (only three years for one whose spouse is an American citizen), and in a state for at least six months.

CIVIL RIGHTS

DEFINITION AND RECENT TENDENCY

Civil rights are the actions of government to protect individuals from interference, arbitrary action, or discriminatory treatment by government itself or by other individuals.

Civil Liberties and Civil Rights[5]

Although the terms "civil rights" and "civil liberties" are essentially synonymous and are usually interchangeably used, subtle distinctions may be drawn between them. The term "liberty' means the freedom of an individual from restraint in personal action—to do what he wants to do, while a "right" is the power or privilege to which one is justly entitled and which should be protected. Civil liberties, therefore, differ from civil rights in that "civil liberties" refer to individual freedom from governmental interference to do certain things, while "civil rights" mean that an individual is entitled to those freedoms guaranteed by the constitution and laws and subject to governmental protection. In other words,

---

[4]The residents of the Louisiana territory were naturalized by the purchase treaty of 1803, the natives of Northern Marianas by a congressional act in 1977, and Texans by joint resolution of the Congress which admitted the independent Republic of Texas to the Union.

[5]American civil liberties are found mostly in the Bill of Rights (the first ten Amendments) in the U.S. Constitution, while civil rights are scattered in the other sections of the Constitution.

civil liberties restrain the government from arbitrary actions that interfere with individual freedom. Civil rights
invoke protection of government to prevent the freedom of
individuals from being abused by other individuals, by private
organizations, or even by the government itself. Briefly,
civil liberty, which denotes personal freedom, is negative in
nature, while civil rights, involving protection of personal
freedom, is positive in action.

Civil rights may fall into two broad categories: substantive and procedural. Substantive rights are basic rights
that confer on an individual the right of some kind of action,
in other words, a right to do something or to be free of some
restrictions, such as the right to freedom of speech and press,
freedom of worship, freedom of association, etc. Procedural
rights seek to attain and protect the substantive rights of
person and property through the establishment of procedures
and methods such as political and legal rights. However, it
is sometimes difficult to determine whether a right is substantive or procedural because it can be either, since it
has both substantive and procedural significance.

Recent Tendency

In constitutions formulated since the early 1940's, a
bill of rights is placed at or near the beginning of the
constitution, often in the first article in some countries
and in some American states. The purpose is to show a high
regard for civil rights. Unlike the time-honored United
States Constitution, but like the modern constitutions of
West Germany, Italy, Mexico, etc., the bill of rights of the
Missouri Constitution is embodied in the first article, immediately after the preamble. Again, like West Germany's
basic law, but unlike the United States Constitution, the
freedoms defined in the Missouri Constitution are immediately
followed by a string of restrictions designed to guard against
abuses of liberty. But unlike many other modern constitutions,
civil rights are not balanced by an array of duties in the
fundamental law of Missouri.

During recent decades in the United States, emphasis in
the area of "civil rights" has been placed on the right to
equal protection of the laws, especially on racial equality
before the law. Since the 1940's, strenuous efforts have been
made by government at all levels to secure for blacks and
other minorities equal rights in voting, employment, housing,
public accommodations as well as in other areas. Consequently, the term "civil rights" has become closely identified with

the movement against racial discrimination, particularly after a series of Civil Rights Acts made by Congress beginning in 1957. Undeniably, equal treatment under the law is a basic civil right, but it is only one of many to which Americans are entitled.

Many recent constitutions adopted in various countries throughout the world include not only personal or civil and political rights characteristic of Western democracies but also economic, social, cultural, or educational rights valued by socialist states. Civil and political rights are now commonly known as the traditional individual-personal rights; while social, economic, cultural, or educational rights are most often spoken of as the modern economic-social rights. Perhaps the most appropriate and popular term today is "human rights,"[6] which is used to embrace the traditional meaning as well as the new emphasis on economic, social, and cultural rights. The United States Constitution, the oldest written constitution in the world today, embraces only the traditional rights. Although it does emphasize the rights of private property, which are protected primarily by the due process of law clause in the Fifth and Fourteenth Amendments, few references are made to social and educational rights. The Missouri Constitution contains a sprinkling of economic, social, and educational rights contrasted with an abundance of civil and political rights. Again following the more recent trend, the Missouri Constitution spells out civil rights in much more

---

[6]On December 10, 1948, the United Nations adopted the Universal Declaration of Human Rights. The Declaration, including 30 articles, consists of a list of inalienable rights of mankind: personal, civil, political, economic, social and cultural. On December 16, 1966, the United Nations unanimously adopted two covenants: the Covenant on Civil and Political Rights; and the Covenant on Economic, Social, and Cultural Rights.
The Russian delegates at the UN downgraded the traditional rights as empty and meaningless without a guarantee of the new economic, social, cultural, or educational rights. They, therefore, insisted that these new rights should take precedence over the traditional ones and be emphasized. However, the American and British delegates, on the other hand, stressed the traditional rights. With civil and political rights as weapons in hand, they argued, people could fight for and finally win other rights. Because of the opposing views on human rights, two separate covenants were therefore written.

detail than the United States Constitution. There are 31 sections in Article I (Bills of Rights) and some educational
rights in Article IX in the Missouri Constitution in compari-
son with only six clauses in the original United States Constitution and 16 amendments.

CIVIL RIGHTS IN MISSOURI

Before proceeding to define specific civil rights, the
Missouri Constitution in Article I first lays down the fundamental principles, upon which the Missouri Government is
built.

Missouri is a free and independent state with a government of the people, by the people, and for the people, subject only to the United States Constitution and with civilian
supremacy over the military.[7] According to the Missouri Constitution, "all political power is vested in and derived from
the people," and "all government of right originates from the
people, is founded upon their will only" (the government of
the people). Meanwhile, "the people of this state have the
inherent, sole and exclusive right to regulate the internal
government and police thereof, and to alter and abolish their
Constitution and form of government" whenever necessary for
their safety and happiness (the government by the people).
The government will promote the general welfare of the people
and give security to their natural right to life, liberty,
the pursuit of happiness, the enjoyment of their earnings,
equal rights and opportunity to which they are entitled under
the law (the government for the people). All federal constitutional amendment proposals which affect individual liberties
or which impair local government shall be submitted to conventions of the people for decisions.

The following are the civil rights safeguarded for Missourians by the Constitution:

I. Personal or civil rights

   A. Substantive rights:

      1. Freedom of religion (Art. 1, Secs. 5-7; Art. 9,
         Sec. 8)

         a. Freedom of worship (Art. 1, Sec. 5)

            All people have a natural and indefeasible

---

[7]Mo. Const. art. 1, sec. 24.

right to worship God according to their own consciences. The rights of conscience shall not be interfered with; eligibility for public office or for juror service shall not be denied, nor shall one's person or estate be molested because of one's religious belief. But there shall be no act of licentiousness, no violation of order, peace, or safety of the state nor infringement of others' rights.

b. Freedom in support of any clergymen or in attendance at any church (Sec. 6)

No person shall be forced to attend a church or support any priest of any religion.

c. Separation between church and state

(1) No preference shall be given to, nor discrimination made against, nor public funds used to support, directly or indirectly, any church, sect, or creed of religion, or priest thereof (Sec. 7);

(2) No public funds shall be used to support, nor shall private property or real estate be donated by the state to, any religious educational institutions (Art. 9, Sec. 8).

2. Freedom of expression or communication (Art. 1, Sec. 8)

Freedom of expression or communication includes freedom of speech, freedom of writing, and freedom of publication. Every person, nevertheless, shall be responsible for all abuses of such liberty. In all lawsuits for libel or slander,[8] the truth thereof may be produced in evidence. In lawsuits for libel, the jury, under the direction of the court, determines both the law and the facts.

3. Rights of peaceable assembly[9] (Art. 1, Sec. 9)

_____

[8] Libel is a written defamation; slander is an oral one.

[9] The freedom of expression, the freedom of religion, and the rights of peaceable assembly and petition are safeguarded by the First Amendment to the U.S. Constitution.

The Constitution safeguards the people's right of peaceable (not violent) assembly. The "assembly" includes not only meetings in private homes or public halls but also rallies in streets, parks, and other public places, and even physical demonstrations such as parades, marches, or picketings.

4. Quartering of soldiers prohibited[10] (Sec. 24)

No soldier is allowed to be quartered in any house without the consent of the owner at any time except as provided by law.

5. Right to keep and bear arms[11] (Sec. 23)

Everyone has the right to keep and bear arms for self-defense or in aid of the civil government. However, no one is allowed to carry concealed weapons such as pistols, daggers, sword-canes, etc.

6. Irrevocable privileges (Sec. 13)

No law shall be made to grant irrevocable special privileges or immunities.

7. Definition of treason (Sec. 30)

Copied from the United States Constitution,[12] "treason" against Missouri is defined by the State Constitution as (1) levying war against it, (2) adhering to its enemies, or (3) giving them aid and comfort.

8. Imprisonment for debt prohibited (Sec. 11)

No person shall be imprisoned because of debt, except for failure to pay fines or penalties imposed by court.

9. Fines or imprisonments fixed by administrative agencies prohibited (Sec. 31)

---

[10]Safeguarded by the U.S. Constitutional Amendment III.
[11]Safeguarded by the U.S. Constitutional Amendment II.
[12]U.S. Const. art. III, sec. 3.

No commission, bureau, board or other administrative authority is allowed to make any rule fixing a fine or imprisonment as punishment.

B. Substantive and procedural rights: Due process of law (Sec. 10)

No person shall be deprived of life, liberty, or property without due process of law. The phrase "due process of law" is not defined in the United States or the Missouri Constitutions, nor has it been exactly defined by the U.S. Supreme Court. In general, it means "fair, reasonable, and just rules or principles" or, in a loose sense, it is equivalent to the phrase "law of the land." Due process of law may be substantive or procedural. Substantive due process of law concerns the contents of law, while procedural due process involves the legal proceedings to be carried out according to established rules and principles.

C. Procedural rights

1. Rights to petition the government for redress of grievances (Sec. 9)

2. No unreasonable search and seizure (Sec. 15)[13]-- right to security

No homes, papers,or belongings shall be unreasonably searched, nor shall persons be unreasonably arrested. No warrant[14] shall be issued without des-

---

[13]Safeguarded by the U.S. Constitutional Amendment IV.

[14]Exceptions to warrant searches and seizures are border searches, consent searches, exigent circumstances (automobile searches), plain view seizures, stop and frisk, searches accident to arrest, abandoned property, second search, administrative inspections, etc. Most warrantless searches and arrests are made under the following conditions:

1. Circumstances do not permit any delay: an airplane, bus, automobile, or boat can be searched without a warrant;
2. A crime is being committed before a policeman or any person who makes a "citizen's arrest";
3. There is probable cause to believe that a crime has been or will be committed, and there is no time to obtain a warrant.

cribing the place or person to be searched or seized, nor without probable cause,[15] supported by written oath or affirmation.

3. Suspension of habeas corpus prohibited[16] (Sec. 12)

Habeas corpus (in Latin: "you have the body") is a court writ ordering the jailer or custodian to bring the arrested person before the court to determine the legality of his imprisonment. In Missouri, no one shall be held more than twenty hours without a warrant;[17] otherwise, he or rather some one on his behalf, has the right to appeal the court having jurisdiction for a writ of habeas corpus, which cannot be denied.

4. Rights of the accused in criminal prosecutions[18] (Sec. 18-a)

The accused has the right to know the nature and cause of the accusation. He also has the right to professional legal counsel. In criminal prosecutions he has the right to appear and defend, in person and by his lawyer,[19] in court. To provide an

---

On April 15, 1980, the U.S. Supreme Court ruled, 6-3, in <u>Payton v. New York</u> and <u>Riddick v. New York</u> that, except in an emergency that requires an immediate arrest, police must first obtain a warrant or consent from the occupant of a house before entering to arrest him. The Court struck down as unconstitutional a New York law authorizing police to enter a house to arrest its occupant without a warrant. Twenty three states adopted a similar law.

[15]Probable cause is reasonable belief based on the existence of facts and circumstances or reasonably trustworthy information that the suspect has committed a crime.

[16]U.S. Const. art. I, sec. 9.

[17]§544.170, RSMo 1959

[18]Safeguarded by the U.S. Constitutional Amendments V & VI.

[19]The following U.S. Supreme Court rulings require states to provide counsels for indigent defendants at public expenses if they so request:

indigent defendant with assistance of counsel, a better and more efficient public defender system was established in Missouri by the State Public Defender Act of 1982.[20] The new law departs from the one of 1976 in three areas: (1) to rely mainly upon full-time public defenders rather than court-appointed attorneys by establishing a statewide public defenders network, (2) to provide adequate funding by removing the $5 million ceiling on expenditures and collecting fees from those who can make partial payments, and (3) to toughen eligibility guidelines by setting up new standards to determine who actually qualifies for state paid legal aid. But private attorneys are still used whenever necessary.

The public defender system provides defense services to any eligible person (1) detained or charged with a felony or a misdemeanor which will probably result in incarceration including appeals from a conviction in such a case, (2) detained or charged with a violation of probation or parole, (3) entitled to the assistance of counsel according to the federal or state constitutions, or (4) entitled to the assistance of counsel according to any law of this state in a case where the defender faces a loss or deprivation of liberty.

5. Indictments and informations in criminal cases (Secs. 16 & 17)

Criminal prosecutions in either misdemeanor or felony cases must be instituted by indictments or informations except in cases arising in the land and naval forces or in the militia when in actual service in time of war or public danger. An indictment or a "true bill" is a formal criminal accusation issued by a grand jury, while an information is a formal statement of charges sworn to by a prosecutor.

1963 - Gideon v. Wainwright (372 U.S. 335): in non-capital as well as capital cases.
1964 - Escobedo v. Illinois (378 U.S. 478): at the time of arrest, not solely for trial.
1966 - Miranda v. Arizona (384 U.S. 436): besides a counsel to be provided, the defendant must be advised by the police, before questioning, of his rights to remain silent and to have the presence of an attorney.
1972 - Argersinger v. Hamlin (407 U.S. 25): for any misdemeanors punishable by jail sentences.

[20] Chapter 600 RSMo Supp. 1982.

In Missouri, a grand jury consists of 12 citizens,[21] who are convened upon an order of a judge of a court having jurisdiction over felonies. Nine of them concurring will find an indictment or a true bill. Once assembled, the grand jury has the power to investigate and return a true bill called "presentment" based upon its own findings. Its investigations into willful misconduct of government officers and indictments against them can never be suspended.

6. Denial of bail and excessive bail prohibited[22] (Secs. 20 & 21)

   No bail shall be denied, nor shall it be excessive, except for capital offenses with evident proof or under great suspicion.

7. Open courts and a speedy public trial by an impartial jury (Secs. 14 & 19-a)

   Courts are open to everyone because fair trials are more ensured before the public than in secret star-chamber court rooms.[23] Rights and justice must be administered without sale, denial, or delay. Certain remedies, such as compensations, are afforded for every injury to person, property, or character.

   The accused has the right to a speedy public trial by an impartial jury of the county. Effective in September 1978, a new state trial act,[24] patterned after a similar federal law,[25] requires

---

[21] Mo. Const. art. 1, sec. 16. Between six (6) and 23 jurors in other states. A federal grand jury consists of from 16 to 23 jurors.

[22] Safeguarded by the U.S. Constitutional Amendment VIII.

[23] A secret court existed in England from 1487 to 1641 to try special cases. It was co-called because the chamber had starred walls and ceilings.

[24] §545.780, RSMo 1978.

[25] In 1974, Congress enacted a law, effective in 1976, requiring defendants in federal criminal cases to be set free if they had not been tried within 100 days of their arrest.

anyone charged with a crime to be brought to trial
within 180 days of his arraignment, subject to
several exceptions.[26]

To sift out biased or unfavorable jurors, the
veniremen (persons who have been determined as
qualified for jury service) are subject to voir dire
("to speak the truth") examinations given by both
the prosecutor and the defense lawyer in court.
There are two kinds of voir dire examinations: challenges for cause and peremptory challenges. Challenges for cause[27] (reasons need to be given) may,
with approval of the presiding judge, be without
limit. Peremptory challenges, for which no reasons
need be given, are limited to from three to twelve
in Missouri.[28]

8. Trial by jury (Sec. 22-a)[29]

---

[26]A period of delay may result from such reasons as an
examination of the defendant and hearing on his mental com-
petency or physical incapacity or a change of venue, etc.
§545.780, RSMo 1978.

[27]Challenges for cause can be general, such as "prior
conviction," "failure to qualify," "unsound mind," or "prejudice."

[28]In all criminal cases the state and the defendant are
entitled to a peremptory challenge of jurors as follows:

1. If the offense charged is punishable by death or
   life imprisonment, the state (prosecutor) may
   challenge 6 and the defendant 12;
2. If the offense charged is punishable by imprisonment in the penitentiary, the state 4, the defendant 8;
3. In all other cases, the state and the defendant
   each 3. §546.180, RSMo 1978

[29]Juries are not used in impeachment trials and equitable
proceedings (equity cases). A jury may be used in the military trial but is composed of military officers (not laymen
as in a civilian court). There was a five-officer military
jury in the court-martial of Marine Pfc. Robert Garwood in
February 1981 on charges of his collaborating with the enemy
during the Vietnam War.

48

A jury for the trial of criminal and civil (cases in courts not of record[30] may consist of less than 12 jurors; a two thirds majority of such number concurring renders a verdict in all civil cases. A jury for the trial of either criminal or civil cases in courts of record consists of 12 jurors. A unanimous vote is required to render a verdict in all criminal cases including misdemeanors, but a three-fourths majority is required in civil cases.[31]

A defendant may, with the approval of the court in any criminal case, waive a jury trial and leave the trial of his case to the judge alone. The judges decision has the same effect as the jury's.

Women are not disqualified from jury service, but they may be exempted upon request before being sworn as jurors.[32]

9. Witnesses and depositions in felony cases (Sec. 18 a & b)

In criminal prosecutions a defendant has the right to face witnesses as well as to compel the at-

---

[30]A court of record is a court "required to keep a record of its proceedings and may fine or imprison." Black's Law Dictionary, 5th rev. ed. (1979), s.v. "Court." The Missouri Supreme Court, Court of Appeals, and circuit courts are the courts of record and keep just and faithful records and their proceedings. §476.010, RSMo 1978. That is, the court of record keeps a written transcript (record) of the oral pleadings, the testimonies of witnesses and the arguments of counsels taken by a stenographer or court reporter during the trial; and the appellant court, in reviewing the case, only reads the record and need not hear the case de novo (anew). All divisions in the circuit courts in Missouri are courts not of record.

[31]Mo. Const. art. 1, sec. 22 (a). John Scurlock, "Basic Principles of the Administration of Criminal Justice with Particular Reference to Missouri Law--Revised," UMKC (University of Missouri in Kansas City) Law Review, Winter 1975, pp. 292-93; 309.

[32]Mo. Const. art. 1, sec. 22 (b).

tendance of witnesses in his favor through compulsory process.

A deposition is a written testimony taken on oath outside the courtroom to be used as evidence at trial. Upon a hearing and finding by the circuit court in any felony case, it is necessary to take the deposition of any witness within the state other than the defendant and spouse so as to preserve testimony. If the court issues such orders as to fully protect the defendant's rights to confront and cross-examine the witness, the state may take the deposition of such witness. The deposition may be used by either party at the trial, as in civil cases, if such orders have been substantially complied with.

10. Self-incrimination prohibited (Sec. 19)

No one can be forced to testify against oneself in a criminal case. This clause is evidently derived from the Fifth Amendment to the United States Constitution. It is based upon an ancient English law prohibiting use of physical torture to exact confession from a person.[33]

11. Double jeopardy prohibited (Sec. 19)

Also safeguarded by the Fifth Amendment is the right not to be tried a second time for the same offense after being once acquitted by a jury. However, if the jury fails to render a verdict,[34] or the court stays its judgment after having found a verdict of guilty on defective indictment or information, or reverses the judgment on a verdict of guilty for error in law, the judge may dismiss the jury and try the accused a second time.

Other exceptions to the prohibition against double jeopardy are:

(1) A person may face civil as well as criminal charges;
(2) He may be tried for each of several offenses

---

[33]Also called the "third degree".

[34]A jury that cannot reach a decision (verdict) because of disaggreement among jurors is called a "hung hury."

growing out of a single act.[35]
  (3) He may be tried by both federal and state courts
      if he has violated both federal and state law by
      one criminal act such as robbery of a federally
      chartered bank;
  (4) Persons in the armed service may sometimes be
      subject to both a military court-martial and a
      regular state court trial for the same offense;
  (5) On appeal by a defendant after conviction, a
      higher court may order a new trial.

12. Excessive fines and cruel and unusual punishment
    prohibited (Sec. 21)

        Excessive fines shall not be imposed, nor shall
    cruel and unusual punishment be inflicted. Fines
    may be considered excessive and punishment cruel and
    unusual if they are out of proportion to the offenses.

        On June 29, 1972, the U.S. Supreme Court, 5-4,
    struck down capital punishment across the nation,
    declaring it unconstitutional on the ground that it
    was cruel and unusual punishment and discriminatory
    in application. In 1977, the death penalty was re-
    stored in Missouri after a new capital punishment
    law was enacted in compliance with the guidelines
    laid down by the United States Supreme Court.

13. Ex post facto law prohibited (Sec. 13, see Chapter I)

14. Bill of attainder for treason or felony prohibited
    (Sec. 30, see Chapter I)

15. Conviction and punishment of treason (Sec. 30)

        No person shall be convicted of treason, unless
    on the testimony of two witnesses to the same overt

---

[35]On August 18, 1980, the Missouri Supreme Court ruled
that "to convict one under the state's armed criminal action
law as well as first-degree robbery violated the constitutional guarantee against double jeopardy, for armed criminal
action and first degree robbery were essentially the same
offense and to try a defendant separately for each offense
constituted double jeopardy." Sours v. Missouri, 603 SW2d.
592 (Mo. banc 1980).

act or on a confession in open court.[36]

Under the old common law a person convicted of
felony or treason by attainder was deprived of the
right to hold or pass on property, rank, or title to
heirs at death. That is, the legal consequences of
guilt were extended beyond the person convicted, for
instance, to his family. Such punishment is called
"corruption of blood," which both the United States
and the Missouri Constitutions prohibit upon any
convicted person. The Missouri Constitution goes
further to include those who commit suicides or die
by accidents.

II. Political rights

Missouri citizens have the right to elect government
officials, initiate, and ratify constitutional provisions
and law; but they have no right to the recall.[37] The
Constitution guarantees free and open elections, prohibiting any power, civil or military, from meddling with
the free exercise of suffrage at any time. (Sec. 25)

III. Economic rights

A. No person shall be deprived of...property without due
process of law. (Sec. 10)

B. Eminent domain--substantive right

1. No private property shall be taken or damaged for
public use without just compensation. Such compensation must be determined by a jury or board of
commissioners of not less than three freeholders[38]
according to law. No property shall be disturbed
nor shall the owner's proprietary rights be divested,
until compensation is paid him or paid to the court
for him (Sec. 26);

---

[36] U.S. Const. art. III, sec. 3.

[37] A procedure enabling voters to remove an elected official from office before his term expires. Approximately 12
states and numerous local governmental units adopt this procedure. It was first used in this country by Los Angeles in
1903 and applied to state officers by Oregon in 1908.

[38] Freeholder is the owner of real estate either in fee
simple or fee tail, or for life.

2. Disposition of excess property acquired by eminent domain is restricted (Sec. 27);

3. With a few exceptions, no private property can be taken for private use without the consent of the owner (Sec. 28);

4. Corporations are also subject to eminent domain. (Art. XI, Sec. 4)

C. Laws impairing the obligation of contracts prohibited (Art. I, Sec. 13)--Substantive right

The United States Constitution[39] forbids any state to make a law impairing the obligation of contracts. While framing the Constitution, the founding fathers intended only that ordinary contracts between individuals be effected, such as contracts of debt. Later, the meaning of the word "contracts" was expanded by court interpretations to cover those made by the states[40] themselves, including franchises granted to corporations.[41]

No contracts shall violate existing law. In exercising police power, the state legislatures may, for the public welfare, make laws to interfere with individual contracts. (Art. XI, Sec. 3)

IV. Social rights--substantive rights

A. Employees have the right to organize and to bargain collectively through representatives chosen by them (Sec. 29);

B. Racial discrimination in employment of teachers is prohibited. (Art. IX, Sec. 3:c)

V. Educational rights (Art. IX, Sec. 1)--Substantive rights

---

[39] U.S. Const. art. I, sec. 10.

[40] Fletcher v. Peck (6 Cranch 87) 1810. The U.S. Supreme Court ruled that the "contract" clause applied to public as well as private contracts.

[41] Dartworth v. Woodward (4 Wheaton 518) 1819. The Court ruled that charters establishing corporations were also contracts.

A. The General Assembly must establish and maintain free public schools for all persons in this state under age 21 (between the ages 6 and 18).

B. The state may provide specific schools for the handicapped and career training for adults

MISSOURI COMMISSION ON HUMAN RIGHTS

In order to protect all people from discrimination in housing, employment, and public accommodations because of race, sex, religion, and physical or mental handicap in Missouri, the eleven-member Commission on Human Rights was created in 1957.

Anyone claiming to be aggrieved by an unlawful discriminatory act may file a written complaint with the commission. The commission will then conduct an investigation and make every effort possible to remove the discriminatory practice by persuasion, conference, and conciliation. If conciliation fails, a public hearing will be held before a panel of three members of the commission or before a hearing examiner, who is a Missouri-licensed lawyer appointed by the commission.

The panel or hearing examiner makes a finding of fact and then reaches a conclusion of law. If the commission finds the alleged illegal discriminatory practice has actually occurred, it will order the respondent to cease and desist such injustice and to take such affirmative steps as the commission deems fitting. Otherwise, the complaint will be dropped.

Each party has the right to appeal the commission's decision to a circuit court within 30 days. If no appeal is made within this period, the commission may obtain a court order to enforce its decision. In the event of appeal for review, the attorney general represents the commission in court.

Among the important statutes enacted by the General Assembly safeguarding human rights are the Fair Employment Practice Act of 1961, extended in 1965; the Public Accommodation Act of 1965; and the Fair Housing Practices Law of 1972.

CHAPTER IV   VOTING

SUFFRAGE

Originally the United States Constitution authorized the states alone to fix voting qualifications in all elections, leaving Congress to make or alter the regulations at any time regarding the times, places, and manner of holding elections prescribed by each state.   Later, because the states abused the power and denied blacks the right to vote, the federal government entered the picture.   The government interferes in state elections under a series of Civil Rights Acts[1] and court

---

[1]The Civil Rights Acts made by Congress in this century:

1957 – empowered the U.S. attorney general to seek court injunctions against any violation of voting rights and made disobedience punishable as civil or criminal contempt of court.

1960 – authorized federal courts to appoint referees to help blacks to register, etc.

1964 – (1) outlawed racial discrimination in employment (later extended to apply to the aged and the handicapped) and voter registration, (2) expedited suffrage lawsuits, and (3) abolished segregation in public accommodations.

1965 – (Voting Rights Act) – (1) authorized federal officials to register any qualified voters in any election if they were rejected, and (2) suspended discriminatory literacy tests.

1968 – outlawed discrimination in the advertising, financing, sale, or rental of houses because of race, religion, or national origin.

1970 – (Voting Rights Act) – extended the 1965 Act, (2) completely abolished literacy tests, (3) set 30 days as the residency requirement in presidential elections, and (4) lowered the voting age to 18 in all elections.   (The last provision was declared unconstitutional by the U.S. Supreme Court in Oregon v. Mitchell (400 U.S. 112) in 1970 on the ground that Congress could not extend this provision to state and local elections without a constitutional amendment.

1975 – extended the 1970 Act to 1982 and broadened it to cover bilingual ballots in certain areas.

1982 – (Voting Rights Act Amendments) – amended the Voting Rights Act of 1965 to extend the effect of certain provisions for 25 years.

Four Civil Rights Acts (or 1866, 1870, 1871 and 1875)

decisions[2] pursuant to a string of Amendments to the United States Constitution.[3] On March 21, 1972, the U.S. Supreme Court declared invalid lengthy state (one year) and local (90 days) residency requirements and suggested 30 days as sufficient.[4] On October 31 of the same year, the three-

---

were enacted by Congress after the Civil War. Some provisions were struck out by the Supreme Court (such as the public accommodations provisions declared unconstitutional in the Civil Rights cases of 1883) or were amended or repealed by Congress. However, the major provisions in the Acts of 1866, 1870 and 1871 still survive and remain on the books today, though the section numbers have been redesignated.

[2]The divices used by the white Southerners to disfranchised have been out lawed by the U.S. Constitutional Amendments, congressional acts, and judicial decisions:

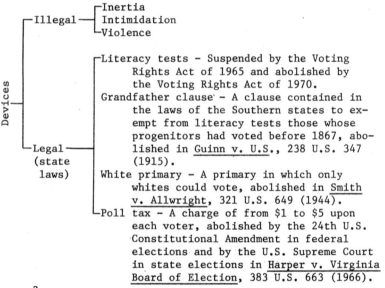

Devices

Illegal
- Inertia
- Intimidation
- Violence

Legal (state laws)
- Literacy tests – Suspended by the Voting Rights Act of 1965 and abolished by the Voting Rights Act of 1970.
- Grandfather clause – A clause contained in the laws of the Southern states to exempt from literacy tests those whose progenitors had voted before 1867, abolished in Guinn v. U.S., 238 U.S. 347 (1915).
- White primary – A primary in which only whites could vote, abolished in Smith v. Allwright, 321 U.S. 649 (1944).
- Poll tax – A charge of from $1 to $5 upon each voter, abolished by the 24th U.S. Constitutional Amendment in federal elections and by the U.S. Supreme Court in state elections in Harper v. Virginia Board of Election, 383 U.S. 663 (1966).

[3]14th Amendment – Penalty to reduce a state's representation in Congress due to denial of suffrage;
15th Amendment – No racial discrimination in voting;
19th Amendment – No sexual discrimination in voting;
24th Amendment – No poll tax in federal elections;
26th Amendment – Voting age at all elections: 18.

[4]Dunn v. Blumstein, 405 U.S. 330 (1972).

judge federal district court in Kansas City formally declared the application of this ruling to all elections in Missouri. Since then all American citizens from other states have the right to vote in any election in Missouri after having resided therein for 30 days.

The Missouri Constitution[5] and court decisions establish six qualifications for voting in Missouri today:

1. U.S. citizenship[6] 2. 30 days' residence in Missouri
3. Age 18   4. No mental incapacity
5. Not convicted of felony or crime connected with voting
6. Pre-registration not later than 28 days before the election

Presently there is no compulsory voting in the United States. However, compulsory voting was required in Kansas City, Missouri, in the 1890's but was abolished by the Missouri Supreme Court[7] in 1896. Since all qualified voters have the right to vote in the United States, universal suffrage prevails.

Registration[8]

To prevent voting frauds, registration before voting is required in Missouri. There are two forms of registration: permanent and periodic. Missouri adopts a permanent registration system. Under this system, a voter, once registered, need not re-register and his name remains on the registration records until he moves, dies, or changes his name. Periodic registration requires all voters to register annually or at fixed intervals; otherwise they will forfeit their voting privileges.[9] All voters must be properly registered by 5:00 p.m. on the fourth Wednesday before an election in Missouri. A voter's name is checked against a roster of registered voters at the polls. A qualified voter may also register by

---

[5] Mo. Const. art. 8, sec. 2.

[6] Ironically at one time aliens could vote in some states. The last state to drop this practice was Arkansas in 1926.

[7] Kansas City v. Whipple, 136 Mo. 475 (1896).

[8] The registration system was first used in Massachusetts in 1800. Registration is required in every state today except North Dakota.

[9] About 36 states use the permanent registration system; all others periodic.

mail in cases of illness, disability, religious practices, incarceration, and so on.

Absentee voting

Any qualified voter in Missouri has the right to vote by mail when away from home, or even outside the United States, or because of illness, religious belief, physical disability, etc. on election day.

Ballots

Missouri, as well as other states, adopts the so-called Australian ballot,[10] which is a secret ballot printed at state expense. With variations based on the voting device available, it is used in all public elections. It lists the candidates' names and ballot issues, usually with a blank line for voters to write in a name not printed on the ballot for an office-- so-called "write-in" votes.[11]

There are two types of ballots: the party-column[12] and office-group.[13] The party-column ballot lists all candidates vertically under the name and symbol[14] of their party but grouped separately under the various offices being sought. In the primary election, each party has a separate ballot. In the general election, all parties are printed on one ballot with each party having one column containing all its candidates nominated in the August primary. Alongside the party columns on the ballot is a "non-partisan" or "independent" column. The office-group ballot is a ballot in which all candidates are grouped or listed under offices sought with each candidate's party indicated alongside his name.

---

[10] Originally used in Australia, the ballot listed the names of candidates without party designations. Since Kentucky first adopted this type of ballot in 1888, all other states followed suit, but with party designations thereon.

[11] In 1954, by means of write-in votes, Strom Thurmond was elected U.S. Senator in South Carolina.

[12] Known as the Indiana ballot because it was first used in Indiana in 1889.

[13] Known as the Massachusetts ballot because it was first used in Massachusetts in 1888.

[14] In Missouri, the symbol of the Democratic Party on the ballot is not a "donkey" but a drawing of the statue of liberty.

Missouri uses the party-column ballot. Both its primary and general election ballots are long ballots. The constitutional, initiative, referendum, and judicial ballots are short ballots. Voting machines or punchcard devices are now used in many cities and counties in Missouri.[15]

"Write-in" Votes in Missouri

In Missouri, a voter wishing to vote for one or more candidates not listed on the ballot may draw a line through the printed name of the candidate for such office and write below the canceled name the name of the person for whom he wishes to vote. He then places a cross mark in the square at the left of such name.

THE ELECTORAL PROCESS

NOMINATION

The electoral process consists of two steps: nomination and election. Nomination is the act of proposing a person as a candidate for election to public office. There are four principal methods of nomination:

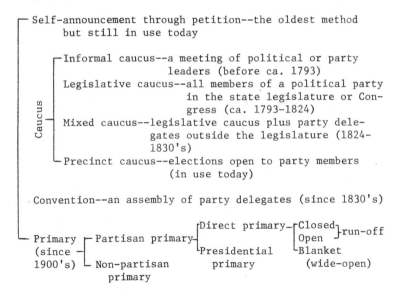

Self-announcement through petition--the oldest method but still in use today

Caucus
- Informal caucus--a meeting of political or party leaders (before ca. 1793)
- Legislative caucus--all members of a political party in the state legislature or Congress (ca. 1793-1824)
- Mixed caucus--legislative caucus plus party delegates outside the legislature (1824-1830's)
- Precinct caucus--elections open to party members (in use today)

Convention--an assembly of party delegates (since 1830's)

Primary (since 1900's)
- Partisan primary
  - Direct primary--Closed, Open }run-off
  - Presidential primary--Blanket (wide-open)
- Non-partisan primary

---

[15]For quick and accurate counting, the IBM votomatic is

Self-announcement

Self-announcement is the oldest form of nomination but is still in use today. Whoever aspires to a public office may just declare his candidacy, though normally his declaration must be endorsed by a petition signed by a stipulated number of voters.[16]

Caucus

However, through the decades of early American history it was King Caucus that flourished as a nominating method. At first a handful of political bosses met informally in a "smoke-filled" room to put forward their favorite choices. After the rise of the political parties, the legislative caucus--all members of a party in the legislature--selected their party candidates for state offices, while congressional caucuses separately nominated their presidential and vice-presidential candidates. Criticized for being unrepresentative and undemocratic, the legislative caucus was soon replaced by the mixed caucus. The mixed caucus was composed of a party caucus plus the party delegates elected from the districts unrepresenated by that party in the legislature. By the 1830's King Caucus[17] had been buried, on both national and state levels, by the convention system as a device to nominate candidates.

---

used in Missouri. A new device features a ballot printed on a punch card, and the voter just punches the spots beside the names of the candidates for whom he votes with a pencil-like stylus. The punched holes on the cards are then counted by computers.

[16] Senator Harry Byrd from Virginia announced his candidacy as an independent for U.S. senator in 1970 and 1976, and was elected twice. The "write-in" candidate need not file a petition.

[17] The major reasons for the demise of King Caucus are (1) its violation of the separation of powers rule, (2) its unrepresentative nature, and (3) manipulation by a small ruling clique with such tricks as "snap caucus" and "packed caucus." The "snap caucus" was held on such a short notice or even without notice that most of the party members could not attend so that the ruling clique might dictate nominations. Caucus packing was that word was passed out in advance to the friends of the ruling clique to come early to occupy the seats in a small meeting room.

Today a variant form of caucus is found in about fifteen states. Whatever its appellation: precinct caucus, primary-type caucus, or nominating caucus, it bears close resemblance to the primary election open to all party members. It is conducted less formally in precincts[18] to elect party candidates to local offices or delegates indirectly to the national convention. On a previously announced day, local party members in these states meet informally in caucuses or mass meetings-- in private homes, public halls, churches, schoolrooms, or even fire stations--to elect precinct delegates to county conventions, which in turn elect delegates to congressional district conventions and then to state conventions. In some states, county conventions may elect delegates to congressional district conventions and to state conventions at the same time. Then from state conventions state delegates are chosen to the national convention. Other state delegates may be elected at large. From the local level up, Democrats, in all states except Illinois, adopt the proportional representation system-- to apportion delegates in proportion to the votes each candidate has received. In other words, the total number of state delegates for each candidate is fixed in the Democratic caucus elections.[19] Republican permit "winner-take-all" voting, except in California where the practice is optional at the state level. In some states the caucus election of both parties is open to all those who will be eligible to vote in the November election.

Convention[20]

---

[18]The precinct is the basic party unit, a district comprising several city blocks or a rural neighborhood and often serving as an election district.

[19]Iowa was the first state to hold a precinct caucus election in 1980 (January 21). There were fifty state delegates from Iowa to the 3331-delegate Democratic National Convention in New York City on August 11, 1980. As Jimmy Carter received 59.1% of the votes in 2531 precinct caucuses and Ted Kennedy only 31.2%, Carter won 29 Iowa state delegates to the August convention, while Kennedy won only 15. The number of Democratic delegates determined for each candidate in precinct elections is binding, but not the Republican delegates.

[20]By 1804, conventions were already used throughout the states in the Atlantic seaboard area. A state convention was held in New York in 1824 and in Missouri as early as 1828. By 1840, state conventions had been widely held in the northeastern states.

A convention is an assembly of party delegates at the
national, state, or local level to nominate candidates for
elective officers and to decide upon party policy and strategy. In most states both parties hold county and state conventions annually. A national party convention is held
every four years to elect presidential and vice-presidential
candidates.[21] The state delegates to the national convention
are chosen either by subsidiary (county or congressional district) conventions[22] or by party voters directly in presidential primaries.

Primary

At the turn of this century the primary[23] was gradually
replacing the convention as a nominating system in states.
There are two kinds of primary: direct and presidential.
The direct primary is so-called because the candidates selected in direct primaries (in Missouri in August), unlike
presidential nominees, can enter the (November) general election races "direct" without any more hurdles on their way.
A presidential nominee, on the contrary, has to be elected
by the party convention, no matter how overwhelmingly victori-
ous he emerges from the presidential primaries. Many presidential primary winners didn't win presidential nominations
at the party conventions such as Estes Kefauver in 1952,
though since 1972 the presidential primary has played an increasingly decisive role in party nomination.[24] Meanwhile,

---

[21]The first party which used the national convention to
nominate presidential and vice-presidential candidates was
the Anti-Masonic party in 1831. Jackson's Democrats and the
new National Republicans followed suit in 1832.

[22]The states which held conventions to pick delegates to
the national conventions in 1980 were: Missouri, Alaska, Arizona, Colorado, Delaware, Hawaii, Iowa, Maine, Minnesota, Mississippi (Democrats only), North Dakota, Oklahoma, South Carolina (Democrats only), Texas (Democrats only), Utah, Virginia,
Washington, and Wyoming.

[23]First used in Crawford County, Pennsylvania, in 1842.
Washington was the first state to establish by law the statewide primary system in 1903 and the presidential primary in
1905. After Connecticut adopted the primary system in 1955,
every state followed with some form of primary.

[24]George McGovern won nomination as the Democratic presidential candidate in 1972 and Jimmy Carter in 1976 because of
their primary victories. The reason for the growing impor-

though all states have adopted the direct primary system to nominate most national, state, and local officials, conventions and caucuses are still used for some nominations in some states.[25]

The primary may be closed, open, or blanket. The closed primary is a primary closed to all voters except a party's own members. In closed primary states, voters usually declare party affiliations and allegiance when they register or when challenged by officers at the polling places. The open primary is one which is open to all voters regardless of their party affiliations and is now used in seven states. Thus the open primary may invite crossovers or raidings,[26] that is, the voters of one party may cross party lines and vote for the weakest candidate of the rival party who they believe would be easily defeated in the general election. In Washington and Alaska, primaries are blanket or wide-open. The names of all party candidates are printed in separate columns on a single long ballot, and a voter may vote for any candidate of any party as he wishes, just as he does in a

---

tance of the presidential primary is a great increase in number in the 1970's. There were 24 presidential primaries in 1972, 30 in 1976, and 37 in 1980, contrasted with 15 in 1968, 17 in 1964, 16 in 1960.

In 1980, 31 states and two territories held presidential primaries for both parties and four states for one party only. The two territories were the District of Columbia and Puerto Rico. The four states were Texas, South Carolina, Mississippi (only Republican primaries) and Arkansas (Democratic primary).

[25]Three states, Connecticut, Delaware, and Indiana, retain the convention system to nominate senators or representatives or state-wide officers. New York dropped the convention system in 1967. There are pre-primary conventions in Colorado, Idaho, and Utah, that is, a party convention held before the primary election nominates candidates to be considered in the primary. Connecticut and Massachusetts have challenge primaries, allowing challenges in the primaries by those failing to win the convention nominations.

[26]For instance, many Republican party voters are alleged to have "raided" the Democratic primaries in 1972 to vote for Democratic candidate George McGovern, because they felt he was the weakest candidate of the Democratic party and would be the easiest one to be defeated by Nixon.

63

general election. In the open primary, however, the voter can only vote for the candidates of one party.

Generally, a candidate who polls the most votes in the primary wins his party nomination. In some eleven Southern states, a candidate who receives the Democratic nomination is almost certain to be elected. Therefore, in those states a majority vote is required in primary elections. If no one polls a majority vote, a run-off primary is held between the top two candidates in the first primary election.

Non-partisan primaries are used to nominate state legislators in Minnesota and Nebraska and judicial and local officers in several other states. In the non-partisan primary all qualified voters may participate and the names of candidates appear on the ballot through voter petitions without party designation. If one candidate receives a majority of the total votes cast, he is declared elected; otherwise, there will be a run-off election between the top two.

NOMINATIONS IN MISSOURI

Direct Primary

State and local elective officers in Missouri are nominated by the direct primary, which is supposed to be a closed one. But actually it is more open than closed. A registered voter may be handed any party ballot upon request without being challenged or asked to show party identification by election officials.

Filing for Candidacy

To seek nomination by either party, a candidate must file a written declaration of candidacy with an appropriate election official--the secretary of state for offices above the county-level; and the county clerk or the board of election commissioners both known as election authorities, for any county office. A board of election commissioners is established in (1) a county with over 900,000 population, (2) a city not situated in a county, (3) a city with over 300,000 population (on January 1, 1978) and situated in more than one county, (4) a first-class county containing part of a city with over 300,000 population, and (5) a first-class county which elects to have such a board. Each candidate seeking nomination by one of the two major political parties must pay a filing fee to the treasurer of the party's state or county committee.

64

Figure 4.1 Where to File and How Much to Pay

Office Sought	Where to File	Fee	To Whom
Presidential elector	Secretary of		
U.S. senator	state	$100	Treasurer of
Statewide office	"	"	the party's
U.S. representative	"	$50	state com-
Circuit judge	"	"	mittee
State senator[27]		"	"
State representative	"	$25	"
County offices	Election	"	Treasurer of
Associate circuit	Authority		the party's
judge		"	county
			committee

There is no cross-filing in Missouri.[28] The state
election law prohibits a candidate from filing for more than
one office or the same office on more than one ballot at the
same election. The deadline for filing is 5 p.m. on the last
Tuesday in April before the August primary. After filing,
the candidate's name appears on the primary ballot. Separate
ballots are printed for each of the major parties.

Vacancy in Candidacy

At the prescribed time, an appropriate party nominating
committee--county, legislative or congressional district, or
state--may select by a majority vote a party candidate for
nomination to an office on the primary ballot if there is a
vacancy in candidacy due to the death, withdrawal, disqualification of all candidates.[29] But if the death, withdrawal,
or disqualification of an incumbent party candidate creates
a vacancy on the primary ballot, filing for the office will
be reopened for five working days for new candidates to

---

[27]The state senator files a declaration of candidacy with
the secretary of state if the district covers more than one
county, but with an election authority if the district is entirely within a county or in St. Louis City.

[28]A few states have permitted "double" or "cross" filing
in the primary elections. California abandoned this system
in 1959 after its 45-year existence. In New York candidates
often get one major and one minor party nominations, but
seldom two major party nominations.

[29]§115.363, RSMo 1978

file.[30] If death or withdrawal occurs after the third Friday
before the primary election, the election and canvass will
still go on with the incumbent's name on the ballot. If he
receives the most votes and is elected as the party candidate,
an appropriate party committee may by a majority vote select
a substitute to run for that office in the general election.

Missouri primary elections are held on the first Tuesday
after the first Monday in August in even numbered years. After
the polls are closed on the primary election day, ballots are
counted. Whichever candidate receives the most votes is nominated as the party's candidate for the general election. The
primary winner is the only candidate of that party for that
office. After the primary, should a candidate die or become
disqualified before the second Monday prior to the general
election or withdraw before the eighth Tuesday prior to the
general election, an appropriate party nominating committee
may select a substitute to run for that office.[31]

No Presidential Primary in Missouri

There is no presidential primary in Missouri, although
several efforts have been made to pass a law mandating one.
The primary is an integral part of the electoral process[32]
and is therefore subject to state regulation. In this con-
nection, all expenses for primary elections are paid by the
state, just as for general elections. As estimated in 1979,
the presidential primary would cost Missouri $325,000 a year.

In 1980, the Missouri Democrats sent 77 delegates to the
national convention in New York City, August 11-14: 53 elected
at congressional district conventions, 17 selected at large
at the Democratic state convention, and seven (7) chosen by
Democratic officials from the party. The Republicans sent
37 state delegates to the national convention in Detroit,
July 14-18: three (3) elected by each congressional district
convention and seven (7) by the state convention.

An Independent Candidate

In filing as an independent candidate for a statewide
office, one must present a petition signed by the number of

---

[30] §115.361,RSMo 1978

[31] §§115.363 & 115.359, RSMo 1978

[32] U.S. v. Classic, 313 U.S. 299 (1941)

registered voters equal to at least (1) 1 percent of the
legal voters in each of the state's congressional districts,
or (2) 2 percent in each of at least five congressional districts. In filing for a district or county office, the candidate must present a petition signed by the number of registered voters equal to 2 percent of the legal voters in the
district or county. No filing fee is required of any independent candidate, a new party candidate, or a candidate for
presidential elector.

CAMPAIGN

The Missouri Campaign Finance Disclosure Law, adopted
by the 79th General Assembly in 1978, took effect on August
13, 1978. The law "provides for pre-election disclosure of
contributions and expenditures concerning candidates and
ballot issues and establishes standards of accountability
for campaign funds." The law requires all expenditures and
contributions to be made through the treasurer of a committee formed by each candidate himself. It limits cash contributions to $49.99 and forbids anonymous contributions of
more than $10. It requires each expenditure of $20 or more
to be paid by a check. It exempts a candidate who receives
no more than $500 from reporting, but requires contributors
of more than $50 to be reported by name and address. "Passing
the hat" fund-raising, under certain restrictions, is permissible. Corporations and labor unions are permitted to
make contributions and expenditures for a political campaign,
but discrimination or intimidation relating to elections is
strictly prohibited. Above all, the law requires each candidate and committee to file a statement of organization along
with disclosure reports of receipts and expenditures for
every election.

The law establishes a six-member bipartisan campaign
finance review board to supervise the enforcement of the
election law. The board is charged with auditing the campaign
reports and statements submitted by candidates and committees
and investigating any law violations. The six members are
appointed by the governor, with Senate consent, for a staggered term of six years. Two members are of the governor's
own choice, while the others are nominated by the state committee chairmen of the two parties, the president pro tem of
the Senate, and the speaker of the House of Representative.

ELECTION

The general election is held on the first Tuesday after
the first Monday in even numbered years unless a different

day is fixed by the General Assembly upon the concurrence of two-thirds of all members in each house. Municipal elections may be held on the first Tuesday after the first Monday in February or March, and in April, June, August and November. The election authority in each county shall choose either February or March date, but not both dates for the same political subdivision. All elections are open and free. To encourage a high turnout in elections, every employee is given a three-hour break for voting without the loss of pay. Voters are privileged from arrest while on their way to, from, or at polling places, except in cases of treason, felony or breach of the peace.

In the general election, if a voter wishes to vote a "straight (party) ticket"--to vote for all Republican or all Democratic candidates for every office--he places a cross (X) mark in the circle immediately below the party designation. If he wishes to vote what is commonly known as the "split ticket"--to vote for some from one party and others from another party--he may mark "X's" in the squares to the left of the names of candidates for whom he wishes to vote. He may also place an "X" in the circle immediately below one party designation and mark "X's" in the squares at the left of the names of candidates on the other ticket for whom he wishes to vote. The squares so marked take precedence over the cross marked in the circle. On short ballots used for voting for judges under the Non-partisan Selection of Judges Plan,[33] for constitutional amendments, or for initiative propositions, the voter marks an "X" in the box opposite "Yes" or "No". Missouri voters also have the option of "write-in" votes.

Final results are formally announced by a verification board within two weeks of the election. The verification board is composed of the county clerk and two judges appointed by him from the two names submitted by the county committees of the two major parties. In an area where there is a board of election commissioners, it serves as the verification board.

The Office of Secretary of State and the Campaign Finance Review Board are responsible for statewide elections. The bipartisan board of election commissioners is composed of four members appointed by the governor with senatorial approval. The election authorities prepare ballots, appoint

---

[33]Commonly known as the "non-partisan court plan". See Chapter XI.

election judges, lay out voting precincts, set up polling
places, appoint precinct officials to preside at the polls
on election days, mail out absentee ballots, issue certificates to the winners of elections within the county, and submit complete election returns to the secretary of state.
Each election authority appoints four election judges or
more (half from each major party) from the persons nominated by each party's county committee for each polling
place and two of them (one from each party) as supervisory
judges. Each board of election commissioners, however, may
appoint election judges for individual elections.

Figure 4.2 A List of Elective Officials in Missouri

National	State	Circuit Districts	County	Munici- pality
Presidential	Governor	Circuit	County	Mayor
Vice-presi-	Lt. Governor	judges	court	Councilmen
dential	Secretary	(most	judges	Aldermen
electors	of state	elected	Associate	Trustees
Senators	Auditor	out-	circuit	Municipal
Representa-	Treasurer	right;	judges	judges
tives	Attorney	some	(some	Assessor
Delegates to	General	under	under	Collector
state con-	Senators	the	the	Attorney
vention to	Representa-	"Non-	"Non-	or prose-
consider	tives	parti-	parti-	cutor
U.S. consti-	Supreme	san	san	Treasurer,
tutional	Court &	Court	Court	etc.
amendment	Court of	Plan")	Plan")	
proposals	Appeals	Circuit	County	
(only once	judges	clerk	clerk	
to date:	(after one-		Recorder	
the 21st	year guber-		of deeds	
Amendment)	natorial		Prosecut-	
	appointment		ing At-	
	under the		torney	
	"Non-partisan		Sheriff	
	Court Plan")		Assessor	
	Delegates to		Collector	
	constitu-		of revenue	
	tional con-		Treasurer	
	vention		Coroner	
	called to		Public ad-	
	revise the		ministrator	
	state con-		Surveyor	
	stitution		Auditor	

INITIATIVE AND REFERENDUM[34]

People not only can hire and fire government officials
by election and recall but also can directly participate in
lawmaking through the initiative and referendum.

The initiative is a procedure whereby a specific number
of voters propose by petition a new statute (statutory initiative) or constitutional amendment (constitutional initiative)
and submit it to popular vote (direct initiative) or submit
a statutory proposal to the legislature first and then to the
electorate if the legislature rejects it (indirect initiative).
The referendum is the process of submitting to popular vote
a constitutional proposal (constitutional referendum) or a
statute passed or proposed by the legislature or by popular
initiative (legislative referendum). Briefly, the initiative
is a device whereby voters propose a measure to the legislature or the electorate for approval, while the referendum
is a device whereby voters approve or reject the measure
passed or proposed by a legislative body or by popular initiative.

The legislative referendum may be mandatory or optional
(advisory). The mandatory referendum requires new legislation to wait for a specific length of time, usually 60 to 90
days, before it goes into effect. If during this period a
referendum is requested by a stipulated number of voters, the
act will not take effect until after it has been approved by
voters at the next election. The optional or advisory referendum permits the legislature to voluntarily refer a measure
to voters in order to ascertain popular sentiments. As the
initiative and referendum on constitutional amendments have
been discussed in Chapter I, the following describes how
statutes are directly proposed and approved or rejected by
the voters in Missouri.

INITIATIVE AND REFERENDUM IN MISSOURI[35]

Initiative petitions for statutes must be signed by at
least 5 percent (8 percent for constitutional amendments) of

---

[34]The initiative and referendum for state legislation
were first adopted by South Dakota in 1898. Today about 23
states have adopted these two devices directly to control
legislation, but Maryland and New Mexico provide for referendum only. There is no initiative or referendum at the
national level in the United States.

[35]Mo. Const. art. 3, secs. 49-53.

the legal voters in each of two-thirds of the congressional district in the state. Each petition shall contain no more than one subject clearly expressed in the title. It must be filed with the secretary of state no less than four months before the election. If approved by a majority of the votes cast thereon at the general election in November or at an earlier special election called by the General Assembly,[36] the law takes effect after the election unless otherwise stipulated in the Missouri Constitution. However, the initiative must not be used for the appropriation of any money not raised by the same proposal or for any other purpose prohibited by the Constitution.

A referendum may be ordered either by a petition signed by 5 percent of the legal voters in each of two-thirds of the congressional districts, or by the General Assembly. Any law enacted by the General Assembly may be subject to the referendum except (1) laws necessary for the immediate preservation of public peace, health or safety; and (2) laws making appropriations for the current expenses of the state government, for the maintenance of state institutions, and for the support of public schools. Legislative reapportionments are not subject to the referendum either.[37]

Referendum petitions must be filed with the secretary of state not later than 90 days after the adjournment of the session of the General Assembly which passed the bill. The referendum may be held at the next general election or at an earlier special election called by the General Assembly.[38] The measure takes effect if approved by a majority of the votes cast thereon and is not subject to the governor's approval.

From 1945 through 1982, six propositions[39] were made, and four statutes ordered, by initiative petitions to be submitted to referenda. Three of the six propositions were adopted in 1974, 1976, and 1982 respectively, while all four statutes were rejected. Two statutes submitted to referenda ordered by the General Assembly in 1955 were both approved, but the one submitted in 1982 was rejected.

In 1980, a controversy arose as to whether the names

[36,38]Ibid., sec. 52 (b). There may be errors. According to Article 12, Section 2 (b), it is the governor who calls for special elections.

[37]Ibid., secs. 2 & 7.

[39]A PROPOSITION is a proposed law.

could be withdrawn from an initiative petition already filed
with the Office of Secretary of State. A petition to limit
government spending had been filed before the July 4, 1980
deadline to be placed on the November 4 election ballot.
Suddenly in September, 1178 signers asked for withdrawal of
their names from the petition. Following the same traditional procedure he had used with other petitions, Secretary of State James C. Kirkpatrick accepted their requests
on the ground that he had not certified the petition yet.
Thereupon, the petition fell short of signatures for ballot status, and the secretary of state declared it invalid.
Immediately the Missouri Farm Bureau and the Taxpayers
Survival Association challenged his stand in the state Supreme Court. On October 9, the Court ruled in the plaintiff's favor,[40] declaring that, since no signature could
be added to the petition after the deadline, no name should
be taken off after the deadline.

Shortly afterwards a law[41] was enacted by the Missouri
legislature allowing withdrawal of signatures by affidavit
and took effect on January 1, 1981.

The law was challenged but upheld at the Cole County
Circuit Court in 1982 when a petition for the creation of a
citizens utility board was taken off the November 2 election
ballot. After over 350 signers had withdrawn their names
from the petition, Secretary of State Kirkpatrick ruled that
the petition fell short of the needed signatures to meet
state ballot requirements. On September 20, the State Supreme Court overturned the circuit court's decision and
ordered the issue to be put back on the ballot.[42] A state
law, declared the state's highest court on October 7, allowing people to withdraw their signatures from initiative
petition is unconstitutional.

---

[40] *Missouri Farm Bureau Federation v. Kirkpatrick*, 603
SW 2d 947 (1980).

[41] §116.110, RSMo Supp. 1980.

[42] *Rekart, et al. v. Kirkpatrick, et al.*, No. 64372 (Mo.
banc), September 20, 1982.

CHAPTER V DYNAMICS OF POLITICS

POLITICAL PARTIES

THE AMERICAN PARTY SYSTEM

Briefly, a political party is a voluntary association of individuals who, with some ideological consensus, organize to gain and maintain control over governmental power. The political party system may be classified as a one-party, two-party or multi-party system.[1] The United States is a two-party system country,[2] because at the national level there are the Democratic and Republican parties dominating the scene and alternating in government. A two-party system does not mean only two parties but only two major parties. There are a bewildering number of third or minor parties in the United States.

American Political Parties

The dominant American political parties are characterized by decentralization of party power, lack of discipline, loose coalition of factions, moderate platforms, and a pragmatic approach to contemporary issues without embracing a hard and fast political creed. True, both the Democratic and Republican parties are actually controlled by their state and local organizations rather than by their national party ma-

---

[1] In an authoritarian or totalitarian state there is only one political party, though sometimes attached to it is a string of minor parties as window-dressing. Multi-party systems are typical of continental European democracies, a system in which more than two major parties exist. However, recent trends have been drifting toward a two-party system in Europe. Totalitarianism is characterized by total control of people in every way of life by the government, while an authoritarian state controls only people's political lives.

[2] The chief reasons behind the American two party system are (1) influence by the British two-party tradition, (2) a single-member district system with plurality vote to elect government officers (one of two major parties invariably wins and the minor parties, unable to gain plurality, always lose), (3) no sharp class consciousness in American society, (4) the inherent dualism of American political issues, and (5) the idea of the two-party system having been part of American political socialization, which is the process of acquiring political ideas, systems and roles from one's family, friends, media, environment, etc.--through involvement in society.

chines, which have prestige but little power. Unlike the
closely-knit and tightly-controlled parties in totalitarian
countries, the two parties each are held loosely together
by an inner group of leaders and organization activists,
the so-called party members being but voters in the strict
sense. Again unlike the German Nazi party founded on racism
or the Communist party built upon anti-capitalist Marxism,
both parties refrain from taking firm and extreme ideological stands to avoid frightening away potential supporters.
Therefore, being more pragmatic than doctrinaire, they wave
moderate-hued flags to attract as many voters as possible
from all sides. However, inside each party there are entrenched a variety of factions constantly at loggerheads on
various ideological grounds.

Though the American Constitution is silent on political
parties, the Missouri Constitution has not left them out.[3]
The Missouri law regulates primaries and elections, campaign
funds, the organization of established parties, the formation of new ones, and many other relevant matters. The
parties, therefore, have a definite legal status in Missouri
as well as in other states. They organize and run governments and dominate politics. So they are at least quasi-
or semi-public legal organizations, by no means entirely
private groups like interest or pressure groups.

Party Functions[4]

The basic functions of the parties in the United States
are to put candidates before voters for election to public
office and to run the government after elections. But they
may also serve as a unifying force to harmonize various
branches of government and to hold together vitally important
but highly divergent interests. They may also crystalize
amorphous and diverse public opinions and channel them into
effective streams of political influence. In parliamentary
democracies, the party in the wilderness serves as a loyal
opposition. It scrutinizes and criticizes the policies and
administration of the government, offers alternate programs
and tactics, and stands ready to pick up the reins of government whenever it wins elections.

Yet in the United States there are still third parties

---

[3]Mo. Const. art. 3, sec. 7.

[4]The totalitarian government uses the party to indoctri-
nate (brainwash) and control the people.

coming and going on the national scene. Consistently kept
off the ballot by state laws with inordinate requirements,
lacking abundant resources for skyrocketing campaign costs,
and meanwhile having no future to attract political talents,
no favors to dispense to supporters, and no moderate platforms (their ideology is generaly radical) to woo voters,
they are doomed to failure from the outset. Yet they still
fight on indefatigably. Waving their bloody shirts and rais-
ing battle cries, they can tip the balance of the two established parties and influence the outcome of elections. They
at least can crystallize dissenting opinions and turn them
into vociferous protests. They may therefore force the major
parties to yield to some of their radical issues. More often
than not, they blaze trails in reforms and the major parties
steal their thunder.

Political Ideologies[5]

Political ideology is a coherent and consistent set of
beliefs and values which lead to specific perceptions and
attitudes about political issues, economic order, social
concerns, and moral values, and, meanwhile, appeal to emotion,
arouse action, and provide strategic guidance for its reali-
zation. Ideology may fall into five basic categories as
follows:

Figure 5.1 Five Basic Political Ideologies

(Radical left)				(Radical right)
Radical	Liberal	Moderate	Conservative	Reactionary
				(Extreme rightism)
Left		Center		Right

The liberals continually seek changes, progress, and reforms; while the radicals are disposed to sweeping or revo-
lutionary changes, astonishing progress and thorough reforms.
The conservatives, in the strict sense, defend and rationalize
the existing order or the status quo. However, they are, by
no means, diametrically opposed to any innovation, change or
reform, but uphold it if such change would not destroy the
fundamental traditional values and bring what they consider

---

[5]The term "ideology" appears to have been coined by
French philosopher Destuit de Tracy in 1796. Its original
meaning is "science of ideas."

to be adverse effects. Put simply, conservatism may make no change or rather slow and cautious changes, gradual progress and absolutely needed reforms[6] as compared with the faster pace of liberalism. But the difference among these ideologies is not merely in velocity of change but also in matters of strategy, approach, and action. Neither as fast as liberalism nor so slow to change as conservatism is moderation, the mainstream of American ideologies. The reactionary tends to return to an older outworn order and is always derogatory.

The terms "left" and "right" are derived from the seating order in most continental European legislatures. There the seats are arranged in a semicircle with the radical party (Communist party) deputies sitting at the extreme left, the reactionary party (Fascist party) at the extreme right, and others in a descending order respectively from the two extremes toward the center according to their political tinges. Products of the French Revolution[7] and of the widespread European tradition, these two terms have now become popular and sophisticated words in politics and history.

There is much truth to the "Tweedledum and Tweedledee" image of the two major parties, because they appear only slightly different in their basic ideologies or even in their general programs. Both of them are cautiously walking the tightrope of the "middle of the road" ideology. They may lean toward liberalism (left of the center) or conservatism (right of the center), but they would never swing too far to either side lest they should alienate potential voters. Nevertheless, these two parties are still not entirely identical in ideologies. The Democrats are slightly more liberal than the Republicans. Stressing the equality of individuals (equalitarianism), the Democrats are more concerned with the lot of the poor and minority groups and for wider social welfare, a bigger governmental role and greater governmental intervention in the economy, particularly regulation of busi-

---

[6] A new term for this kind of conservatism is "reformist ideology." Roy C. Macridis, Contemporary Political Ideologies (Cambridge, Massachusetts: Winthrop Publishers, 1980), p.9.

[7] The terms originated from the seatings in the National Assembly in Paris in the summer of 1789. In the horse-shoe-shaped amphitheatre where the Assembly met, the conservatives sat to the right of the presiding officer, the radicals to the left and the liberals in the center. Reo M. Christenson et al., Ideologies and Modern Politics (New York: Harper & Row Publishers Inc., 1981), p.2.

ness, besides broader international commitment. The Republicans, emphasizing the liberty of individuals, are more for individualism, free enterprise, private initiative and more spending on defense. The Democrats draw more support from labor, blacks, Jews, Catholics, and the low-income class; while the Republicans more from rural, suburban and small town dwellers, the high-income class, Protestants, businessmen, and professionals.

Party Decline

Not only has ticket-splitting increased during recent decades, but party affiliation is also declining. The loosening of family ties in the wake of the widening generation gap has contributed to the decline of party loyalty. But the growing influence of interest groups, the popularity of primaries, the rising interest in issues and candidates, the growth of the merit system to sap party patronage, the socializing effects of mass media to bring voters directly into contact with candidates, the dwindling party cohesion through intense battles fought within, and particularly the increasing disillusionment with the parties after a rash of political scandals, all acount for party decline.

POLITICAL PARTIES IN MISSOURI

Although well entrenched in national politics, the two party system does not fare well in all states. At the state level there are three types of party systems:[8] (1) the two-party states; (2) the modified one party states--only one party wins most elections, though both parties maintain organizations and contend for offices; and (3) the one party states where one of the two parties is merely a pale shadow. The South, which has been known as the "Solid South" since Reconstruction days because of Democratic domination, and Northern New England, which used to be a Republican stronghold, are comprised of one party states. Today, however, the Solid

---

[8]Modified one-party Democratic states: Missouri, Florida, Hawaii, Kentucky, Maryland, Massachusetts, New Mexico, North Carolina, Oklahoma, Rhode Island, Tennessee, Virginia, and West Virginia; modified one-party Republican states: Colorado, Idaho, Kansas, North Dakota, South Dakota, Vermont, and Wyoming; one-party states: Alabama, Arkansas, Georgia, Louisiana, Mississippi, South Carolina, and Texas (so-called the Solid South). Other states are two-party states. Herbert Jacob and Kenneth Vines, eds., Political Parties in the American States, 3rd ed. (Boston: Little Brown, 1976), p. 62.

South is no longer solid, and the New England stronghold is no longer strong, the two rival parties having invaded each other's territory.

Missouri, A Strong Democratic State

Missouri has long been branded as a modified one-party Democratic state. So far Missouri has had only 9 Republican governors out of 47, 10 Republican lieutenant governors out of 41, and 12 U.S. Senators out of a total of 39. In this century, the Republican party has been a majority party in the state Senate only six years and in the House of Representatives only 22. On four occasions, while Republican presidential candidates won elections, Missouri chose Democratic governors. Beginning in 1904, Missouri has gone along with most other states in electing the successful presidential candidates but voted for Democratic Adlai E. Stevenson instead of incumbent Republican President Dwight D. Eisenhower in 1956. In 1980, despite the Republican ascendancy, the Democrats still dominated the 81st General Assembly (1981-1982) with an edge of 23-11 in the Senate and 111-52 in the House of Representatives. They continue to dominate the 82nd General Assembly by a majority of 22-12 in the Senate and by 110-53 in the House of Representatives. There are only three Republicans in the U.S. House of Representatives from Missouri, 1983-1984.

However, Missouri is still far from safe for the Democrats. Both parties are led by prominent leaders, maintain well-established organizations, and fight as fiercely as they can for victories at the polls. The Republicans have been making substantial gains in various offices at the state level since 1964, but have never been so successful as in 1980, and the trend seems to be moving toward their greater success. Nevertheless, the state still remains predominently democratic in local elections. So Missouri is a two-party state today, though undeniably still a strong Democratic one. Jackson county, St. Louis City, and Southeast Missouri are Democratic bastions. Much of southern Missouri, encompassed by the seventh congressional district and containing 17 counties, is a Republican stronghold. At one time, state and local parties were dominated by political machines.[9] Missouri once had a well-known Democratic machine under Boss Thomas J. Pender-

---

[9] A machine is a well-entrenched party organization in a county, city, or even in a state, and headed by a boss or small group of autocratic leaders, who monopolize power in the area. The bosses and machines which once flourished have declined in recent decades.

gast in Kansas City. There are also several minor parties in the state, but they are not strong nor even very visible.

Established Parties in Missouri

Party Organization

In structure, both the Democratic and Republican parties have the same form of pyramid with the national committee at the apex and hundreds of ward and township committees at the bottom. Within each state political party the committees correspond generally to the districts or areas which elect government officers. Thus under a state committee are arranged three layers of various district and local committees: (1) congressional, senatorial (state), judicial, and representative; (2) county and city; (3) township and ward. Though the precinct is the basic unit of party organization, it has lapsed into inactivity except at election time and there is actually no officer in charge.

Figure 5.2   Organization of the Democratic and
Republican Parties in Missouri

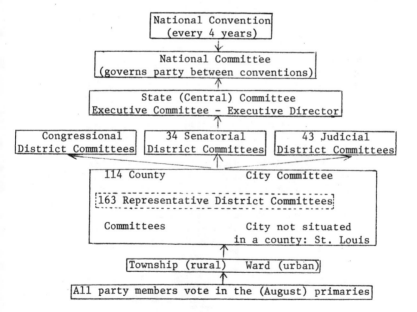

All party members elect township or ward committeemen

and committeewomen in the August primary elections, the only party officers directly elected by party members. Then from each township or ward a man and a woman are elected to a county committee. If a county has more than one representative district, the committee includes also a chairperson and a vice-chairperson from each district, and one must be a woman. Each senatorial, congressional, and judicial circuit district is composed of the chairpersons and vice-chairpersons of all county committees within the district. But if a county within the district contains wholly one or more representative districts, the (senatorial, congressional, or judicial circuit) district committee shall also include the chairperson and vice-chairperson of each representative district within the county. If the senatorial or judicial district is composed wholly or partially of a part of a city or a part of county, the district committee shall include the committeemen and committeewomen of the wards or townships in those parts. Where any district is conterminous with one county, the district committee is the county committee. The sexes are equally represented in committee membership.

All committees elect their own officers--chairperson, vice-chairperson, secretary, and treasurer. The chairperson and vice-chairperson must be committee members, and one must be female. The secretary and the treasurer do not have to be committee members, but one of them must be a woman. The Democratic and Republican state committees each are made up of 68 members, one man and one woman chosen by each of the state's 34 senatorial districts. The Democratic state committee has, besides the above-mentioned four officers, an executive director, a seven-member executive committee, three other officers, and thirteen standing committees. All officers are elected to two-year terms.

Each committee is responsible for party affairs in the area where it functions. Each is charged with planning and conducting election campaigns, advising candidates on strategy and policy, and getting out the vote on election day. In some instances, the committees have authority, pursuant to the state election laws, to nominate candidates to public offices in the event of death or withdrawal of the regularly chosen nominees.[10]

The state committee is charged with writing the party's state platforms as required by the state law, overseeing all party machinery, fostering party harmony in the state, direct-

---

[10]See Chapter IV.

ing campaigns for state officers and U.S. senators, conducting state conventions, and mobilizing state efforts for the
national ticket. The senatorial district committees campaign
for state senators, the judicial circuit district committees
for circuit judges, and the representative district committees
for state representatives. The county committees, the most
significant and vigorous unit in the party machinery, conduct
county conventions, carry on campaigns and supervise party
affairs throughout the county, coordinate the activities of
the precincts, call public meetings, advise candidates on
campaign, and nominate election judges to the county court.
The township and ward committees constitute the very backbone
of the party's working force, since they are in direct contact
with the grassroots.

The Republican National Committee is made up of two committee members from each of the state parties. The Democratic
National Committee includes the chairperson and the vice-
chairperson (the opposite sex) from each state party and also
two hundred other members apportioned to the states according
to the same formula as the delegates to the national convention, in addition to other party members.[11] In 1980, the Missouri Democratic party had seven national committee members,
four men and three women.

Delegate Selection to National Convention

Each party has its own formula to apportion delegates
among states to the national convention.[12]

---

[11]The chairperson and two other members of the Democratic
Governors' Conference, the Democratic leader and one other
person from the U.S. Senate and House, the chairperson and two
other members of the Democratic Mayors' Conference, the president and two other representatives of the Young Democrats, and
up to 25 additional members.

[12]The Democratic apportionment formula: (1) 3 delegates
for each electoral vote, and (2) additional delegates according to the Democratic votes in the last three presidential
elections (victory bonus).

The Republican apportionment formula: (1) 6 delegates
at large, (2) 3 delegates for each congressional district in
the state, and (3) "Bonus" delegates at large if the state
elected a Republican governor or senator or at least half of
its House delegation in 1976 and 1978.

Figure 5.3 Missouri Delegates to Republican
National Convention

1980

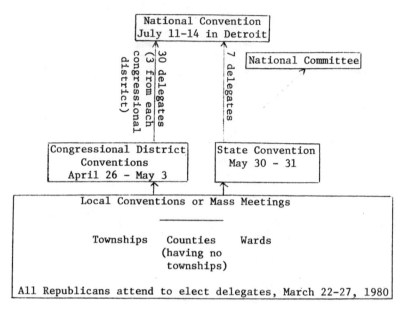

```
                    ┌─────────────────────────────┐
                    │   National Convention       │
                    │ July 11-14 in Detroit       │
                    └─────────────────────────────┘
          ↑              ↑                    ↑
  30 delegates      7 delegates         ┌──────────────────┐
  (3 from each                          │ National Committee│
  congressional                        └──────────────────┘
  district)                                      ↗
┌──────────────────────┐    ┌─────────────────┐
│ Congressional District│    │ State Convention│
│ Conventions           │    │ May 30 - 31     │
│ April 26 - May 3      │    └─────────────────┘
└──────────────────────┘              ↑
          ↑
┌────────────────────────────────────────────────┐
│     Local Conventions or Mass Meetings          │
│     ─────────────────────                       │
│   Townships   Counties      Wards               │
│               (having no                        │
│               townships)                        │
├────────────────────────────────────────────────┤
│ All Republicans attend to elect delegates, March 22-27, 1980 │
└────────────────────────────────────────────────┘
```

Figure 5.4 Missouri Delegates to Democratic
National Convention

1980

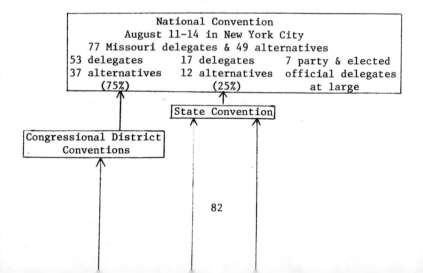

```
┌──────────────────────────────────────────────────┐
│              National Convention                  │
│          August 11-14 in New York City            │
│      77 Missouri delegates & 49 alternatives      │
│ 53 delegates       17 delegates      7 party & elected │
│ 37 alternatives    12 alternatives   official delegates│
│     (75%)             (25%)            at large   │
└──────────────────────────────────────────────────┘
        ↑           ┌──────────────────┐    ↑
                    │ State Convention │
                    └──────────────────┘
┌──────────────────────┐   ↑                ↑
│Congressional District│
│ Conventions          │
└──────────────────────┘
        ↑
```

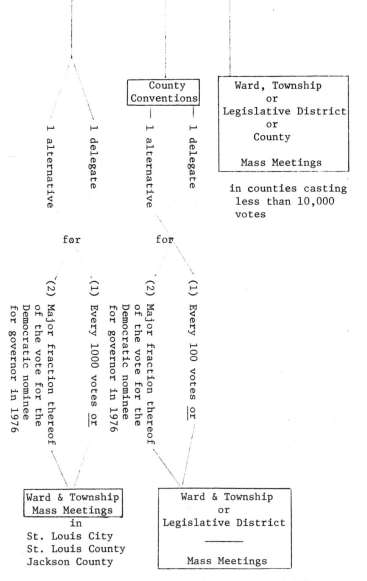

County Conventions

Ward, Township
or
Legislative District
or
County

Mass Meetings

in counties casting
less than 10,000
votes

1 alternative   1 delegate   1 alternative   1 delegate

for   for

(2) Major fraction thereof of the vote for the Democratic nominee for governor in 1976

(1) Every 1000 votes or

(2) Major fraction thereof of the vote for the Democratic nominee for governor in 1976

(1) Every 100 votes or

Ward & Township
Mass Meetings
in
St. Louis City
St. Louis County
Jackson County

Ward & Township
or
Legislative District
_____
Mass Meetings

All counties casting 10,000 or more
votes for the Democratic nominee for
governor in 1976 except St. Louis City,
St. Louis County, and Jackson County

Formation of a New Political Party in Missouri

Parties exist as legal entities if they satisfy the requirements of the state law. Any group of persons wishing
to form a new political party above the county level in Missouri must file a petition with the secretary of state; but
they must file with the election authority of the county, if
they wish to form a new party at the county level. In the
petition, the intention to form a new party must be declared
concisely, and the petition must be signed by the requisite
number of registered voters according to the Election Laws
of Missouri.[13] The political group becomes a new party after
the filing of a valid petition. The names of the new party's
candidates on the petition will appear on the ballot at the
next general or special election. Likewise the names of the
new party's presidential and vice-presidential candidates,
not those of the candidates for presidential electors, will
be placed on the official ballot at the next general presidential election.

If a new party's candidate for a statewide office receives more than 2 percent of all votes cast for the office
at the first election, the new party becomes an established
party in the state. If the candidate for an office receives
more than 2 percent of the votes cast for the office in any
district or county at the first election, the new party becomes an established party only in the district or county.
The new established party shall select all committeemen and
committeewomen necessary for a provisional party organization in the area where it has become established.

INTEREST GROUPS

An interest group is a group of people who organize to
pursue a common interest by influencing the course of public
policy. Union is strength, and so individuals who wish to
advance their interests through governmental action or inaction
must pull together before they can bring pressure effectively
to bear upon the government for the policies or issues they
favor. An interest group is therefore also known as a pressure group.[14] But this term is used less nowadays because

---

[13]§115.315, RSMo 1978.

[14]Some political scientists distinguish "pressure groups"
from "interest groups" in that the former are highly organized
in order to influence government agencies for policies favorable to them, while the latter are organized to secure public

of its slightly sinister connotation. There are thousands of interest groups at the national level in the United States and several hundred in Missouri.

Why Interest Groups?

The overriding reason underlying the rise of interest groups is legislative representation on a geographical basis. That is, our senators and representatives are elected from each district or state. Thus they represent a vast amalgam of interests in their areas in Congress or state legislatures. Since no legislator could represent, and take exclusive care of, a single interest, individuals of shared beliefs, attitudes, and objectives have to band together to look after their interests by exerting influence upon the government. Put briefly, because political parties represent sectional interests, interest groups rise to give functional representation, which cuts across geographical lines. However, though some countries have incorporated the principle of "functional" representation in the organization of their legislative bodies to supplement district representation,[15] such mixed representation still can not end lobbying activities in their capitals. Today interest groups seek to influence not only the legislatures but also the executive bureaucracies and even the judiciary, which are playing an increasingly significant role in policy-making.

Interest Groups, Political Parties, and Lobbyists[16]

---

support for activities or policies they favor. It seems that these political scientists identify special interest groups as "pressure groups" and public interest groups as "interest groups."

[15]The members of the legislative bodies in China are elected on both geographical and functional bases. The representatives in the Seanad (the upper house of the legislature) of the Republic of Ireland are elected on a functional basis, while the members of the lower house are elected on geographical lines.

In contemporary history, two states adopted the principle of functional representation instead of regional or geographical representation in their legislative bodies and established "corporate states." They are Italy (1926-1943) and Portugal (1935-1974). See Chapter VI.

[16]"Lobbyist," as defined by the Missouri law, is "any per-

The basic function of political parties is to capture public offices and to run governments, while interest groups only seek to influence specific public policies without assuming any responsibility for the conduct of government. Once candidates are elected to office, the parties are inside the government; but interest groups are always outside of it. So after all, interest groups are still private, non-governmental institutions, while political parties become somewhat quasi-official organizations. Moreover, major political parties represent broad interests as contrasted with the relatively narrow interests represented by interest groups.

Lobbyists are representatives or spokesmen employed by interest groups to influence government officers through personal contact. Lobbyists are so called because they usually talk with legislators informally in the lobbies, just off the floors of the legislative chambers. Therefore, an effort to influence the decisions of government policy-makers through personal contact is called lobbying. Though often referred to as "the third house" of the legislature or more elegantly as "legislative representatives or counsels," they actually influence executives, administrators, and even judges as well as legislators. Any level of government or any official who makes or implements government policies affecting an interest group is subject to lobbying. It is common and fallacious assumption that interest groups lobby only legislatures.

Types of Interest Groups

Interest groups may be classified as "special," "public," and "government." About two thirds of the interest groups are special groups, which represent economic or professional interests, the earliest interest groups in American history. Public interest groups, also known as citizens' lobbies, seek to represent general public interests rather than specific

---

son, other than any member of the General Assembly or elected state officer but including persons employed by or representing federal or state agencies and all political subdivisions thereof, who acts in the course of his employment or who engages himself for pay or for any valuable consideration for the purpose of attempting to influence the taking, passage, amendment, delay, or defeat of any legislative action by the legislature; or any person who receives any direct or indirect benefits or expenses for lobbying activities...from any state, the federal government or any private not for profit foundation or corporation." §105.470, RSMo 1978.

economic interests. Government groups are governmental units which organize groups to lobby other governmental agencies. Though interest groups are usually thought of as private organizations influencing governmental actions, governments themselves also have conflicting interests and consequently feel compelled to lobby one another.

I. Special (economic) Interest Groups

Business interests: Missouri Chamber of Commerce, Missouri Bankers Association.

Labor unions: Missouri State Labor Council, AFL-CIO; Teamsters Local Union, No. 833.

Agricultural groups: Missouri Farm Bureau Federation.

Professional associations: Missouri Bar Association, Missouri Pharmaceutical Association.

Veteran organizations: American Legion Department of Missouri.

II. Public (political-social) Interest Groups

Ethnic groups: National Association for the Advancement of Colored People (NAACP), Congress of Racial Equality (CORE).

Women's groups: Missouri League of Women Voters, State Women's Political Caucus.

Religious groups: Missouri Council of Churches, Missouri Baptist Convention, Missouri Catholic Conference.

Reform groups: Common Cause in Missouri, American Civil Liberties Union, Missouri Citizens for Life.

III. Government Interest Groups

Missouri Association of Counties, Missouri Municipal League, Mid-Missouri Council of Governments.

Group Targets and Techniques

The activities of interest groups are varied. They include public relations and the education of the public about the goals of the groups, but their technique and target is to influence the government at all levels.

I. Lobbying

   A. Influencing legislators--to offer written reports, to organize and draft bills to testify before committees, to make personal appeals, to speed a bill through or slow it down and defeat it, and to mobilize the organizations back home to deluge the legislatures with a flood of letters, telegrams, and petitions.

   B. Influencing executives and administrative agencies-- to urge the governor to include or delete specific measures from his proposed legislative programs, to sign or veto particular bills, and to increase or decrease an agency's budget request. Since the state legislature tends to grant broad discretionary powers to administrative agencies, interest groups influence them by appearing at their hearings to testify for or against proposed rules.

   C. Influencing courts--to participate in the selection of judges by supporting those sympathetic to their interests and opposing those considered biased against them. Local bar associations may, for instance, withdraw endorsement for elective judges. To influence the judicial process, interest groups finance lawsuits and file class actions (a lawsuit brought by an individual for himself and for all other persons in the same situation) and amicus curiae (friend of the court) briefs. Originally an amicus curiae is one who is not a party to a lawsuit but gives information on some matter of law for the assistance of a court. Utilizing this device, interest groups seek to influence court decisions in favor of the sides they espouse with their persuasive legal arguments, oral or written, in order to pursue their own interests. They also publish articles in legal periodicals, which judges may even sometimes quote as authority for their rulings.

   D. Influencing other governmental units.

II. Electioneering--to help nominate and elect their chosen candidates by mobilizing members to vote for them and making financial contributions to their campaigns.

III. Information--to furnish policy-makers with necessary and detailed information, literature, data, etc.

IV. Mobilizing the public by mass propaganda--to create a climate of favorable public opinion through mail appeals, newspaper advertisements, distribution of literature, and use of radio and television to spread propaganda about their issues.

V. Log-rolling or cooperative lobbying--to cooperate with other interest groups with similar goals so that by presenting views in concert, they are more likely to succeed than by acting alone. Such cooperation cuts across what would generally be felt divergent categories of special interests.

VI. Using the initiative and referendum--to use these two devices to pass laws or constitutional provisions or to defeat unwanted legislation or unwanted constitutional amendment proposals.

VII. Litigation--A good example is that of the NAACP ending major school segregation in the famous Brown v. Board of Education of Topeka[17] case in 1954.

VIII. Social activities--to entertain policy-makers with fancy dinners, luxurious parties, or all-expense paid trips, or even to bribe them with fabulous gifts or even money.

IX. Non-violent and violent political protests--Organized non-violent political protests include passive resistance, picketings, boycotts, sit-ins, strikes, and mass demonstrations. Interest groups may also organize violent protests to press for their issues.

INTEREST GROUPS IN MISSOURI

Though interest groups contribute to democracy and are safeguarded by Missouri constitutional rights of peaceable assembly and petitions,[18] they are still subject to state regulations.[19] A lobbyist is required to register with the chief clerk of the House of Representatives and the secretary of the Senate within five days of beginning lobbying activi-

---

[17]347 U.S. 483 (1954).

[18]Mo. Const. art. 1, sec. 9; U.S. Const. amend. I.

[19]§105.470, RSMo 1978. The U.S. law to regulate lobbying activities is-the Regulation of Lobbying Act, Title III, Legislative Reorganization Act of 1946.

ties in the General Assembly. Registration forms must be filed under oath. Meanwhile, the lobbyist has to file reports with the two houses three times a year: (1) within ten days after the convening of each session, (2) within 45 days before the adjournment of any regular session, and (3) within 30 days of the end of each session. The reports must include (1) total expenditures for lobbying purposes and an itemized statement of such expenditures; and (2) the name of the recipient and amount of each honorarium, gift or loan, service or anything of value exceeding $25; and (3) separate statements of the proposed legislation or legislative action supported or opposed. Any violation is a misdemeanor punishable by a fine of not more than $1,000 or by imprisonment for not more than one year, or both. Moreover, conviction results in the suspension of all lobbying activities for two years.

Lobbying groups have increased in number with the increase in the amount of legislation in Missouri because more bills are introduced in annual rather than biennial sessions.

CHAPTER VI

GENERAL ASSEMBLY: REPRESENTATION, POWERS AND MEMBERSHIP

Patterned after the national government and characterized by the principle of separation of powers and checks and balances, the government of Missouri comprises three branches: the legislature known as the General Assembly,[1] the executive headed by the governor, and the judiciary with the Supreme Court standing at the pinnacle of the legal pyramid. The legislature makes the laws, the executive enforces the laws, and the judiciary interprets the laws and Constitutions, federal and state, and applies them in settling disputes.

In Missouri, the General Assembly is a bicameral type of legislature composed of the Senate[2] and the House of Representatives.[3] Bicameralism, or the two-house legislature, exists in every state except Nebraska[4] where the one-house legislature is known as "unicameralism."[5] The size of both houses

---

[1]The legislature is called "state legislature" in 26 states, "general assembly" in 19, "general court" in Massachusetts and New Hampshire, and "legislative assembly" in Oregon, Montana, and North Dakota.

[2]This term is used in every state. The one-house legislature in Nebraska adopted the name of "Senate" at its first meeting, but it is not used in the Nebraska Constitution.

[3]The term "assembly" is used in California, Nevada, New York, and Wisconsin; "house of delegates" in Virginia, Maryland, and West Virginia; and "general assembly" in New Jersey.

[4]Unicameralism was first used by Vermont but abolished in 1836. In 1934, it was adopted in Nebraska under the late Senator George W. Norris.

[5]Both bicameralism and unicameralism have strengths and weaknesses; and one's strengths are the other's weaknesses. Bicameralism may prevent ill-considered legislative action and provide checks and balances to avoid the concentration of political power in a single house. Moreover, the two-house legislature may be less easily dominated by interest groups than a single house legislature and therefore less susceptible to corruption from the outside. The unicameralism avoids duplicate efforts and time, provides quick legislative action, accepts full responsibility for all legislation and ensures simpler procedure and lower cost.

in the Missouri legislature is fixed by the Constitution and therefore cannot be changed except by a constitutional amendment. There are 34 state senators and 163 representatives.[6] Comparable to the national House of Representatives, the lower or first chamber in Missouri represents population; but unlike the U.S. Senate representing the states, the Missouri upper chamber represents another population group in a different set of districts which overlap the representative districts.

REPRESENTATION[7] AND APPORTIONMENT[8]

---

[6]The size of state legislatures ranges from 20 members in the upper houses of Nevada and Alaska to 67 in Minnesota and from 40 in the lower houses of Nevada and Alaska to 400 in New Hampshire.

[7]Three kinds of legislative representation:

(1) Geographical representation--two electoral systems

    (a) Single-member district (small electoral district) system: The whole constituency (nation, state or city) is divided into as many small electoral districts as the representatives in the legislature, and each district elects one representative by:

        i. A plurality vote--Whoever receives the most votes is elected, for instance, U.S. congressional districts, Missouri state senatorial districts, and so on.

        ii. A majority vote--used in the primary elections of some 11 Southern states. If none receives a majority vote, the top two in the first election run again in a run-off election. The one who receives more votes than the other is elected.

    (b) Multi-member district (large electoral district) by proportional representation system: the whole constituency is not divided into small districts; all representatives are elected at large. Consequently, the seats in the legislature are allotted among the political parties in direct proportion to the votes they each poll in the election. This system is used in continental European countries and in a few American cities, such as New York City, for election to the city councils but never for higher legislative bodies as in Canadian provinces or Australian states.

In Missouri as well as in other states, a single member
district system is used to elect state legislators as well
as U.S. congressmen.[9] Therefore, in order to elect 34 state
senators, 163 state representatives, and 9 congressmen,[10]
the whole state of Missouri is divided into 34 senatorial
districts, 163 representative districts, and 9 congressional
districts. There is a census in the United States every ten
years.[11] After each decennial census, not only the seats in
the U.S. House of Representatives are reapportioned among
the fifty states, but the population of senatorial and representative districts in Missouri is also determined and the
whole state redistricted to reflect shifts in population.
Redistricting is the process of redrawing district lines
or bonndaries.

Drawing new districts, whether congressional, state
senatorial or representative should be based upon three
fundamental rules: contiguous territory, compactness, and

There are three methods of count: Hare system,
list system, and cumulative system.

(2) Professional or functional representation--legis-
lators are elected from economic or occupational
groups rather than from districts, for example,
the corporate state in Italy under Mussolini
(1926-1943) and Portugal (1935-1974).

(3) Mixed (geographical and functional) representation
--China, Spain, and Brazil (1934 Constitution).

[8]The allocation of legislative seats by dividing a state
into voting districts that are approximately equal in population.

[9]Missouri's single-member congressional districts were
first created in 1847. Since then Missouri's congressmen
have been elected from districts except in the 1932 election.
In 1932, the federal court overturned the Missouri redistricting plan and all thirteen congressmen were elected at large.
They were all Democrats.

[10]As a result of the 1980 census, 11 states gained seats
in the U.S. House of Representatives and 10 lost. Missouri
lost one. The gainers were Florida (4 seats), Texas (3),
California (2), and Arizona, Colorado, Nevada, New Mexico,
Oregon, Tennessee, Utah, and Washington (1 each). The losers
were New York (5), Ohio, Pennsylvania, and Illinois (2 each),
Indiana, Massachusetts, Michigan, Missouri, New Jersey, and
South Dakota (1 each).

[11]U.S. Const. art. I, sec. 2.

equality in population as near as practicable. As the Missouri Constitution categorically stipulates, "districts shall be composed of contiguous territory as compact and as nearly equal in population as may be."[12] Equal population or political equality as defined in Gray v. Sanders[13] means "one person, one vote."

To avoid unfairness in redistricting, the federal courts step into what they formerly dubbed a "political thicket" and assume jurisdiction by authority of the equal protection clause of the Fourteenth Amendment after the U.S. Supreme Court reversed itself in 1962 in the Baker v. Carr[14] decision. In 1964, the Supreme Court applied the "one person, one vote" rule to congressional districts in Wesberry v. Sanders.[15] Several months later, the Court again applied the same ruling to state legislative districts in Reynolds v. Sims.[16]

However, despite the Missouri constitutional requirement for equal population in the elective districts, gerrymandering still dominates elections in the state. Gerrymandering is a device used by a majority party in a legislature to divide a state in favor of its own party by including the rival party voters into as few districts as possible and spreading its own strength over as many as it can. To weed out this century-old politics in the state, the Missouri Constitution authorized a special bipartisan commission instead of the General Assembly to redraw senatorial districts after 1945 and state representative districts after 1966, but it still leaves the congressional apportionment in the hands of the state legislature even after a storm brewed over the congressional districting in 1981.

CONGRESSIONAL APPORTIONMENT BY THE GENERAL ASSEMBLY[17]

When the number of representatives to which the state is entitled in the U.S. House of Representatives under each

---

[12] Mo. Const. art. 3, sec. 45.

[13] Gray v. Sanders, 372 U.S. 368 (1963). Congressional Quarterly Service, Congressional Guide, Fall 1969, p.85.

[14] Baker v. Carr, 369 U.S. 186 (1962), which reversed the Colegrove v. Green (1946) ruling.

[15] Wesberry v. Sanders, 376 U.S. 1 (1964).

[16] Reynolds v. Sims, 377 U.S. 533 (1964).

[17] Mo. Const. art. 3, secs. 45, 2 & 7.

census is certified to the governor, the General Assembly shall by law divide the state into districts corresponding with the number of representatives to which it is entitled. The Assembly shall divide the population of the state by the number of the districts and establish each district in compact and contiguous territory with population as nearly equal as possible to the quotient.

In 1965, the year after <u>Reynolds v. Sims</u>, the Missouri Democrat-dominated General Assembly redistricted the state according to the "one person, one vote" rule. However, in the ensuing 1966 congressional election, the Republicans received only 20% of the seats, although they polled 46.3% of the votes. In 1967, after intervention by the three-judge federal district court in Kansas City, the General Assembly redistricted Missouri a second time. But the party gerrymandering still dominated the 1968 election. The Democrats polled only 55.9% of the statewide vote but got nine out of the ten seats in Congress. In 1969, the U.S. Supreme Court in the <u>Kirkpatrick v. Preisler</u>[18] landmark decision struck down the redistricting plan. The Court declared it unconstitutional on the ground of excessive disparities in population, as the most populous district was 3.13% above the population of average district, while the least populous district was 2.83% below. Some districts were over-represented, while others were markedly under-represented. Upholding Preisler's argument that the plan violated the "one person, one vote" doctrine, the Court ruled that no geographical or political deviations from the doctrine could be allowed to stand.

In November 1969, about seven months after the Court decision, the Missouri General Assembly drew up another congressional district map. In the ensuing election in 1970, the Democratic party still received proportionately more seats than the votes it polled—nine seats for 58.4% of the vote. At this point, the three-judge federal district court in Kansas City stepped in again. It remapped Missouri itself and drew new congressional district lines on February 22, 1972. Though the new map received approval from the U.S. Supreme Court, the Democrats still won nine out of ten seats with popular votes of 59.7%, 67.1% and 56.7% respectively in the 1972, 1974, and 1976 elections. In 1978, the Democrats won eight congressional seats for 62.5% of the total popular vote. But in 1980, the Republicans won four congressional seats for 45.9%, the biggest share of the total won by the Republicans since 1952.

---

[18]<u>Kirkpatrick v. Preisler</u>, 394 U.S. 526 (1969).

As a result of the 1980 census, Missouri was compelled to relinquish one of its ten seats in the U.S. House of Representatives because of population loss, that is to say, the state lagged behind most other states in population growth during the past ten years. In 1980, the 81st General Assembly made strenuous efforts to draw the state's nine new congressional districts, but failed. The bone of contention was whether the new map should maintain all three (1st to 3rd) congressional districts in the St. Louis area, all held by Democrats, especially the first district of Democratic incumbent William L. Clay, who was Missouri's only black congressman. The Democrats contended that the area had about 37 percent of the state's population and should therefore keep its current three districts. But the Republicans argued that the greatest population loss came in the St. Louis area, particularly Clay's district. Under the Republicans' pressure, Governor Bond called the legislature back into special session on November 6 to plow ahead with congressional districting. After six weeks' deliberations and debates, the legislature ground to a halt and adjourned on December 17. After the failure of the legislature in its remapping efforts, the federal district court in Kansas City stepped in and, with Democrats in a two-to-one majority, drew a nine congressional district map on December 28, 1981. The new map still preserved the three original St. Louis congressional districts, but made major shifts in some district boundaries.

To avoid further storms over the congressional redistricting, the General Assembly proposed a constitutional amendment to authorize a bipartisan commission to apportion Congress like the one apportioning the state legislature and meanwhile to empower the State Supreme Court instead of the federal district judges to redraw the lines in case the commission fails. But this proposed amendment was unfortunately defeated in the November 2 election of 1982. In 1982, three Republicans and six Democrats were elected to the U.S. House of Representatives from Missouri.

APPORTIONING THE STATE LEGISLATURE BY BIPARTISAN COMMISSIONS

Senate Apportionment Commission[19]

Within 60 days after the population of this state is reported to the President for decennial census of the United States and within 60 days after notification by the governor that a reapportionment has been invalidated by a court of

---

[19]Ibid., sec. 7.

competent jurisdiction, the state committees of the two major political parties shall each select by vote and submit to the governor a list of ten persons. Within 30 days thereafter, the governor shall appoint a commission of 10 members, five from each list, to apportion the 34 senatorial districts and to establish the numbers and boundaries of said districts. If a party committee fails to submit a list within such time, the governor shall appoint five members of his own choice from that party. On the 15th day after the governor's appointment, excluding Sundays and holidays, the commissioners shall meet in the capitol building to organize themselves and to adopt an agenda establishing at least three public hearing dates. A copy of the agenda shall be filed with the secretary of state within 48 hours after its adoption. The commission shall reapportion the senatorial districts by dividing the whole population of the state by the number 34 and establish districts with the population as nearly equal as practicable to the quotient, even if county lines need to be crossed.

Within five months after its appointment, the commission shall file with the secretary of state a tentative plan of apportionment and map of the proposed districts and shall hold as many public hearings as necessary in the ensuing 15 days. Within six months after its appointment, the commission shall file with the secretary of state a final statement of the numbers and boundaries of the districts together with a map of the districts, which must be approved by at least seven members. If the commission fails to file a final statement within such time, it shall stand discharged. The State Supreme Court shall appoint six state appellate court judges to organize a commission to apportion the Senate. Within 90 days after the discharge of the first apportionment commission, the judge-commission shall file with the secretary of state its plan and map, which must be signed by at least a majority of six judges.

House Apportionment Commission[20]

Within 60 days after the population of this state is reported to the President for decennial census of the United States and within 60 days after notification by the governor that a reapportionment has been invalidated by a court of competent jurisdiction, the congressional district committees of the two major parties shall each select by vote two members of their party, who must be residents from different legislative districts within their (congressional)

---

[20]Ibid., sec. 2.

districts, as apportionment commissioners. Within 30 days
after receipt of the lists of nominees, the governor shall
appoint a commission consisting one name from each list to
reapportion the state into 163 representative districts and
to establish the numbers and boundaries of said districts.
If any congressional committee fails to submit its nominees
within such time, the governor shall make his own choice
from that party in that district.

On the 15th day after the governor's appointment, excluding Sundays and holidays, the commissioners shall meet
in the capitol building to organize themselves and to adopt
an agenda establishing at least three public hearing dates.
A copy of the agenda shall be filed with the clerk of the
House of Representatives within 24 hours after its adoption.
The commission shall reapportion the representatives by dividing the state into 163 representative districts with
population as equal as possible in each district. Not later
than five months after its appointment, the commission shall
file with the secretary of state a tentative plan of apportionment and map of the proposed districts and hold as many
public hearings as necessary in the ensuing 15 days. No
later than six months after its appointment, the commission
shall file with the secretary of state a final statement of
the numbers and boundaries of the districts together with a
map, which must be approved by at least seven-tenths of the
commission. If the commission fails to file a final statement within such time, it shall stand discharged. The State
Supreme Court shall appoint six state appellate court judges
to organize a commission to apportion the House of Representatives. Within 90 days after the discharge of the first
apportionment commission, the judge-commission shall file
with the secretary of state its apportionment plan and map,
which must be signed by at least a majority of six judges.

No reapportionment shall be subject to the referendum.
No apportionment commissioner shall hold office as a member
of the General Assembly for four years following the submission of his commission's final statement.

POWERS AND FUNCTIONS

In performing its essential policy-making function, the
General Assembly has a wide range of powers. Besides lawmaking power, the Assembly also has non-legislative powers,
which fall into five categories: constituent, executive,
judicial, investigative, and supervisory.

I. Legislative powers

A. Powers limited by the Missouri Constitution[21]

All funds received by the state must go to the
treasury and cannot be withdrawn except by legal appropriations. All appropriations must be made according
to the following order: (1) payment of principle and
interest on public debt, (2) public education, (3) the
cost of assessing and collecting the revenue, (4) the
civil lists,[22] (5) charitable and other state institutions, (6) public health and welfare, (7) all other
state purposes, and (8) the expense of the General
Assembly.

Meanwhile, the General Assembly is restricted to
incur debt, or to issue bonds therefor, not exceeding
(1) a total sum of $75 million for repairing, remold-
ing, or rebuilding state buildings and properties; or
(2) a total sum of $150 million for the protection of
the environment through the control of water pollution.

B. Powers denied by the Missouri Constitution

Apart from the restrictions imposed upon the General Assembly, the Missouri Constitution also denies the
state legislature certain powers:[23]

1. To violate civil rights;

2. To incur any debt, or to issue bonds therefor except
   (a) to refund outstanding bonds, and (b) to meet, on
   the governor's recommendation, a temporary liability
   caused by unforeseen emergency or deficiency in revenue, not to exceed $1 million for any one year and
   to be paid within five years. Any debt above that
   amount must be submitted to the people for approval;

3. To grant public money or property or to lend credit
   to, or to guarantee liabilities of, any private
   person, association or corporation except for public calamity, pension for the blind, old age assistance, aid to dependent or crippled children or

---

[21]Ibid., sec. 36.

[22]The salaries and expenses of civil officers and the
government. In Britain, civil lists cover the personal income of the sovereign, any allowance for other members of
the Royal Family, and the expenses of the Royal Household.

[23]Mo. Const. art. 3, secs. 37-44.

the blind, direct relief, adjusted compensation, and bonus or rehabilitation for discharged veterans;

4. To give extra compensation to public employees or contractors after they have rendered services or even have entered into contracts;

5. to pay any claim against the state or any county or municipal corporation of the state under ultra vires contracts--contracts made without express authority of law;

6. To relinquish debts, liability or obligation due the state or any county or city without consideration;

7. To pay for certain war debts of Missouri;

8. To act upon, in a special session, any subjects other than those for which the special session is called;

9. To remove the capital from Jefferson City;

10. To authorize lotteries or gift enterprises with an exception;

11. To impose use or sales tax on political subdivisions;

12. To pass 30 specified types of local or special laws where a general law can be made applicable in order to avoid favoritism and interference with local governments and judicial proceedings:

Among the 30 particular subjects which the Constitution forbids the legislature to deal with by special legislation are:

a. Limiting civil actions; regulating liens; granting divorces; enforcing invalid wills or deeds; changing the names of persons or places; affecting the estates of minors or disabled persons; changing the law of descent or succession; granting to any individual, association, or corporation any special right, privilege, or immunity; fixing the rate of interest; authorizing the adoption or legitimation of children, and so on;

b. Changing the venue in civil or criminal cases; summoning or empaneling grand or petit juries; regulating the practice or jurisdiction of, or changing the rules of evidence in any judicial proceeding or inquiry before courts, sheriffs, arbitrators; providing or changing methods for the collection of debts or the enforcing of judgments; remitting fines, penalties, and forfeitures, and so forth;

c. Changing county seats; creating new townships or changing the boundaries of the townships or school districts; incorporating cities, towns, or villages or changing their charters; creating local offices or prescribing the powers and duties of local officers or regulating local affairs; regulating or maintaining roads, highways, streets or alleys, ferries or bridges except for the erection of interstate bridges; regulating the management of public schools and school buildings; and legalizing the unauthorized or invalid acts of state officers or of any county or municipality;

d. Regulating labor, trade, mining, or manufacturing; conducting elections, fixing, or changing the voting place; and extending the time for the assessment or collection of taxes;

13. To indirectly enact a special or local law by partial repeal of a general law, except a law repealing local or special acts;

14. To tax or interfere with the U.S. lands or property in Missouri;

15. To impose higher tax upon land not owned by Missourians;

16. To fix discriminatory interest rates.

C. Powers reserved to Missouri by the U.S. Constitution or delegated by the U.S. or Missouri Constitution:

1. To protect and foster the health, safety, morals, and welfare of the people. This is called police power, the principal reserved power of the state. Though in the American federal system police power belongs to the states, the national government also plays a limited but effective and significant police role;

2. To tax and borrow money (power concurrently exercised by the national government);

3. To enact laws for counties, cities, towns, villages, and other local units of government;

4. To maintain and train a militia;

5. To establish courts and fix their jurisdiction;

6. To regulate intrastate commerce;

7. To maintain peace and order;

8. To charter banks and other corporations;

9. To provide for education;

10. To define crimes and prescribe punishment;

11. To exercise the power of eminent domain;

12. To exercise emergency powers on enemy attack;

13. To draw up new congressional districts and new judicial circuit districts;

14. To conduct elections.

It is impossible to enumerate all legislative powers, but those listed above are among the most important the General Assembly exercises.

II. Non-legislative powers and functions

A. Constituent powers

1. To request Congress to call a convention to propose a U.S. constitutional amendment. Amendments may be proposed by a national constitutional convention called by Congress upon request of two-thirds of the state legislatures.

2. To act on proposed amendments to the U.S. Constitution. The U.S. constitutional amendment requires the ratification by legislatures or by special ratifying conventions in three-fourths of the states.

3. To propose state constitutional amendments.

4. To submit to the voters the question whether to call a convention to revise and amend the State Constitution every twenty years beginning in 1962.

B. Executive powers

Certain appointments by the governor are subject to senatorial confirmation. This process is not applicable to civil service appointments under the state merit system, or to officials elected by popular vote or judges appointed by the governor under the non-partisan court plan. In some states removal

of state officials from office[24] by the governor requires senatorial approval, or the governor exercises
removal power only on announcement of the legislature.
The Missouri governor has the exclusive power to remove appointed executive officers, except those who
have fixed terms such as commissioners or members of
boards.

C. Judicial powers: impeachment[25]

According to the Missouri Constitution, all
elective executive officers and judges are liable to
impeachment for crimes, misconduct, habitual drunkenness, willful neglect of duty, corruption in office,
incompetency, or any offense involving moral turpitude or oppression in office.

In impeachment, the House of Representatives
files charges and acts as prosecutor. The State Supreme Court[26] tries all impeachment cases except
those involving the governor or a Supreme Court judge,
who is tried by a special commission of seven eminent
jurists chosen by the Senate. Conviction requires
the concurrence of five-sevenths of the court or of
the special commission. The only penalty upon conviction is removal from office and disqualification
from holding any public office in the future. After
impeachment the impeached may be tried and punished
in a regular court of law for the same criminal act
for which he was impeached. Legislators and the
military are not subject to impeachment. Each house
in the Missouri legislature has the power to punish
its own members.

D. Investigative power

The power to investigate was first used by the
British House of Commons as early as the 16th century and was later adopted by American colonial

---

[24] Several state constitutions explicitly enumerate the
causes of removal such as incompetency, neglect of duty,
and malfeasance in office.

[25] Mo. Const. art. 7, secs. 1-4.

[26] In the national government, the U.S. Senate tries all
impeachment charges; but in trying the U.S. President, the
U.S. Supreme Court chief justice presides.

legislatures and the Continental Congress. Today the state legislatures as well as the U.S. Congress[27] have relied upon these parliamentary precedents to carry out investigative functions. The investigative power has thereby become a traditional legislative function, though the state legislatures do not use it as extensively as Congress. Most often a standing or select committee conducts investigations, but sometimes both houses work together through a joint committee.

In order to make possible future legislation, to test the effectiveness of existing statutes, to throw open the truth to the public, and to lay the groundwork for impeachment proceedings, lawmakers have to explore every possibility of unearthing facts and gathering information. They call for papers, look into records, subpoena witnesses, interrogate government officers and lobbyists and even punish them for contempt, though in practice the General Assembly leaves trial and punishment to courts. Committee witnesses are not accorded all the safeguards of the judicial process, because legally they are not in jeopardy of life or limb, though they may seek shelter under the Constitution against self-incrimination. However, in order to improve the quality of laws, law-makers have to understand the situation thoroughly, and nothing short of an investigation can accomplish this mission.

E. Directory and supervisory functions

Direction, oversight, and control of administration, which is the historical and essential practice of the American system of checks and balances, has become one of the principal functions of the legislature. Because of a drastic increase in the role of the administration in policy decisions within the framework of the law and because of the crucial effect of its economic and social programs upon the state or even the whole nation, the legislature cannot leave the administration alone and adrift on an uncharted sea without sufficient guidance and close surveillance. Investigation, which may unearth

---

[27]First used by the U.S. House of Representatives to inquire into the St. Clair military disaster in Indian territory in 1792.

instances of callous, arbitrary, or capricious administrative actions or corruption, malfeasance or
inefficiency of administrative officers, is but one
way by which the General Assembly asserts its supervisory authority; there are still many others, explicitly expressed or implied in the Constitution.

As the legislature may leave the bureaucracy
considerable discretion in interpreting and applying
the law, it must regularly examine the substance of
government policy and implementation by systemati-
cally and rationally reviewing administrative programs, performance, and impact. It may therefore
wade into the governmental policy-making process by
requiring governmental agencies to submit reports
and other data for approval before their acting on
time. It may hold regular hearings on governmental
programs and operations and exercise a variety of
informal contacts with administrative officers.
Above all, it determines the basic organization and
powers of the administration; it creates or abolishes
agencies and enlarges or diminishes their authority.
It controls state personnel by making laws governing
the civil and military services. It loosens or ties
up the purse strings to executive branch appropriations by increasing or reducing their funds. The
Senate confirms major gubernatorial appointments and
the House of Representatives institutes impeachment
proceedings.

Indeed, along with investigations, committee
hearings, constant assessment of programs and operations, reorganization of the administration, withdrawal of authority from governmental agencies, control of personnel and the purse strings of the state,
senatorial confirmation of appointments, and House
impeachment charges all combine to make the General
Assembly a "powerful" watchdog over the administration.

MEMBERSHIP

Terms[28] and Qualifications

---

[28] Senators are elected for four years in 36 states and
for two years in 13 states. The term of members of Nebraska's unicameral legislature is four years. Members of lower
houses serve for two years in 45 states. In only four

The term of a General Assembly is two years. The one running from 1983 through 1984 is the Eighty-second General Assembly. The members of the House of Representatives are elected at each regular election for a two-year term, while senators are elected for staggered four-year terms, half of them elected every two years. The senators from the odd-numbered districts are elected in presidential election years, while the senators from the even-numbered districts are chosen in off-year elections. Vacancies in either chamber are filled through special elections called by the governor.[29] There are 22 Democrats and 12 Republicans in the Senate and 110 Democrats and 53 Republicans in the House of Representatives in the 82nd General Assembly, 1983-1984.

State senators must be at least 30 years of age, a qualified Missouri voter for three years and a one-year resident of the district which he is chosen to represent.[30] Qualifications for state representatives are a minimum age of 24, a qualified Missouri voter for two years and a one-year resident of the district he is chosen to represent.[31] During their terms neither senators nor representatives can hold other government jobs (whether federal, state, or local) except in the militia, the reserve corps, on local school boards, or as notaries public.[32] They each receive a salary of $15,000 per year and an allowance of $35 per diem while attending sessions, plus mileage to and from their residence to the State Capitol in Jefferson City. The Senate president pro tem and the House speaker are paid an additional $2,500 each year. The House speaker pro tem and the majority and minority leaders of both houses are paid an additional $1,500.

Legislative Privileges and Immunities

Like all other state and federal legislators, Missouri senators and representatives are entitled to legislative privileges: immunity from arrest in all cases except treason, felony, or breach of the peace during the session of the

---

states--Alabama, Louisiana, Maryland, and Mississippi--both Senate and House terms are four years.

[29]Mo. Const. art. 3, sec. 14.

[30]Ibid., sec. 6.

[31]Ibid., sec. 4.

[32]Ibid., sec. 12.

General Assembly and for the 15 days before the commencement
and after the termination of each session. Furthermore, they
cannot be questioned for any speech or debate[33] made in their
official capacities in an official setting.

Occupations

Traditionally, lawyers have been the largest occupational
group in the Missouri General Assembly as well as in other
state legislatures, with farmers running closely behind. But
during recent years their proportion of the total membership
has declined. Businessmen, particularly real estate salesmen
and insurance brokers, have become a dominant occupational
force in the present-day Missouri state legislature. During
1981-1982, there were 14 lawyers, 14 businessmen and 1 farmer
in the 34-member Senate; and 44 businessmen, 19 lawyers and
21 farmers in the House of Representatives. Besides these
three predominant groups, the remaining members come from all
other walks of life. Most of them have received college education, and many have earned college degrees.

There are few women and blacks in the state legislatures
as well as in the U.S. Congress. There are only two women
and three blacks in the Missouri Senate and 23 women and 12
blacks in the House of Representatives in 1983.

State legislators enjoy far less prestige and power than
their national counterparts. They do not receive handsome
perquisites and lucrative pensions as the lawmakers on Capitol
Hill; their pay is rather meager. Because of low salary, the
pressure of personal business, the lack of influence, and the
insecurity of their positions, the turnover among legislators
is rather high in state legislatures.

The First Day in The General Assembly

Immediately after the November elections in even-numbered
years, the two parties in each house bustle to organize themselves for the coming session, nominating candidates for house
offices and electing their own party officers.

The General Assembly meets on the first Wednesday after
the first Monday in January. At the noon commencement of the
regular session following each general election, the lieutenant governor as president of the Senate or the president
pro tem of the last session calls the Senate to order. After
prayer by the Senate chaplain, temporary officers are named,

---

[33]Ibid., sec. 19.

a roll call is taken, and new senators are sworn in by a state court judge. Then follows a flurry of elections of permanent officers in the Senate: president pro tem, secretary, enrolling and engrossing director, sergeant-at-arms, doorkeeper, and chaplain. The president pro tem is sworn in by a state court judge immediately after his election.

The House of Representatives is called to order by the secretary of state. After the oath has been administered by a state court judge to all members and a roll call taken, a temporary speaker is elected to preside until permanent officers are chosen. The House then elects a speaker, a speaker pro tem, a chief clerk, a sergeant-at-arms, a doorkeeper, and a chaplain. After having been elected, these permanent officers are sworn in, the speaker and the speaker pro tem by a state court judge and all the other officers by the speaker. All other non-elective officers and employees in the House and the Senate are appointed by the speaker and the president pro tem respectively in each house. After both houses have been duly organized, traditionally the House of Representatives adopts a resolution to invite the senators to receive the governor's address at a joint meeting, usually at 2 p.m. on the first day of the session.

CHAPTER VII

GENERAL ASSEMBLY: STRUCTURE AND ORGANIZATION

The General Assembly in Missouri is patterned after the United States Congress, which inherited its structure, organization, and traditions basically from the British Parliament.

ORGANIZATION

Figure 7.1   Organization of the General Assembly

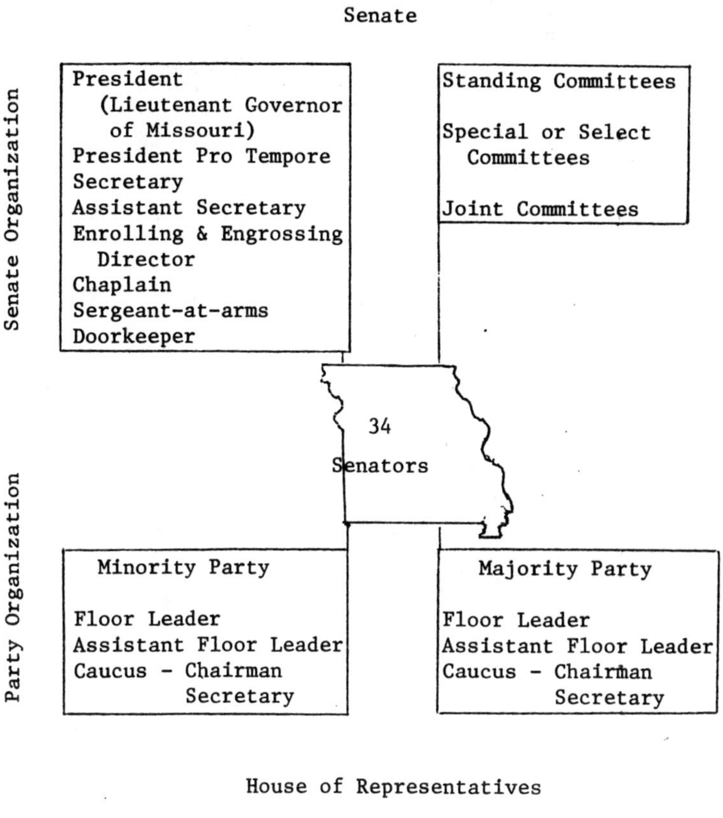

Senate

Senate Organization	President
	   (Lieutenant Governor
	   of Missouri)
	President Pro Tempore
	Secretary
	Assistant Secretary
	Enrolling & Engrossing
	   Director
	Chaplain
	Sergeant-at-arms
	Doorkeeper
		Standing Committees
		
		Special or Select
		   Committees
		
		Joint Committees

34
Senators

Party Organization	Minority Party
	
	Floor Leader
	Assistant Floor Leader
	Caucus - Chairman
	             Secretary
		Majority Party
		
		Floor Leader
		Assistant Floor Leader
		Caucus - Chairman
		             Secretary

House of Representatives

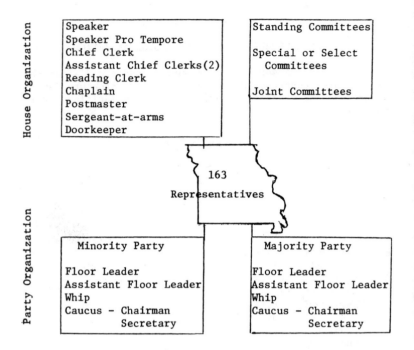

House Organization

Speaker	Standing Committees
Speaker Pro Tempore	
Chief Clerk	Special or Select
Assistant Chief Clerks(2)	Committees
Reading Clerk	
Chaplain	Joint Committees
Postmaster	
Sergeant-at-arms	
Doorkeeper	

163 Representatives

Party Organization

Minority Party	Majority Party
Floor Leader	Floor Leader
Assistant Floor Leader	Assistant Floor Leader
Whip	Whip
Caucus – Chairman	Caucus – Chairman
Secretary	Secretary

ORGANIZATIONS OF TWO HOUSES

Officers

Both the Senate and the House of Representatives have six officers elected respectively by the members thereof but also hundreds of appointive officers and employees. Though the Constitution limits employees to 75 in the Senate and 125 in the House of Representatives,[1] both houses may hire as many additional employees as they need. The duties and powers of all elective and some appointive officers are stipulated in the rules of both houses as follows:

Senate

President[2]

---

[1] Mo. Const. art. 3, sec. 17.

[2] In 41 states having a lieutenant governor, that officer is, except in Hawaii and Massachusetts, president of the Senate

Just as the U.S. Constitution makes the American Vice-President the President of the U.S. Senate, the Missouri Constitution makes the lieutenant governor the ex officio president of the Missouri Senate.[3] He presides over the Senate and joint sessions of the General Assembly, conducts the business according to the rules, debates only procedural questions and votes only in case of a tie. But he may debate all questions in the Committee of the Whole. He signs all acts, joint resolutions, and addresses for the Senate and all writs, warrants, and subpoenas issued by order of the Senate and attested by the secretary.

President Pro Tempore[4]

In the absence of the president of the Senate, the president pro tem performs the president's duties. The president pro tem is formally elected by the Senate at the beginning of each General Assembly but is usually chosen by the majority party caucus in the Senate before election. Besides presiding over the Senate during the president's absence, he is parliamentarian,[5] decides all points of order[6] and refers bills and resolutions to committees after their introduction. In his absence, points of order may be ruled on by the chairman of the Committee on Judiciary, but in either case points of order may be referred to the Committee on Parliamentary Procedure[7] for decisions. Above all, the president pro tem appoints committees including chairmen and vice-chairmen, but the minority caucus chooses minority party members to the committees. Moreover, the president pro tem is the second in the line of succession to the governor after the lieutenant governor.

---

[3]Mo. Const. art. 4, sec. 10.

[4]The term "pro tempore," meaning "temporary," is usually shortened to "pro tem."

[5]An expert in the rules and usuages of a legislature.

[6]An objection raised by a member at a meeting when another member is departing from the rules thereof. The objector cites the rule violated, and the chair upholds his objection if correctly made, but the ruling is subject to appeal to the floor.

[7]The Committee on Parliamentary Procedure is composed of three members, namely, the president pro tem, the chairman and the ranking minority member of the Committee on Judiciary. Missouri, General Assembly, Senate, Rules, 81st G.A., 1981-1982, Rule 28. Hereafter cited as "Senate Rule."

In 1973, a storm broke out in the Senate when Democratic President Pro Tem William J. Cason prohibited Republican Lieutenant Governor William C. Phelps from presiding over the Senate on the last day of the session, June 15.[8] Cason's action was based upon the new rule, adopted at the start of the 1973 legislative session, that the president pro tem had complete jurisdiction over who would preside over the Senate. The lieutenant governor should, according to Cason, preside over the Senate at the pleasure of the president pro tem, since the Senate has the constitutional right to "determine rules of its own procedure."[9] Moreover, allowing the lieutenant governor, an officer of the executive branch, to chair the Senate would violate the constitutional separation of powers. In refuting Cason's allegation, Phelps argued that "constitutionally the lieutenant governor is the ex officio president of the Senate," which means "he has the right to preside over the Senate whenever he wishes." By a vote of 6-1, the State Supreme Court sustained Phelps' interpretation that the lieutenant governor is the presiding officer of the Missouri Senate. The Court held that "each house may determine the rules of its own proceedings except as herein provided," and one of the exceptions is that the Constitution makes the lieutenant governor the president of the Senate, that is, presiding officer of the Senate. But the Court did not elaborate his powers. Several months later, another wrangle boiled over. On April 8, 1974, the Court ruled that the president pro tem has authority under the rules to refer bills to committees and to rule on points of order in the Senate.

Secretary

The secretary keeps a journal of the proceedings of the Senate and performs other duties as the Senate directs. He certifies all acts and joint resolutions passed by the Senate and all writs, warrants, and subpoenas issued by order of the Senate. He is aided by an assistant secretary.

---

[8] The dispute began at 1:45 p.m. on June 15. When the sergeant-at-arms blocked Phelps' way to the dais to take the chair, the lieutenant governor shouted "I object, I object. I am president of the Senate. This denies my constitutional right to preside." Cason then had the sergeant-at-arms escort him from the Senate chamber. Immediately thirteen Republican senators walked out of the chamber in protest.

[9] Mo. Const. art. 3, sec. 18.

Enrolling and Engrossing Director

The enrolling and engrossing director certifies the final copy of a bill passed by the Senate or by both houses and is responsible for seeing that all amendments and substitutes have been exactly incorporated in the bill. He also performs such other duties as the Committee on Rules, Joint Rules, Resolutions and Miscellaneous Bills directs.

Sergeant-at-arms

The sergeant-at-arms attends the Senate during its sittings, executes its commands, maintains order, makes arrests, and serves subpoenas.

Doorkeeper

The doorkeeper enforces the commands of the Senate and its presiding officer and controls access to the floor or galleries. He is also present at committee hearings.

Chaplain

The chaplain opens every meeting of the Senate with prayer.

House of Representatives

Speaker[10]

Nominated by the majority party caucus and elected by the House, the speaker is, like his national counterpart, the presiding officer of the House of Representatives. He

---

[10] In all state legislatures, the presiding officer of the lower house is called "speaker." The title originated in the House of Commons in England. After the commons began to assemble separately from the Lords in the late thirteenth century, they elected a member from among themselves to preside over debate and to report their decisions to the king. Because he spoke to the king on behalf of the whole house, he was therefore called speaker.

In Britain the speaker is impartial and judicious, while in the United States the speaker in either Congress or state legislatures is still partisan, using the power of his office to promote his party programs.

recognizes the members wishing to speak, interprets and applies the rules of procedure, conducts the business of the House according to the rules, puts questions to a vote, rules on points of order, and preserves order and decorum in debate. He may vote in all cases of election in the House and to break a tie. He signs all bills, joint resolutions, addresses, writs, warrants, and subpoenas attested by the chief clerk. He refers bills or resolutions to appropriate committees; but, most important of all, he has the power to appoint all committees including chairmen and vice-chairmen.[11] He has general direction and supervision of the Hall and superintending control over all employees of the House. He follows the lieutenant governor and president pro tem in the order of succession to the governorship.

Speaker Pro Tem[12]

A speaker pro tem is elected to perform the duties of the speaker during the latter's absence. In the absence of the speaker pro tem, the speaker may appoint any member of the House to perform his duties.

Chief Clerk

The chief clerk serves as chief administrator of the House of Representatives. He attends meetings regularly, keeps its journal of proceedings, transmits all its messages and documents, keeps regular files and attests all writs, warrants, and subpoenas issued by order of the House. He may be authorized to act for the Committee on Accounts and is the repository of the minute book after each General Assembly.

Assistant Chief Clerk

---

[11]Missouri, General Assembly, House of Representatives, Rules, 81st G.A., 1981-1982, Rule 25. Hereafter cited as "House Rule."

Before 1911, the speaker in the U.S. House of Representatives had the power to appoint standing committees, including chairmen, but lost this power after the revolt of 1911 when Joseph Cannon was speaker. But the national speaker still has the power to appoint select and joint committees and chairmen.

[12]There is no such office in the U.S. House of Representatives and many state legislatures.

There are two assistant chief clerks: one for administration and the other for procedure. The duties of these two assistant chief clerks are to assist the chief clerk in performing his duties and to take charge of his office during his absence.

Reading Clerk

Appointed by the speaker, the reading clerk attends the House during its sittings and reads all bills, resolutions, and communications to the House and performs other duties related to his office.

Sergeant-at-arms

The sergeant-at-arms preserves order in the galleries and lobby and keeps the entry to the aisle cleared during the sessions of the House.

Chaplain

The chaplain opens every meeting of the House with prayer and preaches in the House chamber whenever requested by the House.

Postmaster

Appointed by the speaker, the postmaster or postmasters take care of all received mails for the House members.

Doorkeeper

The doorkeeper announces all messages or communications from the governor or from the Senate and admits no one inside the bar except the message bearers and those permitted by the rules or orders of the House.

Committees

There are three types of committees in each house: standing, special or select, and a Committee of the Whole. There are also joint committees between the two houses and interim committees between two sessions.

Standing Committees[13]

---

[13] In the legislatures of 46 states, each house has its own set of standing committees, but the legislatures in three

The standing committees are regular committees created at the beginning of the General Assembly and provided for by the rules of each house to consider bills within their areas. Like their counterparts in Congress, the standing committees are set up according to functions,[14] corresponding somewhat to the departments or agencies in the executive branch. They are composed, as nearly as possible, of both party members in proportion to their total membership in each house. Though seniority is not observed so rigidly in the General Assembly as in Congress, it still plays a signigicant role in the appointment of committee chairmen and assisgnments to important committees and even to offices and seats in the Senate chamber. Seniority is determined by each party caucus on the basis of length of service.[15] Standing committees may establish subcommittees to study bills, hold hearings, and report their findings. But only the full committees can report bills to the floor for consideration.

Always a member of the majority party, the committee chairman presides over all sessions of the committee, votes on any measures, and sees that a minute book is kept. He can exercise great influence over the destiny of bills assigned to his committee. He determines when and if the committee will meet, which bills it will consider, and whether public hearings will be held or subcommittees appointed. He is customarily appointed to a conference committee established to iron out the differences between the two houses over a bill originating in his committee.

Select or Special Committees[16]

A select or special committee is temporarily created for a special purpose, such as investigation or consideration of a particular subject or a bill not appropriate to any

---

New England states (Maine, Massachusetts, and Connecticut) have the system of joint standing committees. The committees, composed of both house members, consider bills jointly in order to save time and efforts.

[14] The standing committees in the British Parliament are designated A, B, C, D, E, and Scottish.

[15] Senate Rule, 30.

[16] Called ad hoc (a Latin word which means "for this special purpose") committee in the British Parliament or in other organizations such as the United Nations.

standing committee.

Committee of the Whole[17]

The Committee of the Whole is the entire membership of the house sitting as a committee to consider specific bills or matters in order to expedite business. A majority of the members constitutes a quorum. The chairman is appointed by the president pro tem in the Senate and by the speaker in the House of Representatives. The rules and procedures are observed in the committee when applicable; otherwise, it functions as any other committees. But bills must have first passed through the regular committees and be on the calendar for perfection before they go to the Committee of the Whole.

Interim Committees[18]

The term "interim committees" is used when standing committees meet during the interim between the odd-numbered year and the even-numbered year sessions to consider bills or to perform other necessary legislative functions.

Joint Committees

A joint committee is a committee comprising a specific number of members from each house. There are temporary and permanent joint committees. A conference committee to iron out differences between the two houses over a bill is a temporary joint committee. A permanent joint committee is established to administer business concerning both houses or the state, performing executive, investigative, advisory, or supervisory rather than legislative functions.

Statutory Committees

Usually special and standing committees are created by simple resolutions in one house and joint committees by concurrent resolutions between the two houses. But sometimes they may be established by law and thus are known as statutory committees. Among the statutory (joint) committees or commissions in the 81st General Assembly are the Missouri Commission on Interstate Cooperation, created in 1941; the Joint Committee on Correctional Institutions and Problems, in 1957; the Atomic Energy Commission, in 1959; the Committee

---

[17] Senate Rules 37-44; House Rules 99-105.

[18] Mo. Const. art. 3, sec. 22.

on State Fiscal Affairs, in 1965; and the Committee on Legislative Research, in 1943 but provided by the Constitution two years later.

The Interstate Cooperation Commission promotes cooperation between this state and other states. The Correctional Institutions and Problems Committee and the Fiscal Affairs Committee make studies, analyses, inspections and investigations for improvement in correctional and fiscal matters respectively. The Atomic Energy Commission keeps the governor and the General Assembly informed of developments in the field of nuclear energy. The Legislative Research Committee drafts bills and revises and publishes statutes. Statutory (joint) committees may include members from the outside. For example, the Interstate Cooperation Commission includes five members of the Governor's Committee on Interstate Cooperation and the Atomic Energy Commission includes seven members from the community at large.

Senate

In the 81st General Assembly the Senate has 24 standing committees, three less than the last Senate. Several Senate committees were merged, but the Committee on Criminal Jurisprudence and Corrections was split into two separate committees. The 24 standing committees are:

1. Accounts, Assignments & Clerical Force (9 members)
2. Agricultural, Conservation, Parks & Tourism (9)
3. Apportionment, Elections, Military & Veterans Affairs (9)
4. Appropriations (10)
5. Banks, Banking & Financial Institutions (10)
6. Constitutional Amendments & Reorganization (9)
7. Corrections (9)
8. Criminal Jurisprudence (9)
9. Education (9)
10. Gubernatorial Appointments (9)
11. Insurance (9)
12. Interstate Cooperation (5)
13. Judiciary (9)
14. Labor & Management Relations (9)
15. Legislative Research (10)
16. Local Government, Fees & Salaries (9)
17. Municipal Corporations, Railroads, Private Corporations, Urban Affairs & Housing (9)
18. Public Health, Mental Health, Developmental Disabilities, Welfare, Medicaid & Consumer Protection (9)
19. Roads, Highways, Industrial Development, Energy & Environ-

ment (9)
20. Rules, Joint Rules, Resolutions ,& Miscellaneous Bills (7)
21. State Budget Control (9)
22. State Departments & Government Affairs (9)
23. State Fiscal Affairs (7)
24. Ways & Means (9)

Among the 24 standing committees the most powerful one is the Committee on State Budget Control. Comparable to the Rules Committee in the U.S. House of Representatives, it considers all bills, both Senate and House, after they have been approved by other regular committees and perfected and ordered printed by the Senate, with the exception of regular appropriation bills which require new appropriations or expenditures of appropriated funds exceeding $50,000 or which reduce such funds by that amount during either of the first two full years of operation.[19] It also considers any such Senate or House bill amended to increase expenditures or reduce revenue exceeding $50,000 during either of the first two years of operation and re-referred to it upon timely motion.

The other powerful committees are the Committee on Appropriations, which considers general appropriations and disbursement of public funds; and the Ways and Means Committee, which considers all issues about the state revenue, debt, and interest thereupon. Serving as an administrative unit is another powerful committee, the Committee on Accounts, Assignments and Clerical Force, which controls all financial obligations and business affairs, supervises certain employees, and assigns offices and seats in the Senate. The duties of the other committees are self-explanatory.

House of Representatives

The speaker appoints all committees, their chairmen and vice-chairmen. The speaker, the speaker pro tem, and the majority floor leader are ex officio members of all committees for the purpose of a quorum and discussion but have no vote unless they are regular members thereof. There are 44 standing committees in the House of Representatives in the 81st General Assembly.

1. Accounts (10 members)
2. Agri-business (16)
3. Appropriations

---

[19]Senate Rule 29 (11).

4. Appropriations--Education & Transportation (16)
5. Appropriations--General Administration (16)
6. Appropriations--Mental Health (16)
7. Appropriations--Natural & Economic Resources (16)
8. Appropriations--Social Services (16)
9. Banks & Financial Institutions (24)
10. Bills Perfected & Passed (5)
11. Budget (19)
12. Civil & Criminal Justice (13)
13. Commerce (16)
14. Consumer Protection (16)
15. Correctional Institutions & Problems (6)
16. Education--Elementary & Secondary (22)
17. Education--Higher (21)
18. Elections (13)
19. Employment Security & Fair Practices (10)
20. Energy & Atomic Energy (10)
21. Ethics (13)
22. Federal-state Relations & Veterans Affairs (10)
23. Fees & Salaries (10)
24. Governmental Organizations (10)
25. Governmental Review (13)
26. Insurance (13)
27. Judiciary (18)
28. Labor (16)
29. License & Related Matters (10)
30. Local Government & Related Matters (13)
31. Mines & Mining (10)
32. Miscellaneous Resolutions (10)
33. Motor Vehicle & Traffic Regulations (10)
34. Municipal Corporations (10)
35. Public Health & Safety (16)
36. Retirement (10)
37. Revenue & Economics (19)
38. Rules & Joint Rules (13)
39. Social Services & Medicaid (12)
40. State Institutions & Property (10)
41. State Parks, Recreation & Natural Resources (13)
42. Transportation (16)
43. Urban Affairs (13)
44. Workmen's Compensation (10)

In the 81st General Assembly, while the Senate reduced its standing committees from 27 to 24, the House of Representatives expanded them from 36 to 44, eight more than the last House and 20 more than the Senate. But what characterizes the House of Representatives most in the 81st General Assembly is the creation of a new budget committee and five appropriations committees in the fields of general administration, education and transportation, natural and economic resources, mental health, and social services. Playing a pivotal role in appropriations in the House of Representatives, the budget committee files all appropriations, assigns those bills to appropriate appropriations committees for study and then reports all bills recommended by them. It also considers any other bills, measures, or questions about the appropriation and disbursement of public funds referred to it.

Above all, the House Budget Committee is responsible for considering (1) all bills, House and Senate, requiring new appropriations or expenditures of state money in excess of $100,000 or reducing state revenue by more than that amount after they have been approved by the regular standing committees and perfected and ordered printed, but before their submission for third reading and final passage; (2) any such House or Senate bill after having been legitimately released from any standing committee[20] but before its submission to the House floor; and (3) any such House or Senate bill amended to increase expenditures or reduce revenue and re-referred to it upon timely motion.[21] The creation of a budget committee, parallel to the Budget Control Committee in the Senate and supported by five specific appropriations committees, fully reflects the House's vigorous efforts to control the state's purse strings in the face of shrinking revenue.

Other committee changes included the creation of the Committee on Correctional Institutions and Problems and the division of the Committee on Education into the Committee on Higher Education and the Committee on Elementary and Secondary Education. The establishment of a corrections committee in the House, coupled with the separation of the Committee on Criminal Jurisprudence and Corrections in the Senate, symbolizes the General Assembly's special attention to the penal and correctional problems in the state. The division of the original education committee indicates the House's growing concern for education.

The speaker may also appoint such special committees as he sees necessary. There are eleven extra (some statutory) committees in the House of Representatives in the 81st General Assembly. A majority of all committees consisting of 30 members or less, and 15 members of all committees of more

---

[20] See Chapter VIII.

[21] House Rule 29 (11).

than 30, make a quorum for transaction of business.[22]

Majority and Minority Floor Leaders

Elected by the majority party caucus, the majority leader
on the floor of the Senate or the House of Representatives
controls the calendar of daily business. The chief spokesmen
and major strategists of the majority party in each house, as
well as the leading program architects, are the president pro
tem and the speaker. The floor leaders seek to implement
party policies and programs and marshall party forces in debate, usually with themselves taking the lead. They supervise their party members and, with the help of assistant
floor leaders or whips, strive to maintain party solidarity
in the chambers. In the House of Representatives only the
speaker is more influential than the majority floor leader.
In the Senate the majority floor leader is second only to
the president pro tem as the leader of his party.

Minority floor leaders are also elected by their party
caucuses. Like the majority floor leaders in both houses,
they direct their party strategies and spot and criticize
the inconsistencies in the majority party policies or programs and arguments. Sometimes they offer alternatives to
the programs of the majority floor leaders.

In Missouri the majority party leaders in both houses
are more powerful and influential than minority floor leaders.
For instance, the majority leaders are members of the governor-disability board to decide whether the governor has actually recovered from illness and is able to resume his duties.
Along with the House speaker and the speaker pro tem, the
majority floor leader in the House of Representatives is the
ex officio member of all committees of the House for the
purpose of a quorum and discussion, but not the minority
floor leader.

Assistant Floor Leaders

Majority and minority assistant floor leaders assist
their floor leaders in discharging their duties and act for
them in case of their absence. They serve as whips in the
Senate.

---

[22]House Rule 32.

Whips[23]

Also elected by the party caucuses, the whips are often referred to as assistant floor leaders whose functions are to help rally party forces behind their party strategies and to serve as a channel or pipelines of communication between the party leaders and members in the chamber. They maintain close contact with individual party members, sound out their opinions, relay them between the caucuses and the floor leaders, and help develop and coordinate party programs. They advise party members of pending legislation, urge their attendance, and round up votes at crucial moments. They also sometimes arrange pairs[24] and conciliate dissidents.

Caucuses

A caucus is a meeting of party members in each house for the purpose of nominating party candidates for house offices, electing their own party officers, and mapping out party policies or programs. The Republicans sometimes call their party meeting a "conference" instead of "caucus."

SESSIONS AND RULES OF PROCEDURE

Sessions

The General Assembly convenes every year.[25] Each house generally meets at 9:30 or 10:00 a.m. every legislative working day.[26] A majority of the members in each house constitutes a quorum. The first period of the day is designated

---

[23] The terms "floor leaders" and "whips" are also inherited from the British Parliament. The British system derived the term "whips" from fox-hunting, where the "whippers-in" keep the hounds from running astray from the pack while chasing a fox.

[24] Two legislators, holding opposing views on a bill, agree in advance not to vote so that the absence of one from voting will not affect the outcome.

[25] Before 1971, the Missouri General Assembly held a regular session every two years. Today about eight states still hold biennial legislative sessions.

[26] The legislative working days are Tuesday, Wednesday, and Thursday of each week, with additional days toward the end of the session. Legislators sometimes hold night sessions.

as "morning hour"[27] for the conduct of regular routine business. The Assembly adjourns on June 30 in odd-numbered years
but considers no bills after midnight on June 15. In even-
numbered years, it adjourns on May 15, but considers no bills
after midnight on April 30. A special or extra session may
be called solely by the governor[28] but lasts no more than 60
calendar days. It considers only the business for which the
session is specifically called.[29] Another kind of extra
session automatically convenes on the first Wednesday after
the first Monday in September in even-numbered years for no
more than ten calendar days to consider gubernatorial vetoes.[30]

Neither house is allowed to adjourn for more than ten
days at any time without the consent of the other. Each house
is required to keep a daily journal of its proceedings. At
the end of the session all journals are bound by the Office
of Secretary of State. The journals are not records of the
debate but only of the actions taken, including recorded votes.
The business to be considered at the executive sessions[31] are
not always pre-announced. Today the executive sessions are
no longer secret; all sessions, except the party caucus meet-

---

[27] House Rule 2. Time set aside at the beginning of each
legislative day for the conduct of such routine matters as
messages from the governor or from the other house, communications from executive officers, committee reports, and introduction of bills and resolutions. The term "morning
hour" is also used in the U.S. Congress.

[28] In all states special sessions are called by the governor, but with the advice of the executive council in Massachusetts, New Hampshire, and North Carolina or at the request
of specific number of the legislators in several other states.
The legislators in about 1/3 of the states may call themselves together for such meetings. But the legislators in
Georgia and New Mexico, and the lieutenant governor or the
speaker of the House of Representatives in Louisiana call
special sessions if the governors fail to do so.

[29] Mo. Const. art. 3, sec. 39 (7). The U.S. Congress can
consider any subject in a special session once called by the
President.

[30] See Chapter VIII.

[31] Because the U.S. Senate, until June 18, 1929, regularly
considered all executive business in secret, the term is
therefore used to apply to any secret session.

ings, must be held with open doors[32] in the General Assembly, especially after the state sunshine law or "open meetings and open records" law was enacted in 1973. On June 17, 1982, the existing sunshine law was strengthened. Under the new state law, officials who violate the open meetings law could be fined up to $100 and any decisions made could be nullified by a court.[33] In an executive session the public cannot participate in any action as in an ordinary meeting such as giving oral testimonies. Active participation in the executive session is restricted only to committee members.

Rules of Procedure

Each house elects its own officers and is sole judge of the qualifications, elections and returns of its own members. Each house makes its own rules and procedures except as provided by the Constitution. In both houses, any member wishing to speak must rise from his seat and respectfully address himself to the chair; otherwise, he will not be recognized. He must confine himself to the subject under debate, avoid addressing others by their private names, and behave with decorum. In the House, no one shall speak more than twice on the same subject without permission of the House and more than once until any other members wishing to speak have spoken. No member shall, except while reporting a bill or resolution from a committee, speak longer than 15 minutes, unless unanimously approved by the House.[34] In the Senate no senator shall speak more than once on the same subject without permission of the Senate unless he is the introducer, proposer or mover of the subject pending. In such cases, he is allowed to speak or reply before any other senator who wishes to speak. After he has been recognized to close, no other senator is allowed to speak on the pending matter unless he is the proponent of the amendment or author of the bill or resolution.[35]

In both houses, the previous question rule[36] is used

---

[32] Mo. Const. art. 3, sec. 20.

[33] Public Governmental Bodies--Open Meetings, Records and Votes (§610.027, RSMo Supp. 1982).

[34] House Rule 82.

[35] Senate Rule 81.

[36] The previous question means a "question" is subject before the house for a vote, and it is "previous" when some other subject has superseded it. It is a debate-limiting device at a meeting.

to cut off debate and to force a vote on the subject pending. In the House, the previous question is, just like
any other question, moved by a single member and carried
with the consent of a majority of the House. But in the
Senate, it must be proposed in writing by five senators and
carried if voted favorably by a majority of senators without debate.[37]

The attendance of absent members may be compelled under
pain of penalties.[38] Each house may also punish its own
members for disorderly conduct and, with the concurrence of
two-thirds of the whole house, expel them. But no member
shall be expelled a second time for the same cause. The
House of Representatives may order the censure, fine, or
custody of delinquent members by a majority of those present.
Meanwhile, each house may arrest and punish any person, not
a member, by fine not exceeding $300 or imprisonment in a
county jail not exceeding 10 days, or both, for any disorderly or contemptuous behavior in its presence during its
sessions.[39]

---

[37] House Rule 72; Senate Rules 85 & 86.

[38] Mo. Const. art. 3, sec. 20.

[39] Ibid., sec. 18.

CHAPTER VIII   LEGISLATIVE PROCESS

In normal legislative procedure, a legislative proposal must be passed by both houses in a bicameral legislature and signed by the chief executive of the government before it becomes law.

LEGISLATIVE PROPOSALS

Bills and Resolutions

In Missouri, "No law shall be passed except by bill."[1] That is, only a bill can become law. In other words, a bill is a proposed law. There are two kinds of bills: public and private. Public bills become public laws and private bills become private law.[2]

Besides bills, there are resolutions, which are used to express the opinions, purposes and policies of one house or both houses, make proposals or request actions. There are three kinds of resolutions in the General Assembly as well as in the U.S. Congress and other state legislatures: simple, concurrent and joint. A simple resolution or just "resolution," designated "HR (House resolution)" or "SR (Senate Resolution" and passed by one house, not requiring passage by the other, concerns the business of that house alone, House or Senate, depending on which house it passes. A Senate or House resolution merely states facts, makes or amends rules applicable to that house only, expresses opinions or sentiments such as congratulations, condolences, appreciation or honors, or censures house members.

A concurrent resolution, passed by both house, concerns the business of the whole legislature. It is used to make or amend rules applicable to both houses or relates to both houses on such matters as questions of adjournment, going into joint sessions,[3] creating a joint committee, providing for an investigation, fixing the time of adjournment of the legislature,

---

[1] Mo. Const. art. 3, sec. 21

[2] See page 30. Another kind of private law enacted in the U.S. Congress but not in Missouri or other state legislatures is concerned only with specific individual matters such as an alien seeking entry into the United States as an exception to the immigration rules. This kind of private law applies only to the specific individuals or groups or localities named in the acts.

[3] Mo. Const. art. 4, sec. 8.

memorializing Congress on particular matters, calling upon Congress to propose a federal constitutional amendment, expressing sentiments such as commendations or condolences, requesting actions of government officials or departments, setting elections dates for referenda, and so on. Since neither simple nor concurrent resolutions have the force of law, they do not require the approval of chief executives such as the U.S. President or state governors. In Congress, either house or both houses may also nullify or validate executive branch proposals, regulations, or actions by simple or concurrent resolutions, known as "legislative veto."

In the Missouri General Assembly, simple (or concurrent) resolutions which are used to formally recognize special persons or occasions, to offer congratulations, to extend sympathy, or to confer honors are designated as "courtesy resolutions." These resolutions are not read or printed in the journal unless so requested by the sponsors of the resolutions.[4]

But in Missouri, some concurrent resolutions "shall be presented to the governor...proceeded upon in the same manner as in the case of a bill."[5] For example, a rule, prescribed by the Personnel Advisory Board but later suspended by the Joint Committee on Administrative Rules, may be reinstated by the General Assembly with a concurrent resolution signed by the governor.[6] Apparently there are two kinds of concurrent resolutions in Missouri, signed and unsigned by the governor. The kind which does not require gubernatorial signature not only is purely "administrative or procedural" as the State Supreme Court ruled[7] but also purely concerns the General Assembly without an effect upon other branches of government.

The joint resolution is another form of legislative proposals in Congress, which, except proposals for constitutional amendments, go through the same legislative labyrinth as bills and have the same force as law, therefore requiring presidential action. A joint resolution, designated as SJR or HJR, is used for transient or temporary situation or for a limited or minor purpose or for a specific matter, usually containing one subject matter such as a single appropriation and dying as soon as its purpose is served or the situation is over. Therefore, perhaps with the exception of constitutional amendment proposals, joint resolutions rank below bills in formal dig-

---

[4]Senate Rule 72.

[5]Mo. Const. art. 4, sec. 8.

[6]§36.070, RSMo Supp. 1980.

[7]State v. Atterbury, 300 S.W. 2d 806 (Mo. banc 1957).

nity and generally less important. So in Missouri, "No resolution shall have the effect to repeal, extend or amend any
law."[8]

In Missouri, practically joint resolutions are, it seems,
exclusively used for three purposes: (1) to propose Missouri
Constitutional Amendments,[9] (2) to direct the secretary of
state to enroll as laws the bills passed by the two houses
but not returned by the governor within the constitutional
time limit,[10] and (3) to ratify the U.S. Constitutional Amendments. Therefore, though according to Article III Section 31
of the Missouri Constitution, "All...joint resolutions passed
by both houses shall be presented to and considered by the
governor," actually joint resolutions in Missouri are used
for the above-mentioned three purposes and do not require
gubernatorial action.

It is clear that in Congress the joint resolution has
the full force of law and requires presidential approval,
while the simple or concurrent resolutions concern only the
business of one or both houses and do not require presidential action. According to the State Constitution, there
is no such clear-cut distinction between joint and concurrent resolutions in the Missouri General Assembly.

Figure 8.1   Bills & Resolutions in the U.S. Congress

Sources	Measures	Presidential Approval
Executive branch Interest groups Legislators	Private bills Public bills Joint resolutions	Required
	Concurrent resolutions Simple resolutions	Not required

Sources of Legislation

Ideas for legislation originate from several sources.
Some, of course, are conceived by individual legislators,
who author bills based upon their compaign pledges, or on
their experiences in office, or in response to demands from
their constituencies. But an overwhelming majority of bills
flow in from sources outside the legislative halls. They
are mostly from the executive branch of the government and
interest groups. The bills from the executive branch, known

---

[8] Mo. Const. art. 4, sec. 8.

[9] Ibid.

[10] Ibid., art. 3, sec. 33.

as administrative bills, come in the form of the Governor's
messages or letters directed to the speaker of the House of
Representatives and/or the president of the Senate or from
the elective executive officers of the state. But almost
half of the bills originate with interest groups, which not
only help legislators with ideas but also draft bills for
them to sponsor. Sometimes counties and cities, or even
private citizens outside the government, author bills. However, it must be borne in mind that only legislators can
introduce bills in their own houses, even though legislative
proposals bearing their names are not necessarily authored
by them or even contain ideas contrary to their own. Every
year sees some 1,500 proposed laws introduced in the Missouri
state legislature--usually more than 500 in the Senate alone.

HOW A BILL BECOMES LAW IN MISSOURI

I. A BILL IN THE GENERAL ASSEMBLY

A Bill in Either House

Introduction and The First Reading

A bill may be introduced in either house, but traditionally (not constitutionally nor statutorily) appropriation
bills originate in the House of Representatives.[11] No bill
other than general appropriation bills contain more than one
subject clearly expressed in the title. The style of law is
"Be it enacted by the General Assembly of the State of Missouri as follows." No bill shall be so amended in its passage through either house as to change its original purpose.
Every bill must be read by title on three different days in
each house.[12] The title of the measure is read for the
first time when introduced and for the second time when referred to a committee, but the measure is usually read at
length on the floor before a vote is taken. However, in the
House of Representatives, if further reading is called for
without objection, it shall be read in full; otherwise, the
question is determined by a majority vote in the House.[13]

No bill, except an appropriation bill, can be introduced

---

[11]Revenue bills may originate in either house in Missouri.
In Congress, constitutionally, revenue bills originate in the
House of Representatives; traditionally appropriation bills
are also first introduced in the House.

[12]Mo. Const. art. 3, sec. 21.

[13]House Rule 40.

in either house after the 60th legislative day in an odd-numbered year session, or after the 30th legislative day in an even-numbered year session unless consented to by an absolute majority[14] of each house or the governor makes a special request.[15] In the Senate no bill except an appropriation bill shall be introduced after March first of any regular session unless consented to by an absolute majority of the Senators.[16] The governor must submit the budget within 30 days after the beginning of each regular session.[17]

Bills may be pre-filed with either house at any time between December 1 and the day before the opening of the Assembly session in January.[18] In the Senate, as early as July 1 of each year, senators and senators-elect may file bills for the following regular session with the secretary of the Senate. These pre-filed bills will automatically be introduced and read on the first day of the session.

Upon introduction, a bill is read by title by the reading clerk in the House of Representatives or by the secretary in the Senate. This is the first of three readings[19] required by the legislative procedure. The sponsor of the bill usually makes a brief statement of its intended purpose. Then the bill is assigned a serial number and placed on the calendar. Hundreds of copies of the bill are printed and distributed among the members of the General Assembly and to other interested persons. A calendar is a list of bills, resolutions, or other items (such as appointments by the governor in the Senate), in chronological order, to be taken in sequence for consideration and action in a committee or on the floor in either house of the legislature. On the next legislative day, the bill is read by title for the second time. After the second reading, the speaker in the House or the president

---

[14]Absolute majority is a majority of the total membership regardless of the number in attendance or voting.

[15]Mo. Const. art. 3, sec. 25.

[16]Senate Rule 49.

[17]Mo. Const. art. 4, sec. 24.

[18]Missouri, <u>Official Manual</u> (1981-1982), p.126.

[19]The three reading procedure was also inherited from the British Parliament. It was inaugurated because in the early days in England there was no printing, or printing and paper were bad; meanwhile, many country squires sitting in the House of Commons could neigher read nor write well.

pro tem in the Senate refers the bill to an appropriate committee in his own chamber. If the bill seems to fit more than
one committee, the speaker or the president pro tem determines
where it goes unless his decision is overruled by a majority
vote in his chamber. Courtesy resolutions are not referred
to any committee for consideration.

The Bill in Committee

At an announced time, the committee holds a public hearing on the bill. Both supporters and opponents of the bill,
including lobbyists or interest groups, executive officers,
and private citizens, gather before the committee to present
their views. Before the public hearing, a committee sometimes assigns the bill to a subcommittee for study and recommendation. After the public hearing or hearings, the committee meets in open executive session for consideration and
action--debate, amendment, and vote. The Constitution requires every committee to file "the recorded vote of the
members of the committee"[20] in order to disclose how each
member has voted. After its vote, the committee takes one
of the following actions:

1. Reports the bill "Do Pass."

2. Recommends its passage together with its amendments
   known as "committee amendments."

3. Writes a "committee substitute" bill under the original title if many changes are recommended. The original purpose of the bill, however, cannot be changed.
   New copies of the amended or substitute bill are
   printed and distributed.

4. Reports the bill with no recommendation (an unusual
   action).

5. Reports the bill "Do Not Pass."

6. Does not report the bill at all (in effect killing
   it).

However, after a bill has been referred to a committee,
one-third of the members in each house may (after ten legislative days in the House of Representatives)[21] release the

---

[20] Mo. Const. art. 3, sec. 22.

[21] House Rule 37. In the U.S. House of Representatives a

committee of consideration and place it on the perfection
calendar on the floor.[22] In the House of Representatives
the discharged bill is placed on a separate calendar, at the
foot of the existing House Calendar, and will not be considered until after all bills ahead of it on the entire House
Calendar have been disposed of.[23] In the Senate, the discharged bill may, before its final passage, be referred to
the same committee or some other committee for consideration,
if approved by a majority of senators present but not less
than one-third of the entire membership. Furthermore, no
bill or resolution can be reported adversely to the floor
until its sponsor has a chance to appear and be heard before
the committee.[24]

Perfection Calendar

After a bill has been reported out of a committee favorably ("do pass" or "without recommendation") or a substitute
is recommended, it is placed on the calendar in the chamber
for perfection. If the bill is of non-controversial nature,
it goes upon a Consent Calendar for Third Reading so that it
may pass the floor without amendment. But if any member objects in writing, it goes back to the foot of the Perfection
Calendar.

In the House of Representatives, any bill other than the
one reducing state revenue or increasing state expenditures
may be submitted to the Committee on Rules and Joint Rules
for placement on the Consent Calendar, if passed unanimously
by a committee as non-controversial. If the Rules Committee
agrees it is non-controversial and concurs with the original
committee on such placement, the bill may be ordered perfected
and goes upon the Consent Calendar for Third Reading. If one-
third of the members object in writing within five legislative
days after its submission, the bill goes back to the original
committee.[25]

---

bill may be discharged by a motion signed by a majority of
the congressmen after it has been held up for 30 days in a
standing committee or more than seven legislative days in
the Rules Committee.

[22]Mo. Const. art. 3, sec. 22.

[23]House Rule 37.

[24]Senate Rule 51.

[25]House Rule 46.

In the Senate, the sponsor of a bill may request in writing three days before a committee hearing that it be placed on the Consent Calendar. If the committee accepts the request unanimously, the bill goes upon the Consent Calendar. If any member in the committee files written objection within four legislative days, it goes back on the regular calendar and is placed where it would have been, had it not been placed on the Consent Calendar.[26]

In the Senate, certain bills may be called out of the order on the Calendar for early or immediate consideration, such as regular appropriation bills, congressional or legislative redistricting bills, bills increasing state revenue by more than $3 million, bills implementing amendments to the Missouri Constitution adopted at the immediately preceding state election or bills involving federal funds.[27]

Any bill reported adversely ("do not pass") from a committee in either house is not placed on the Calendar for Perfection. But if it, upon the motion of its sponsor, receives a majority vote of members within two legislative days in the Senate or within three legislative days in the House of Representatives after it is reported, it will be placed on the Calendar for Perfection. If no such vote is taken within that time, it will lie on the table.[28]

Committee of the Whole[29]

Either house may resolve itself into a Committee of the Whole to consider any business coming before it. The Committee is presided over by a chairman appointed by the speaker in the House of Representatives and by the president pro tem in the Senate. The house rules and procedures are observed, if applicable, except the rule limiting the number of times of speaking in the House of Representatives. A majority of the members constitute a quorum. The bill is read at length by the secretary in the Senate or by the clerk in the House of Representatives, and then read again and debated upon by clauses or sections, leaving the preamble to be last considered. After the report, the bill is subject to further debate and amendment by clauses as before. Then a vote on the

---

[26] Senate Rule 46.

[27] Senate Rule 6.

[28] Senate Rule 54; House Rule 42.

[29] Senate Rules 37-44; House Rules 99-105.

question to perfect and print it is taken. Upon completion of its action on the bill, the committee dissolves itself by "rising," and the regular presiding officer resumes his seat. The full house returns to hear the recommendations from the committee.

Perfection

Perfection is the debate and amendment of a bill on a house floor in order to put finishing touches to it. When the bill's turn comes up for perfection, the committee amendments or substitutes are taken up first. Upon call of the bill by the sponsor, the amendments or substitutes are presented, read, and voted upon. If adopted, they are still subject to further consideration and amendments on the floor before final adoption. If they are rejected, the original bill will be brought upon the floor.

These amendments, if adopted, are designated as "Senate or House Amendments" to distinguish from "Senate or House Committee Amendments." Upon completion of amendments to the bill and cessation of debate, a vote is taken, often by voice, unless a member requests a roll call vote. The speaker may also call for a roll call vote if he is in doubt on a voice vote. If a majority of the members vote favorably, the bill is declared perfected and ordered printed. Then the clerk in the House or the Senate Committee on Bills Perfected and Ordered Printed incorporates the adopted amendments into the bill. Then the bill is proofread and printed.

Filibuster in the Missouri Senate?

Filibuster is a dilatory tactic used by a minority (a small group of senators usually from both parties, not a minority party, in the Senate) in an effort to delay or prevent a vote on a bill which probably would pass if put to a vote. This tactic is often employed in the U.S. Senate. Many U.S. Senators have successfully talked bills to death. Because the American upper house has the cherished tradition of freedom of speech, debate is therefore unlimited, and the closure rule[30] to cut off endless talk is hard to invoke in the U.S. Senate. Though in the Missouri Senate the strict

---

[30] To close off debate in the U.S. Senate is the cloture or closure rule or Rule 22, which requires (1) motion by 16 senators or 1/6 of the entire Senate membership, (2) a roll call vote on the second day, and (3) approval by 3/5 of the entire Senate membership.

rules make filibuster difficult, it is not entirely impossible for senators to resort to this time-delaying device. Unlike the Missouri House of Representatives where no member shall speak more than twice on the same question and more than 15 minutes each time without permission of the House,[31] state senators are not subject to time limit, though they are restricted to speak only once on the subject under consideration, unless permitted by the Senate.[32]

Obviously at least two rules in the Missouri Senate can prevent senators from bogging down in endless debate: Rules 81 and 85 (the previous question rule). The previous question rule is a device to cut off debate and to force a vote on the subject pending. Though a petition must be signed by five senators, it is voted upon immediately (not on the second legislative day as in the U.S. Senate) and requires an absolute majority vote (not "three-fifths" as in the U.S. Senate). Furthermore, by prohibiting other senators from speaking on the pending matter "after a senator has been recognized to close," Rule 81 can cut off the so-called "organized" or "collective" filibuster, the most effective tactic used by a bill's opponents. By joining together to control the scene, gaining the floor and then yielding it among themselves, they keep the debate going on and on until the bill's proponents finally give in or give up the whole bill.

The Senate Committee on State Budget Control and The House Budget Committee

Subject to certain conditions or exceptions, both Senate and House bills are referred to these two committees for consideration (see Chapter VII).

Third Reading and Final Passage

After perfection and reprinting, the bill goes upon the Calendar for Third Reading and Final Passage, but it must lie over one day before a third reading. When its calendar order comes up the next day, the bill is read again by title only. The bill is subject to further debate but not to further amendment except that its title may be altered to fit its contents. At the close of debate, a recorded vote is taken. A constitutional or absolute majority vote (18 in

---

[31] House Rule 82.

[32] Senate Rule 81.

the Senate and 82 in the House of Representatives) is required for final passage of the bill.

If a bill contains an emergency clause, action is taken first on the bill excluding the emergency clause. If the bill receives an absolute majority vote, a roll call vote is taken on the emergency clause without debate. If it receives a two-thirds vote, the bill will become law at the time of the governor's approval, unless another date is specified in the bill.[33]

The Informal Calendar

When a bill or resolution comes up for perfection or for third reading and passage in the House of Representatives, the sponsor of a House bill (or the sponsor of a Senate bill in the House) may request it to be laid over informally for one of the following reasons: absence of the sponsor, or not his right time for debate, point of order, prolonged unyielding floor debate (filibuster), and a challenge of the bill's content or title by another member in the chamber. The "informally laid over" bill is not taken up for consideration on the same day but appears in order on the informal calendar for the following legislative day. If it has not been taken up for consideration within ten legislative days, it is tabled and dropped from the calendar without further action.[34]

An Engrossed Bill in the Other House

The final copy of a bill passed by one house, including all amendments or substitutes, and certified by the secretary of the Senate or the clerk in the House of Representatives, is an engrossed bill. Since a bill must be passed by both houses in identical form and signed by the governor before it becomes law, an engrossed bill is automatically sent to the other house for consideration.

In the other house, the legislative procedure is similar. The reading of the message of transferral is counted as the first reading of the bill. After the second reading, the bill goes through almost the same legislative maze as in its house of origin: committee action followed by the perfection stage on the floor. In the House of Representatives, if a Senate bill is reported out of a committee un-

---

[33]Mo. Const. art. 3, sec. 29.

[34]House Rules 43-45.

favorably (with recommendation that it "do not pass"),it
will not go upon the House floor for third reading and
final passage unless ordered by a constitutional majority
of the House.[35]

If the other house approves the bill without any amendment, it is returned to the originating house with an appropriate message indicating approval. Otherwise the other
house has to inform the originating house of the amendments
it made with request for concurrence in these changes. After
having received the message from the other house, the house
of origin places the bill and amendments on the Calendar
for the Third Reading and Final Passage. It may either con-
cur in or reject the amendments. Concurrence requires a
majority vote by roll call on each amendment. Rejection may
be by voice vote upon motion. If the amendments are accepted
by the originating house, the other house is so notified. If
there are differences between the two houses, a conference
committee may be requested to iron out the differences.

In the Conference Committee

All conference committees are composed of five conferees
from each house, appointed by the House speaker and the Senate president pro tem respectively. The conference report
or the compromise version of the bill must be approved by an
absolute majority of the committee with not less than two
conferees from each house signing it.[36] Then the conferees
of each house report to their own house the compromise bill.
Usually the house of origin acts first. If accepted, the
bill goes to the other house. Upon approval there it is
declared Truly Agreed To and Finally Passed. If either house
rejects the compromise bill, further conferences may be held
by the same committee or by newly appointed committees for
further negotiation. Some bills die in conference committees.

Final Action by Each House: An Enrolled Bill

Upon final passage of the version of the bill agreed to
by both houses, it is ordered enrolled. It is typed in its
finally approved form and designated as a Truly Agreed To and
Finally Passed Bill. After having been circumspectly checked
and proofread for errors, it is signed by the president or

---

[35] House Rule 62.

[36] Joint Rule 23.

the president pro tem and the secretary of the Senate and the speaker and the chief clerk of the House of Representatives in open session of each house. The Constitution authorizes any member in either house at this time to file written objections, which are sent together with the bill to the governor.[37] The final authoritative copy of a bill passed by both houses of legislature and signed by their presiding officers is called an enrolled bill.

Concurrence by one house in the other house's amendments, the adoption of conference committee reports in each house, and the final passage of bills all require the approval of an absolute majority in each house with recorded votes.[38] All bills in either house remaining on the calender after midnight on June 15 in odd-numbered years or after midnight on April 30 in even-numbered years are tabled. The last fifteen days in each session are devoted to the engrossing, enrolling, and signing of bills by the presiding officers of both houses.[39]

II. ACTION BY THE GOVERNOR AND REACTION BY THE GENERAL ASSEMBLY

After having received a bill, the governor may take one of the following actions or no action at all:

1. If the governor approves a bill, he signs it and returns it to the originating house within 15 days if the General Assembly is still in session. The General Assembly then passes it on to the Office of Secretary of State. If the General Assembly has adjourned, the governor sends the bill directly to the Office of Secretary of State.

2. If the governor disapproves the bill, he sends it back to the house of origin within 15 days with an explanation of his objection, if the General Assembly is still in session. The veto may be overridden if the bill is passed by a two-thirds majority vote in each house. In this case, the bill becomes law without the governor's signature.

3. If the General Assembly recesses for 30 days or ad-

---

[37] Mo. Const. art. 3, sec. 30.

[38] Ibid., sec. 27.

[39] Ibid., sec. 20.

journs sine die, the governor has 30 more days (altogether 45 days) to act upon the bill. After acting upon a bill, he forwards it to the Office of Secretary of State with his approval or disapproval, accompanied by his reasons.

4. If the governor vetoes a bill within five days before the last day on which the legislature may consider bills in odd-numbered years (June 11-15), the bill is placed at the top of the calendar for the General Assembly to consider when it reconvenes the following January. If the governor vetoes a bill within five days before the last day on which the legislature may consider bills in even-numbered years (April 26-30), the General Assembly reconvenes automatically on the first Wednesday in September for no more than ten calendar days to consider the vetoed bill or bills.[40]

5. If the governor has not returned a bill to its originating house within 15 days while the General Assembly is still in session, it becomes law if both houses adopt a joint resolution by an absolute majority vote in each house directing the secretary of state to enroll the bill as an authentic act.[41] The joint resolution is not submitted to the governor for approval.

6. Theoretically the governor may use pocket veto (or veto by inaction) power to kill a bill. It is likely that a bill will die a natural death if the legislature adjourns before the allotted time for the governor to return a bill expires, especially at the close of the second session. Bills may be carried over from the first session to the second, but not from one General Assembly to another. So far no such constitutional question has ever arisen in Missouri.

7. The governor can reduce (but not increase) any appropriation or strike out any appropriation items or sections in any appropriation bill and sign the remainder into law. The "item veto" power is used to

---

[40] Mo. Const. art. 3, sec. 33.

[41] If the U.S. President has not returned the bill to Congress within 10 days excluding Sundays while it is still in session, the bill automatically becomes law.

get rid of undesirable riders,[42] curtail pork barrel legislation,[43] and fight legislative extravagance. The only exception is that the Missouri governor can "not reduce any appropriation for free public schools, or for the payment of principal and interest on the public debt."[44]

III. A NEW LAW IN EFFECT

After having received newly enacted laws from the General Assembly or from the governor when the Assembly is not in session, the Office of the Secretary of State binds them together into one volume known as <u>Session Laws</u> at the end of each session and preserves the finally typed copies in the state archives. No law takes effect until 90 days after adjournment of the session of the General Assembly in which it was enacted except appropriation bills, which become effective on July 1. A bill containing an emergency clause goes into effect immediately upon approval by the governor unless another date is specified in the bill.

At the end of every ten years, in the year ending in "9", the general statutory laws are revised and promulgated by the Committee on Legislative Research as the <u>Revised Statutes of Missouri</u>. The committee also publishes supplements to the statutes every year to report changes in Missouri law since its previous revision.

---

[42] A bill, unlikely to pass by itself in the legislature, is therefore attached by its sponsor to an important bill, especially appropriation bill, and thus becomes an item to that bill (called a rider) even though they are entirely irrelevant. The rider becomes law if the major bill becomes law.

[43] Acts appropriating public funds for local projects, which politically benefit the legislator who sponsors the bill.

[44] Mo. Const. art. 4, sec. 26.

Figure 8.2

How a Bill

HOUSE

Introduction	Standing or Select Committee		

A bill intro-
    duced by a
    represen-
    tative
First Reading
(Bill on the
    calendar;
    next legis-
    lative day)
Second Reading
	Speaker bill refers to the	Subcommittee
		
		Public Hearing
		Action
		  Consideration
		  Amendment
		  Vote
		  Reports back
			Public Hearing
			
			Action
			  Disapproval
			  Amendment
			  Approval
			
			Reports to the
			  floor

Introduction	Standing or Select Committee		

A bill intro-
    duced by a
    senator
First Reading
(bill on the
    calendar;
    next legis-
    lative day)
Second Reading
	President pro tem refers the bill to re-	Subcommittee
		
		Public Hearing
		Action
		  Consideration
		  Amendment
		  Vote
		Reports back
			Public Hearing
			
			Action
			  Disapproval
			  Amendment
			  Approval
			
			Reports to the
			  floor

A bill first introduced in the Senate follows the same process as in the House of Representatives except that the two house action is reversed.

...... ═══ This procedure does not apply to every bill.

142

The Legislative Process

Becomes Law in Missouri

OF REPRESENTATIVES

Floor				Floor	
Bill on the Perfec- tion Calendar	Perfection		Budget Committee	Bill on the Third Read- ing Calendar	Third Reading & Final Passage
	Committee of the Whole	Debate			
	Debate Amendment Vote (Rising to report back to the floor)	Amendment Vote (Bill re- printed)			

SENATE

Floor				Floor	
Bill on the Perfec- tion Calendar	Perfection		Committee to Amend Bud get on Consent or Control Calendar	Bill on the Third Read- ing Calendar	Third Reading & Final Passage
	Committee of the Whole	Debate			
	Debate Amendment Vote (Rising to report back to the floor)	Amendment Vote (Bill re- printed)			

143

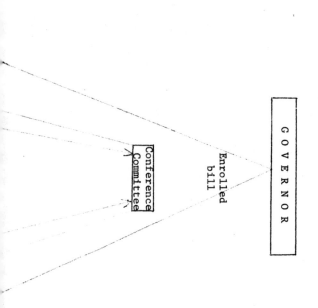

Conference Committee

Enrolled bill

GOVERNOR

CHAPTER IX   STATE ELECTIVE EXECUTIVES

The executive branch of the Missouri government consists of all state elective and appointive officials and employees except the personnel of the General Assembly and courts. There are six executive officers elected by and accountable to the people and thirteen departments and one office under the governor's direct control in the executive branch.

The six elective officials are the governor, lieutenant governor, secretary of state, auditor, state treasurer, and attorney general.

SIX ELECTIVE EXECUTIVES

THE GOVERNOR

Like the President of the United States, the governor of Missouri is not only the chief of state representing Missouri on ceremonial occasions and communicating with the federal government and other states but also the head of the government exercising overall administrative direction. The Constitution specifies in Article IV, Section 1 that "the supreme executive power shall be vested in a governor." But compared with his national counterpart, the Missouri governor is in a much weaker position as administrator of state functions. The United States President may have a humble Vice President, pliable cabinet members, subservient independent agency heads and like-minded judges. Although these appointments are subjected to senatorial confirmation, they are always approved. But in Missouri five additional state executive officers are elected by the people. Frequently, some of them come from the other party and may challenge the governor's authority despite his towering stature in the state.[1]

Qualifications and Election

The governor must be at least age 30, a United States citizen for at least 15 years and a Missouri resident for 10 years before he is elected. He is elected in the presidential election years, sometimes on a presidential candi-

---

[1] Governor Joseph P. Teasdale dared not leave the state to attend the Democratic National Convention in New York in 1980 for fear that Lieutenant Governor William C. Phelps might, in the capacity of acting governor, sign the bills he disapproved.

date's coattails, for a term of four years. Unlike the
American President and Vice President and their counterparts
in other twenty-one states, the governor and lieutenant governor in Missouri are not elected on the same ticket as a team.
They run separately in the November elections every four years
after having won their own primary victories in August. In
the 1976 gubernatorial election, incumbent Republican Governor
Christopher S. Bond was defeated, while Republican Lieutenant
Governor William C. Phelps was re-elected for a second term.

Tenure, Removal, and Succession

The governor's term begins on the first Wednesday after
the first Monday in January following each gubernatorial
election. Patterned after the 22nd Amendment to the United
States Constitution,[2] the Missouri Constitutional Amendment
of 1965 makes the governor eligible for immediate re-election
but limits his tenure to two terms. However, he may hold
office for two more years--altogether ten years including two
elective terms--if he has filled out his predecessor's unexpired term for no more than two years. Such may be the
case with a lieutenant governor who succeeds a governor removed from office by death, resignation, or impeachment.
The same rule applies to the tenure of the state treasurer.

Before 1965, no governor in Missouri had served two full
consecutive terms. John Miller was elected governor at a special election to fill the vacancy on December 8, 1823 and was
re-elected two years later. Governor Lilburn W. Boggs, who
had been lieutenant governor since 1832, succeeded Daniel
Dunklin upon his resignation and was elected in his own right
in 1836. Only Governor Phil M. Donnelly served twice as a
full-term governor but not in succession (1945-1948, 1953-
1956). The first governor who served two consecutive full
terms was Warren E. Hearnes (1965-1972). Beginning in 1981,
the salary of the governor is $55,000 a year. He is fur-
nished with free residence in the Executive Mansion at 100
Madison Street, Jefferson City, and his office is in the
State Capitol.

The governor can be removed from office by death, resignation, impeachment,[3] disability, or nepotism.[4] In Missouri,

---

[2] Adopted on February 26, 1951.

[3] All state governors can be removed by impeachment except
the governor of Oregon who can be removed only by recall.

[4] Any public officer or employee who, by virtue of his

one governor[5] was deposed by the state convention in July
1861, two governors[6] resigned, and four[7] died in office. In
the absence of the governor from the state, the lieutenant
governor acts on his behalf and succeeds him if he is removed from office for any reason. The second in the line of
succession is the president pro tem of the Senate, followed
by the speaker of the House of Representatives, the secretary
of state, the state auditor, the state treasurer, and the
attorney general.[8] In Missouri only five lieutenant governors[9]
and one president pro tem[10] have become governors. There have
been 47 governors in Missouri since it was admitted to the
Union as a state in 1821: 2 Unionists, 9 Republicans, and 36
Democrats.

Disability

Whenever the governor is unable to discharge his duties,
he declares his disability in writing to the Senate president
pro tem and the House speaker. The lieutenant governor then
acts in his behalf until the governor submits a written declaration to the above-mentioned two officers that he is able
to resume his duties. If there is no lieutenant governor or
the lieutenant governor is incapable of acting, the Senate
president pro tem, the House speaker, the secretary of state,
the state auditor, the state treasurer, or the attorney general in succession will be acting governor until the governor's disability is removed.

But sometimes it happens that the governor is disabled
and cannot attend to his office but refuses to declare his
disability. In such a case, In Missouri a disability board
steps in. The board is composed of nine members: the lieu-

---

office or employment, appoints to public office or employment any relative within the fourth degree, by consanguinity
or affinity. Mo. Const. art. 7, sec. 6:

[5] Claiborne F. Jackson.

[6] Daniel Dunklin and Trusten Polk.

[7] Frederick Bates, Thomas Reynolds, Hamilton R. Gamble,
and John S. Marmaduke.

[8] Mo. Const. art. 4, sec. 11 (a).

[9] Lilburn W. Boggs, Merdith M. Marmaduke, Hancock L.
Jackson, Williard P. Hall, and Albert P. Morehouse.

[10] Abraham J. Williams in 1825.

tenant governor, the secretary of state, the state auditor, the state treasurer, the attorney general, the Senate president pro tem, the House speaker, and the House and Senate majority floor leaders. If a majority of the board declares the governor's disability in writing to the Senate president pro tem and the House speaker, the lieutenant governor will be acting governor. Later when the governor submits his written statement to the disability board declaring that his disability no longer exists, he may resume his office on the fourth day, unless a majority of the board declares to the contrary within four days to the State Supreme Court. If the Court, within 21 days after receipt of such declaration, decides by an absolute majority that the governor is unable to discharge the duties of his office, the lieutenant governor will continue to be acting governor; otherwise, the governor will resume his office.[11] This provision is patterned after the 25th Amendment to the United States Constitution.[12]

Duties and Powers

The governor, as the chief executive of the state, usually has most of the powers his national counterpart has, except the power to deal with foreign nations. According to the Missouri Constitution, "The governor shall take care that the laws are distributed and faithfully executed, and shall be a conservator of the peace throughout the state."[13] To discharge his duties, the governor is vested with the following powers:

I. Executive Powers[14]

---

[11]Mo. Const. art. 4, sec. 11 (b), adopted on August 6, 1969.

[12]Adopted on February 10, 1967. In American history two Presidents could not discharge their duties but refused to declare disability. James A. Garfield was shot on July 2, 1881 and died on September 19 after having lingered on the sickbed for eighty days. Woodrow Wilson suffered a nervous breakdown in September 1919 and stayed in office till the end of his term. Vice President Thomas R. Marshall even dared not enter the White House during Wilson's illness to avoid the suspicion of attempting to usurp power. Though President Dwight D. Eisenhower suffered a heart attack twice in office, his ambitious Vice-president Richard M. Nixon didn't have a chance to become acting president.

[13]Mo. Const. art. 4, sec. 2.

[14]In three New England states, Maine, Massachusetts, and

A. Appointment

    1. The governor appoints all department heads, including boards and commissions, such as the Conservation Commission, the State Board of Education, the Board of Probation and Parole and so forth. He also appoints the members of local boards and commissions, such as the Boards of Election Commissioners for St. Louis County, St. Louis City, Kansas City, Jackson County, and Clay County; and the Boards of Police Commissioners for Kansas City and for the City of St. Louis. Many appointments are subject to the advice and consent of the Senate.

    2. The governor appoints judges for the Supreme Court and the Court of Appeals, and also circuit court judges in St. Louis, Jackson, Platte and Clay Counties and St. Louis City under the Non-partisan Selection of Judges Plan.[15]

    3. The Governor appoints the boards of curators or regents of state universities and colleges.

    4. The governor fills vacancies in most public offices including the U.S. Senate,[16] state offices, and judgeships, and also vacancies in county offices except for home rule counties and sheriffs. Appointees serve until their qualified successors are duly elected or appointed.[17]

B. Calling elections to fill vacancies

    The governor calls elections to fill vacancies in either house of the General Assembly[18] and in the U.S. House of Representatives.[19]

C. Commissioning state officers

New Hampshere, the executive council shares certain executive powers with the governor.

[15] See Chapter XI.

[16] U.S. Const. amend. XVII.

[17] Mo. Const. art. 4, sec. 4.

[18] Ibid., art. 3, sec. 14.

[19] U.S. Const. art. I, sec. 2.

The governor commissions all public officers except those whose commissions are otherwise provided by law.[20]

D. Removal

The Missouri Constitution grants the governor a general or unrestricted power of removal, as it stipulates that "All appointive officers may be removed by the governor."[21] In other words, the removal of such officers is not subject to the address of the legislature, or approval of the Senate or of an executive council, nor restricted to the causes enumerated in the Constitution as in other states. However, it seems that the Missouri governor is not entirely free in exercising his removal powers. According to Article VII, Section 4 of the Constitution, "Except as provided in the Constitution, all officers not subject to impeachment shall be subject to removal from office in the manner and for the causes provided by law." The governor cannot in fact remove those having fixed terms except on the ground of incompetence or bad behavior.

E. Calling special elections for referenda

The governor calls for special elections to vote on proposed amendments to the Missouri Constitution.[22]

F. Signing all patents for lands issued by the authority of the state.

G. Control of state finances

1. The governor, along with the state auditor, approves the banks recommended by the state treasurer for the deposit of state funds.

2. Control over state spending

   a. Item veto power

---

[20]Mo. Const. art. 4, sec. 3.

[21]Ibid., sec. 17.

[22]Ibid., art. 12, sec. 2 (b). According to Article III, Section 52 (b), the General Assembly may order a special election for legislative referendum.

To regulate the spending of state funds, the governor has the power, which the United States President has not, to strike out any item in any appropriation bill or any appropriation item in any bill, to which he objects.

b. Reduction in appropriation

The governor may control the spending rate by allotment or other means. He may reduce the expenditures of any agency even after an appropriation law has gone into effect, whenever the state's actual revenues are less than the estimates or are slow in coming to the state treasury.[23]

But the governor cannot cut appropriation for free public schools or for the payment of principal and interest on the state debt.[24]

II. Military Power

The governor is the commander-in-chief of the militia[25] in the state except when it is called into actual national service and becomes part of the National Guard, of which the United States President is the commander-in-chief.[26] The militia is primarily the volunteer armed forces of the states. Since 1916, state militias have been formally organized as the National Guard, an auxiliary of the regular army under federal control. Therefore, the governor of Missouri is the commander-in-chief of the Missouri National Guard. When the Missouri National Guard is called out for defense of national security, enforcement of federal law,[27] or preservation of order in national emergencies by the United States President, it becomes part of the U.S. regular army and its subjection to state

---

[23]Ibid., art. 4, sec. 27.

[24]Ibid., sec. 26.

[25]Ibid., sec. 6.

[26]U.S. Const. art. 2, sec. 3.

[27]For instance, in September 1957, President Eisenhower federalized the Arkansas National Guard and called out regular army units to Little Rock, Arkansas, to enforce the federal court order to desegregate schools, which Arkansas Governor Orval Faubus challenged.

jurisdiction ceases.

Through the adjutant general, the governor of Missouri appoints officers to train the National Guard or militia according to the disciplines prescribed by Congress. Congress also provides for its organization and arming.[28] The governor may call out the National Guard to enforce the state law, prevent threatened riot, suppress actual insurrection, and repel invasion.

III. Legislative Powers

The governor of Missouri has three kinds of legislative powers vested by the Constitution,[29] namely, to recommend messages, to approve or veto bills, and to call special or extra sessions.

A. Recommendation of messages

The governor is required to keep the General Assembly informed from time to time of the status of the state and to make recommendations he deems necessary to be introduced in the General Assembly. He may therefore send messages to the state legislature at any time he wishes. But by law he must deliver the "state of the state" message at the opening of each session of the General Assembly. The message spells out his policies and sets forth proposals to solve problems,

He must also send a budget message to the General Assembly within 30 days after the opening of its regular session. Neither house is allowed to pass any new appropriations other than emergency ones recommended by the governor until the General Assembly acts on all the appropriations recommended in the budget.[30] The governor may recommend "any laws necessary to provide revenues sufficient to meet expenditures."[31]

B. Action on bills:

1. Approval

---

[28]U.S. Const. art. I, sec. 8.

[29]Mo. Const. art. 4, sec. 9 & art. 3, sec. 31.

[30]Ibid., art. 4, sec. 25.

[31]Ibid., sec. 24.

If the governor approves a bill passed by the General Assembly, he will sign it into law.

2. Veto

a. Regular and item vetoes[32]

Like forty-three other state governors, the Missouri governor has both regular and item veto powers. But his item veto power is limited to appropriation bills or appropriation items in any bill.

b. Pocket veto?

It is unclear as to whether the Missouri governor has pocket veto power. The Constitution specifies the action to be taken by the General Assembly to override his inaction—adoption of a joint resolution—if it is still in session, but is silent on any action the Assembly may take after adjournment or just lets the bill die automatically as in Congress. Perhaps, traditionally the Assembly may take a similar action to override the governor's inaction at the beginning of the second session. But what if the governor has not returned a bill after the close of the second session?

C. Calling special or extra sessions

The governor of Missouri has the sole power[33] to call the General Assembly into an extra or special session, which lasts no longer than 60 calendar days. Unlike Congress, the General Assembly, once in a special session, is not allowed to act upon any item other than those specified in the governor's proclamation calling said session.[34]

IV. Judicial Powers

The Missouri governor has a variety of judicial powers,

---

[32]Only the governor of North Carolina has no veto power. Only the governor of Washington can veto any item or clause in any bill, monetary or non-monetary.

[33]Mo. Const. art. 4, sec. 9.

[34]Ibid., art. 3, sec. 39 (7).

namely, commutation, reprieve, pardon,[35] and authorization
of rendition or extradition.

A. Commutations, reprieves, and pardons[36]

Except in cases of treason and conviction in impeachment, the governor of Missouri may, in accordance
with law, grant commutations, reprieves, and pardons
to anyone convicted of a crime. A commutation is a
reduction in punishment. A reprieve is a temporary
postponement in the execution of a sentence usually to
allow time for an appeal because of new evidence discovered or new grounds found. A pardon is a release
from the punishment or from the legal consequences of
a crime or remission of the penalty imposed.

A pardon may be absolute or conditional.[37] A pardon is granted generally after conviction but sometimes
before it or even before trial.[38] The Missouri governor grants pardon only after conviction. He also has
the power to remit fees and forfeitures which he re-
gards as unjust. But he has no power to parole. This
function has been assigned to the Board of Probation
and Parole, which may parole any person confined in the
institutions under the Division of Adult Institutions
except those under death penalty.

---

[35]Ibid., art. 4, sec. 7. Reprieves, commutations, and
pardons are usually referred to as "executive clemency."

[36]In about 30 states, the governor has the full power to
pardon, while in others the governor has to share such power
with a pardon board or with the state senate.

[37]An absolute (or full or complete) pardon absolves the
offender from the penalty or other legal consequences and even
restores the rights or privileges lost because of conviction,
such as enfranchisement or eligibility for public office. In
other words, absolute pardon sweeps away all charges and restores the conditions existing before conviction. A conditional or partial pardon leaves certain obligations or disabilities
on the pardonee. The pardon becomes effective if certain obligations are fulfilled or the stipulated conditions are satis-
fied. For instance, the recipient must be and remain in the
state as a law-abiding citizen or he must leave the state.

[38]President Gerald Ford pardoned former President Richard
M. Nixon even before prosecution.

154

B. Renditions

Interstate rendition involves the return of a fugitive from justice to the state where he has been accused or convicted of a crime. In requesting the return of a fugitive, for instance, from Illinois, the Missouri governor issues a formal requisition, accompanied by a certified copy of indictment or other essential documents concerned, to the Illinois governor. In honoring the requisition, the Illinois governor issues a warrant of rendition ordering his law enforcement officers to arrest the fugitive and hand him over to the officers from Missouri.

In addition to the duties and powers vested by the Constitution, the Missouri governor has many other duties assigned him by statutes and custom. He is an ex officio member of various boards and commissions. Furthermore, like the American President, who is the leader of his party in the United States outside Congress, the Missouri governor is the leader of his party in the state outside the General Assembly.

THE LIEUTENANT GOVERNOR[39]

Like the governor, the lieutenant governor of Missouri is elected for a four-year term, but he is elegible for indefinite re-elections. As he may succeed the governor at any time, he is therefore required to possess the same qualifications as the governor: age 30, 15-year American citizenship, and 10-year state residence.[40] He will be governor for one term if the governor-elect dies before taking office, and for the remainder of the term if the incumbent governor is removed from office by death, failure to qualify, resignation, or conviction in impeachment. The lieutenant governor will be acting governor during the governor's absence from the state or during his disability. Beginning in 1981, his salary is $30,000 a year, but he receives pay at the same rate as the governor while he is acting governor. There have been forty-one lieutenant governors including Kenneth J. Rothman.

---

[39] In the United States there are eight states having no lieutenant governors. In five of them (Maine, Tennessee, New Hampshire, New Jersey, and West Virginia), the president of the Senate is the governor's successor. In Tennessee, the title is lieutenant governor and speaker of the Senate. In other three states (Arizona, Oregon, and Wyoming), the secretary of state succeeds the governor.

[40] Mo. Const. art. 4, sec. 10.

Under the Constitution, the lieutenant governor is ex officio president of the Missouri Senate. By law, he serves as secretary and member of the Board of Public Buildings. Lieutenant Governor William C. Phelps (1972-1980) gained the distinction of being Missouri's first full-time lieutenant governor, who gave up his law practice in Kansas City and devoted full time to his office.[41]

THE SECRETARY OF STATE[42]

The secretary of state is the custodian of the state seal, public records, and official documents, such as legislative acts and the governor's proclamations. He is also the state's chief election official. He accepts declarations of candidacy for all public offices above the county level, supervises official elections, and certifies the results, including the votes on ballot issues regarding constitutional amendments and initiative and referendum proposals. He receives campaign finance disclosure reports from candidates and political committees and ascertains whether they have conformed to state campaign finance laws. He also collects, compiles, and publishes a variety of data and statistics on state government, particularly the journals of the General Assembly, laws, and the Official Manual.

The secretary of state administers the state's corpo-

---

[41] Like his counterparts in five other states (Colorado, Illinois, New Mexico, Wisconsin, and New York), Lieutenant Governor Phelps was also the first lieutenant governor in Missouri who served as ombudsman or "grievance man" to hear and investigate the complaints from the aggrieved individuals against public (not private) agencies or officials and to recommend corrections, if the complaints are justified. The office of "ombudsman" is a Swedish innovation, established in 1809 and later adopted by other European countries (England in 1966), Africa, New Zealand, Australia, and Canada. Originally, this office is appointed by a legislative body.

[42] The office of secretary of state is found in 47 states. Except in 10 states, the office is elective. The 10 states where the secretary of state is appointed are Delaware, Maine, Maryland, New Hampshire, New Jersey, New York, Pennsylvania, Tennessee, Texas, and Virginia. In Alaska, Hawaii, and Utah, the lieutenant governor serves as secretary of state. In Oregon, the secretary of state also serves as state auditor.

ration laws and regulates the issuance and sale of such securities as stocks, bonds, and debentures through the Uniform Securities Act. His office provides centralized filing for perfecting security interests in all business and professional loans. Furthermore, the secretary of state presides over the House of Representatives at the opening session after each election until it is organized. By use of the state seal, he authenticates all proclamations, executive orders, appointments and commissions, extraditions, commutations, and restorations of citizenship made by the governor. He also prepares the commissions of elected state, district, and county officials.

His office is divided into ten units: eight divisions and two services. The Campaign Finance Review Board is assigned to his office only for budgeting purposes. The six-member bi-partisan board was created under the Campaign Finance Disclosure Law of 1978 to assist the secretary of state in enforcing the new law. The law requires preelection reports of contributions and expenditures by candidates and ballot issues, and the board is charged with conducting audits and investigations.

THE STATE AUDITOR[43]

The chief duty of the state auditor is to supervise and audit the receipt and expenditure of public funds. He post-audits[44] the accounts of all state agencies, audits the state treasury at least once a year, and establishes appropriate accounting systems for all public officials of the state. He

---

[43]Mo. Const. art. 4, sec. 13. This official is elected in 31 states and appointed by the governor or legislature in others.

[44]Primarily the state auditor has both pre-auditing and post-auditing duties. He checks on the legality of proposed expenditure and availability of funds before spending to determine if such spending will conform to the appropriate law (pre-auditing) and also on the legality and fidelity of expenditures after spending (post-auditing). Recently this pre-auditing function has been shifted from the elective auditor to an appointive comptroller in many states. About 3/4 of the states now provide for the office of comptroller, and therefore in those states the auditor is concerned only with post-auditing. In Missouri, the Office of Administration is responsible for pre-auditing.

also makes other audits and investigations as required by law. Moreover, he establishes appropriate accounting systems for the political subdivisions of the state, supervises their budgeting systems, and regularly audits third and fourth class counties and other political subdivisions when requested by popular petitions. Together with the governor, he approves the banks selected by the state treasurer for the deposit of state funds.

THE STATE TREASURER[45]

The Constitution assigns the state treasurer three basic duties, namely, receipt, investment or custody, and disbursement of state funds. His office is therefore responsible for (1) receiving all state funds from any source, (2) investing funds not needed for current operation in any Missouri bank selected by the state treasurer and approved by the governor and the state auditor or in short-term U.S. government obligations or other U.S. obligations, both maturing and payable within one year, and (3) paying out these funds on warrants from the commissioner of (the Office of) Administration. His office functions essentially like a bank to the state.

Therefore, the state treasurer has the heavy responsibility of exercising his good judgment to determine the amount of state funds not needed for current operating expenses of the state government and to invest these funds in such banking institutions in the state as can give security satisfactory to the governor and the auditor for safekeeping and payment.

The state treasurer is a member and secretary of the State Board of Fund Commissioners, which is responsible for all transactions regarding the bonded indebtedness of the state. He is also a member of the Missouri Housing Development Commission. By law, he is charged with the administration of Missouri's Abandoned Funds Act.

THE ATTORNEY GENERAL

Perhaps because most of the attorney general's powers and functions are traditional and inherent within the common law, they are not mentioned in the Missouri Constitution nor fully elaborated in the state law.[46] The attorney general

---

[45] Mo. Const. art. 4, sec. 15. This office is popularly elected in 41 states and appointed by the governor or legislature in others.

[46] §§27.010-27.060, RSMo 1978.

is the state's chief representative, advisor, and prosecutor
on legal matters.

As the state's chief legal representative, the attorney
general, on behalf of the state, institutes in trial courts
all civil suits and other proceedings at law or in equity
necessary to protect the rights and interests of Missouri.
He thereby represents Missouri in federal courts in any liti-
gation in which the state is involved. In appellate courts
he represents the state in all appeals to which Missouri is
a party except in misdemeanor cases or those cases in which
the name of the state is used as nominal plaintiff in the
trial court. He or his assistant attorneys also appear in
courts on behalf of state officials or agencies who sue or
are sued in an official capacity.

As the state's chief legal advisor, the attorney general
may give official legal opinions in writing, without fee, to
the General Assembly, the governor, all elected state officers,
any state department heads, commissioner of election, grain
warehouse commissioner, insurance division director, finance
division director, or any circuit or prosecuting attorney
upon any question of law regarding their respective offices
or duties. Though his legal opinions do not have the force
of law, his interpretations stand authoritative until overturned by court decisions.

In his capacity as the state's chief prosecutor, the attorney general supervises or, when directed by the governor,
assists, through one of his assistant attorneys, any prosecuting or circuit attorney in discharging his duties in trial
courts or in examinations before grand juries. "When so directed by the trial court, he may sign indictments [sic] in
lieu of the prosecuting attorney."[47]

Moreover, the attorney general represents the state in
habeas corpus proceedings filed by penitentiary inmates or
in declaratory judgment proceedings when the constitutionality of a statute is challenged. He represents the public
in proceedings affecting the administration of charitable
funds. He initiates legal proceedings to enforce the liquor
laws, collect delinquent taxes, and prohibit illegal practices
in the sale of securities. He administers the Consumer Protection Act to prohibit fraud in the sale of goods or in
services, malpractices, errors or other professional negli-

---

[47]§27.030, RSMo 1978. There may be an error. The formal
accusation filed by the prosecuting attorney should be "information."

gence. He enforces the State Anti-trust Law against monopolization of trade. He may institute quo warranto[48] proceedings against: (1) any corporation having abused its franchise or violated the state law in Missouri, or (2) any office or franchise illegally held. He may move to remove any public official for malfeasance in office.

QUALIFICATIONS, TERMS, AND IMPEACHMENT

All these executive officials are elected for terms of four years. All of them are eligible for indefinite re-elections except the governor and the state treasurer, whose tenures of office are limited to two terms. But both of them may hold office for a maximum of ten years if they have filled a predecessor's unexpired term not exceeding two years. All these officials are elected at the presidential election years (1976, 1980, 1984) except the state auditor who is elected in off-years (1978, 1982, 1986). All except the governor are members of the governor-disability board.

While silent on other statewide officials' qualifications, the Constitution specifies that the lieutenant governor and the state auditor must possess the same qualifications as the governor: at least age 30, 15-year U.S. citizenship and 10 years of state residency. The 10-year state residency requirement has been in the Constitution since 1945 to ensure that candidates have close ties with the state so as to prevent frivolous, fraudulant, or unqualified candidates. But on June 26, 1978, U.S. District Court Judge Elmo Hunter struck down the 10-year state residency requirement for the state auditor's post, thus paving the way for Republican candidate James Antonio[49] to enter the primary race in August.

---

[48] Quo Warranto (Latin: with what authority or right) is a proceeding in which a court questions the right of a person (usually a public official) to hold an office or a corporation to exercise its franchise. Franchise is the right to form, and to exercise the powers of, a corporate body.

[49] Antonio, a deputy state auditor under the previous three state auditors, had lived in Missouri for eight of the past twelve years before the primary election in 1978. Judge Hunter agreed with Antonio that certified public accountants frequently moved from state to state in their jobs. The judge ruled that certified public accountants are professionally well-qualified to serve as state auditors and the 10-year residency requirement would exclude the best suited persons from that office.

All elective executive officials and court judges in the state are subject to impeachment for "crimes, misconduct, habitual drunkenness, willful neglect of duty, corruption in office, incompetency, or any offense involving moral turpitude or oppression in office."[50] The House of Representatives has the sole power to bring charges, and the Supreme Court tries all impeachments except in the case of the governor and Supreme Court Judges, who are tried by a special commission of seven eminent jurists chosen by the Senate. In trial, the House also acts as prosecutor. No one can be convicted without the concurrence of five-sevenths of the court or special commission.[51] The only punishment after conviction is removal from office. Impeached officials can be tried and punished by regular courts of law for the same criminal acts for which they are impeached.[52] No governor of Missouri has been charged for impeachment. In fourteen states the governor may be removed by popular recall, but not the governor of Missouri.

---

[50]Mo. Const. art. 7, sec. 1.

[51]Ibid., sec. 2.

[52]Ibid., sec. 3.

CHAPTER X   ADMINISTRATION

The governmental process includes two fundamental steps: the formulation of public policy and policy implementation. Theoretically, the "executive" is concerned with the former of these two steps, while the "administration" with the latter, though through implementation policy is really or finally shaped. Policy implementation or administrative process involves two essential components:administrative organization and personnel.

ADMINISTRATIVE ORGANIZATION

There are thirteen departments[1] and the Office of Administration, each headed by a director or commission appointed by the governor with the advice and consent of the Senate. The thirteen departments are: Department of Agriculture, Department of Conservation, Department of Consumer Affairs, Regulation and Licensing, Department of Corrections and Human Resources, Department of Elementary and Secondary Education, Department of Higher Education, Highway and Transportation Department, Department of Labor and Industrial Relations, Department of Mental Health, Department of Natural Resources, Department of Public Safety, Department of Revenue, and Department of Social Services.

OFFICE OF ADMINISTRATION[2]

Roughly comparable to the Executive Office of the United States President, the Office of Administration serves as the state's administrative control and general service agency under the governor. It was created on January 15, 1973 to coordinate the central management functions of state government.

---

[1]The new structure of the Executive Department, effective July 1, 1974, was established by the Omnibus State Reorganization Act of 1974, pursuant to the Constitutional Amendment of 1972. In order to achieve effective centralization in administration, the Constitutional Amendment created thirteen departments by name out of the 87 sprawling boards, commissions, and bureaus and meanwhile authorized the General Assembly to establish an additional department. On January 2, 1980, as a result of the Constitutional Amendment adopted in November 1979, the Department of Transportation and the Department of Highways were emerged into one department. In September 1981, the Department of Corrections and Human Resources was established by the state legislature.

[2]Mo. Const. art. 4, sec. 50.

Today, the office not only renders purchasing, managerial, and planning services to all departments but also coordinates policies and programs, designs and maintains the state's general accounting systems, and keeps custody of all public accounting records of the state. Most important of all, the office pre-audits all requests for payments before certifying the state treasurer for payment, prepares the governor's budget for presentation to the General Assembly, and administers the state merit system. Moreover, the Office of Administration is responsible for state construction projects, maintenance and security of state buildings, and promotion of data processing services for the entire state government.

Headed by a commissioner appointed by the governor with Senate confirmation, the Office of Administration comprises eight divisions: (1) Accounting, (2) Budget and Planning, (3) Design and Construction, (4) Electronic Data Processing Coordination, (5) Flight Operations, (6) General Services, (7) Personnel and (8) Purchasing. The commissioner appoints a deputy commissioner and the directors of the eight divisions who are responsible to him through the deputy commissioner.

THIRTEEN DEPARTMENTS

Department of Agriculture[3]

For the purpose of Promoting Missouri agricultural products and stimulating markets, domestic and international, the Department of Agriculture is charged with improving the quality of agricultural products and protecting food producers, distributers, and consumers through fair competitive practices. The department is also required to protect, foster, and develop the agricultural resources of the state. In addition to inspection for quality control on poultry, dairy, and grains, the department has some unique duties such as surveillance of commercial weighing and measuring devices, motor fuel inspection, and inspection of retail gasoline pumps, taxicab meters and odometers.

To carry out these responsibilities, the department is divided into seven major divisions: (1) Agricultural Development, (2) Weights and Measures, (3) Grain Inspection and Warehousing, (4) International Marketing, (5) Fairs, (6) Plant Industries and (7) Animal Health. Affiliated with the Department of Agriculture is the quasi-autonomous State Milk Board, which standardizes regulation, inspection, and grading of milk

---

[3]Ibid., secs. 35 - 36.

and milk products. It is supported by revenue from inspection fees.

Department of Conservation[4]

The basic functions of the Conservation Department are to conserve and develop the state's forest and wildlife resources, such as bird, fish, and game, including hatcheries, sanctuaries, refuges, reservations, and all other property owned, acquired, and used for these purposes. The department is headed by a bi-partisan four-member commission appointed by the governor and approved by the Senate. The commissioners must have knowledge of and interest in wildlife conservation and serve without compensation for staggered terms of six years each. The commission appoints a director of conservation, who, with its approval, in turn appoints assistants and employees.

The department consists of four line divisions and eleven support sections. The four divisions are (1) fisheries, (2) wildlife, (3) forestry, and (4) protection. The protection division enforces all legislative acts concerning wildlife and forestry and rules and regulations made by the department.

The Conservation Commission's basic plan to better fish, wildlife, and forest resources begins with the soil itself. Thereupon, the department cooperates with agricultural and soil agencies in fulfillment of its broad program of forest and wildlife habitat restoration, which tends to improve water quality and to control soil erosion.

The major financial resources of the department come from the sale of hunting and fishing permits, sale of property, the 1/8 of one percent sales tax earmarked for conservation, revenue from administration of wildlife and forest resources, and federal aid on a matching basis.

Created in 1937 at the request of Missourians for professional management of the state's wildlife resources outside politics, the department has survived repeated legislative intrigues to gain political control of the conservation program and the funds collected for its operation.

Department of Consumer Affairs, Regulation and Licensing[5]

---

[4]Ibid., secs. 40 (a) - 46.

[5]Ibid., sec. 36 (a).

The Department of Consumer Affairs, Regulation and Licensing, one of the most diverse departments created by the Constitution, seeks to protect and improve the interests and well-beings of Missourians as well as to promote state economy. Headed by a director appointed by the governor with senatorial consent, the department consists of various units grouped under three main functional categories: the Community and Economic Development Group, the Regulatory Divisions, and the Division of Professional Registration.

Since community development is indispensable to the economic growth of the state, the Community and Economic Development Group not only develops facilities and services throughout the state but also conducts marketing efforts in order to attract new business and new industry for economic development of communities. Meanwhile, it also helps expand existing business and industry to provide more job opportunities for Missourians. The Group includes eight units, among which the division of Commerce and Industrial Development and the Division of Community Development play major roles in developing community economy.

Under the Regulatory Division are the Missouri Commission on Human Rights, the Public Service Commission, the Office of Public Counsel, the Administrative Hearing Commission, and the Divisions of Insurance, Finance (State Banking Board), Savings and Loan Supervision, and Credit Unions. The Public Service Commission regulates the safety, services and rates of privately owned electric, gas, sewer, water, and telephone utilities as well as transportation facilities such as bus lines. The Office of Public Counsel protects the interests of residential customers and others unable to hire lawyers, particularly utility users, and represents them before the Missouri Public Service Commission. Though by law the public counsel is required to represent customers in every proceeding before the commission, yet the heavy volume and complexity of cases added to the small staff in the Office of Public Counsel make representation in all cases infeasible. So the Public Counsel focuses its efforts on major utility rate cases, the cases affecting most Missouri customers, and those of state-wide importance.

The Administrative Hearing Commission conducts impartial adversary hearings over disputes between citizens and certain state agencies, such as licensing disputes between applicants for licensure and a state licensing agency or between a taxpayer and the Revenue Department, or over challenges to agency authority. The Commission issues written findings of fact and conclusions of law and decisions. Its decisions in li-

censing disputes is reviewed by the circuit court, while
the Court of Appeals reviews its decisions in tax cases and
challenges to agency authority.

The most significant commission under the Regulatory
Division is the Missouri Commission on Human Rights. Created
in 1957, the Commission enforces Missouri's discriminatory
practices acts to protect individuals from discrimination in
housing, employment, and public accommodations because of
race, color, national origin, creed, religion, sex, and physical or mental handicap. The commission consists of 11 members,
one from each congressional district of the state, and one of
them is chairman appointed by the governor with senatorial
consent.[6]

The Division of Professional Registration is in charge
of 16 relatively autonomous professional boards assigned to
it by the Omnibus State Reorganization Act of 1974. These
boards license various vocations and callings such as accountants, architects, engineers, land surveyors, barbers,
chiropractors, cosmetologists, dentists, nurses, physicians,
surgeons, pharmacists, real estate agents, psychologists,
optometrists, podiatrists, veterinarians, embalmers and fu-
neral directors and so on.

Department of Corrections and Human Resources

In an effort to improve the administration of penal and
correctional programs in the state, the Department of Corrections and Human Resources was established by law on September 28, 1981. Composed of two units transferred from the
Department of Social Services (the Division of Corrections
and the Board of Probation and Parole) together with the new
Division of Administration, the newly created department assumes the whole responsibility of supervising and managing
all penal, correctional, training, rehabilitation and reformatory institutions, and probation and parole[7] of the state

---

[6]Despite reduction of the state's ten congressional districts to nine because of the 1980 census, "it does not appear that the total number of Commissioners will be affected
by the change....the law merely states the Commission shall
consist of eleven members, one from each Congressional District and does not say that only one commissioner can be selected from a Congressional District." Alvin A. Plummer,
executive director of Missouri Commission on Human Rights,
personal letter, September 13, 1982.

[7]Probation is the placing of a convicted offender under

of Missouri. No longer under the huge umbrella of a social welfare agency, the new department now independently administers Missouri's uniform policies and procedures governing inmates and prepares them, through education, vocation-training, counseling and guidance, to go back to society as law-abiding and productive citizens.

Headed by a director, the Department of Corrections and Human Resources is the only department created by law in the state. The Division of Adult Institutions (formerly the Division of Corrections) supervises the state's ten correctional institutions[8] and programs thereof. The Board of Probation and Parole has authority to parole any prisoners from these ten correctional institutions except those under death penalty. It also receives all applications for pardon, commutation, reprieve or restoration of citizenship and reports to the governor with appropriate recommendations after investigation.

Department of Elementary and Secondary Education

To achieve universal education in Missouri, the State Constitution requires the establishment of free public schools for all persons in the state under age 21. Twenty-five percent of the general revenue of the state, exclusive of interest and sinking fund, is set apart annually for the support of these schools.[9] For special emphasis upon public education,

---

supervision after suspended sentence in order to give him a chance to show he can live freely without committing other crimes. Parole is the release of a prisoner before the completion of his maximum sentence.

[8]There are ten adult correctional institutions in Missouri: Missouri State Penitentiary (Jefferson City--Maximum security facility), Missouri Training Center for Men (Moberly--Medium), Missouri Eastern Correctional Center (Pacific--Medium), Missouri Intermediate Reformatory (Algoa--Medium/Minimum), State Correctional Pre-release Center (Tipton--Minimum), Central Missouri Correctional Center (formerly known as Church Farm near Jefferson City--Minimum), Ozark Correctional Center (formerly the Fordland Honor camp southeast of Springfield--Minimum), Ka-Cee Honor Center (Kansas City--Minimum), St. Mary's Honor Center (St. Louis--Minimum), and Renz Correctional Center (co-correctional institution near Jefferson City--Minimum security facility for men, but a full range of security facilities for women). Renz is the only women's correctional institution in Missouri.

[9]Mo. Const. art. 9, secs. 1 (a) & 3 (b).

a specific article (Article IX) is provided in the Constitution, and a separate department of elementary and secondary education was established in 1974 by the Omnibus State Reorganization Act of the same year.

Headed by a commissioner appointed by the State **Board** of Education, the Department of Elementary and Secondary Education coordinates and supervises the administration and operation of local school districts and improves the administration and instruction in public schools. Its foremost functions consist in improvement of curriculum, certification of teachers, and apportionment of state funds in accordance with the State School Program. The department is also concerned with career, adult, and special education. It provides adults and the disadvantaged with skill training and maintains special schools for the deaf, the blind, and the mentally retarded and physically handicapped by special education.[9] It also provides planning and consultative assistance directly to the large urban areas of the state to meet their unique educational concerns and needs, such as prevention of crime, violence, and vandalism in schools; student motivation and discipline; absenteeism and dropouts; and also equal access to quality education so as to assure the complete education of urban students.

The State Board of Education is a lay board consisting of eight members appointed on a bipartisan basis by the Governor and confirmed by the Senate for staggered eight-year terms. They receive only actual expenses incurred and a per diem fixed by law. The board is especially entrusted by the Constitution with the supervision of instruction in the public schools.[10] A commissioner of education, as the chief administrative officer of the department, must be a citizen and resident of the state, subject to removal at the discretion of the board. The department is organized into six divisions: administration, instruction, career and adult education, vocational rehabilitation, special education, and urban and teacher education.

Department of Higher Education[11]

Headed by the Coordinating Board for Higher Education,

---

[9] The Missouri School for the Deaf at Fulton, the Missouri School for the Blind at St. Louis, and the state schools for severely handicapped throughout the state.

[10] Mo. Const. art. 9, sec. 2 (a).

[11] Ibid., art. 4, sec. 52.

the Department of Higher Education is responsible for co-ordinating operations of the state's institutions of higher education. It approves new degree programs to be offered by colleges and universities, recommends a budget for each of the state institutions of higher education, approves new senior colleges, establishes admission and transfer guide-lines, and administers a student grant program. Under the jurisdiction of the board are ten state universities and colleges,[12] each controlled by its own board of curators or regents. Other agencies under the board are the state li-brary, the State Anatomical Board, and the public junior colleges. The board also plans and coordinates all federal 1202 activities for post-secondary education in Missouri.

The Coordinating Board for Higher Education is a non-salaried bipartisan board appointed by the governor with Senate consent. The board selects the Commissioner of Higher Education who is chief administrative officer of the department and serves at its pleasure.

Highway and Transportation Department[13]

The Highway and Transportation Department is charged with maintenance, operation, and improvement of five trans-portation services in the state, namely, highway, aviation, waterway, transit, and railroad. It also helps in develop-ing and improving airports, railroads, ports, and transit systems in cooperation and coordination with their owners and operators. Meanwhile, it administers state and federal programs and funds for these modes of transportation.

The department is headed by a six-member bipartisan commission. The commissioners are appointed by the governor with Senate approval to staggered terms of six years. With the chief engineer as the chief administrative officer ap-pointed by the commission, the department is composed of 11 divisions and four transportation units. Eight of these di-visions are concerned with highways and bridges: Divisions of Bridges, Construction, Equipment and Procurement, Main-tenance and Traffic, Materials and Research, Planning, Right

---

[12]University of Missouri, Lincoln University, Central Missouri University, Northeast Missouri University, North-west Missouri University, Southeast Missouri University, Southwest Missouri University, Missouri Southern College, Missouri Western College, and Harris-Stowe College.

[13]Mo. Const. art 4, secs. 29-34.

of way, and Survey and Plans. Four transportation units
are responsible for planning for four state-wide modes of
transportation: waterways, transit, aviation, and railroads.

Under the supervision of the department are ten highway
districts throughout the state, each encompassing about 12
counties and containing about 10 percent of the total road
mileage. Each district is under the direction of an engineer. There are several units assigned to the department,
but the department has no budgetary or directional control
over them. They are separate units of state government.[14]

The construction of the state highway network began in
1917. Having since then been continuously revamped and extended under the Centennial Road Law of 1921, subsequent
legislation, and State Constitutional Amendments, the network covered 32,182.776 miles throughout the state as of
December 31, 1981. The major source of revenue for the
department are motor vehicle fuel taxes, license fees and
part of one-half of the motor vehicle sales tax.

Department of Labor and Industrial Relations[15]

The overriding responsibility of the Department of Labor
and Industrial Relations is to foster workers' welfare through
employment security and fair treatment. To achieve this mission, the department, through its six units, promotes employment security, provides compensation or fringe benefits to
unemployed or injured workers, develops occupational safety
and health standards, ensures prevailing fair wage, offers
mediation to settle labor disputes, and encourages the advancement of women in all occupations and the employment of
the handicapped. The six units are: Division of Employment
Security, Division of Workmen's Compensation, Division of
Labor Standards, Board of Mediation, Commission on the Status
of Women, and Committee on Employment of the Handicapped.

The Division of Employment Security, a kind of federal-
state-local partnership, increases job opportunities, provides for the payment of compensation or insurance benefits
to those temporarily unemployed through no fault of their
own, and provides the unskilled with training in order to

---

[14]The units are: Missouri Mississippi River Parkway Com-
mission, Missouri St. Louis Metropolitan Airport Authority,
Bi-state Development Agency, Kansas City Area Transportation
Authority, etc.

[15]Mo. Const. art. 4, sec. 49.

help the public obtain economic security. The Division of
Workmen's Compensation is responsible for compensation payments, medical treatment, benefits to workers injured during work or suffering from occupation-related diseases, and
rehabilitation. The Labor Standards Division administers
wage law to ensure fair wages, develops occupation safety
and health programs and conducts inspections in industries
and mines. The Board of Mediation mediates labor disputes
arising in public utilities. The Commission on the Status
of Women helps Missouri women realize their full basic
rights and encourages their advancement in all vocations
and occupations. The Governor's Committee on Employment
of the Handicapped secures jobs for the handicapped.

The department is headed by a bipartisan commission
appointed by the governor and approved by the Senate. The
Labor and Industrial Relations Commission consists of three
members: one representing employers, another employees, and
the third (who must be a state licensed lawyer) the public.
It performs some quasi-judicial duties in addition to supervising and controlling the department. It receives appeals
from all decisions and awards in workmen's compensation, unemployment compensation and prevailing wage cases. It holds
hearings and renders written opinions according to the Missouri Administrative Procedure Act and subject to judicial
review by the State Supreme Court or Court of Appeals. It
nominates and the governor appoints, subject to Senate approval, a director of the department as its chief administrator.

Department of Mental Health[16]

The Constitution assigns the Mental Health Department
to "provide treatment, care, education and training for persons suffering from mental illness or retardation," to "have
administrative control of the state hospitals and other institutions and centers established for these purposes" and
to "administer such other programs as provided by law."

The department administers three mental health centers,
four state school-hospitals, seven state hospitals, eleven
regional centers for the developmentally disabled,[17] and

----

[16] Ibid., sec. 37 (a).

[17] Three mental health centers: Malcolm Bliss, Mid-Missouri, Western Missouri.

Four state school-hospitals: Higginsville, Marshall,
Nevada, and St. Louis.

172

the St. Louis Developmental Disabilities Treatment Center.

The director of the department is appointed by a seven-member commission with senatorial consent. The commission is appointed by the governor with Senate confirmation but serves in an advisory capacity to the department director, who is directly accountable to the governor. The department is organized into three divisions: (1) Mental Retardation, (2) Alcoholism and Drug Abuse, and (3) Comprehensive Psychiatric Services.

Department of Natural Resources[18]

While the Conservation Department is devoted to the management of wildlife and forest resources, the Department of Natural Resources is charged by the Constitution with "environmental control and conservation and management of natural resources" to protect, maintain, and develop the state's air, water, land, mineral, energy, recreational, and cultural resources, such as state parks and historical sites.

The state's chief environmental protection agency carries out its responsibilities through five divisions: Energy, Environmental Quality, Geology and Land Survey, Management Service, and Parks and Historic Preservation. There are 71 parks and historic sites in the state, covering approximately 97,000 acres.

The department is headed by a director appointed by the governor with Senate approval.

Department of Public Safety[19]

Headed by a director appointed by the governor with senatorial confirmation, the Department of Public Safety is responsible for coordinating and directing criminal in-

---

Seven state hospitals: Fulton, St. Joseph, Farmington, Nevada, St. Louis State Hospital Complex, Woodson Children's Psychiatric Hospital, and Howthorn Children's Psychiatric Hospital.

Eleven regional centers: Albany, Hannibal, Joplin, Kansas City, Kirksville, Marshall, Poplar Bluff, Rolla, St. Louis, Sikeston, and Springfield.

[18]Mo. Const. art. 4, sec. 47.

[19]Ibid., sec. 48.

vestigations, law enforcement, and public safety activities in order to "protect and safeguard the lives and property of the people in the state." These functions are carried out by six main units: Office of the Adjutant General, Division of Highway Safety, Missouri State Highway Patrol, Missouri State Fire Marshal, Division of Water Safety, and Division of Liquor.

The Adjutant General is the administrative head of the military establishment of Missouri and serves as military secretary and chief of staff to the governor, who is the commander-in-chief of the state militia or Missouri National Guard. The National Guard includes both the army and the air guard. The Missouri militia has been in existence since 1808, while the Missouri Air National Guard was organized in 1946 and called into federal service during the Korean War. They are represented by 95 company-sized units located in 63 communities throughout the state. They have a two-fold mission: to serve as the reserves to the U.S. Army and Air Force and to preserve peace, order, and safety in the state. The Office of the Adjutant General is charged with disciplining, training, and mobilizing the National Guard in the state in addition to administration.

Affiliated with the Office of the Adjutant General is the Division of Veterans' Affairs.[20] The division administers two programs: service of veterans and Missouri Veterans' Home. Under the Service to Veterans Program, the division provides information, counsel, and assistance to veterans and their dependents or survivors regarding their benefits and acts as their attorney or agent in their claims for compensation, pension, education, rehabilitation and other benefits due them. It even provides the Veterans Administration with all necessary evidence and documentation for its clients. The Missouri Veterans' Home in St. James provides care to Missourian veterans and their spouses and parents who are unable to support or adequately care for themselves.

The Highway Safety Division is responsible for the administration and supervision of a comprehensive statewide

[20]Established by law in 1931, the Division of Veterans' Affairs was originally affiliated with the Office of the Adjutant General, but it was transferred to the Division of Social Services by the State Omnibus Reorganization Act of 1974. In February 1981, by Governor Bond's executive order, it was transferred back to the Adjutant General's Office.

highway safety program. The State Highway Patrol not only enforces traffic laws for public safety on highways but also renders a general police service for the state. The State Fire Marshal's Office investigates suspicious fires and bombings and collects evidence for prosecution of arsonists. The Water Safety Division promotes boating safety by patrolling the major lakes and waterways in the state. The Division of Liquor controls licenses and regulates the sale of alcoholic beverages under the Liquor Control Law and Non-intoxicating Beer Law.

Department of Revenue

The major responsibility charged to the Department of Revenue by the Constitution is the collection of "all taxes and fees payable to the state...."[21] Its subsidiary duties are to title and register all motor vehicles and license drivers. To fulfill these duties, the department has three divisions organized along functional lines: Taxation, Motor Vehicles and Licensing, and Information Systems.

Affiliated with the Department of Revenue are two relatively autonomous agencies: the Highway Reciprocity Commission and the State Tax Commission. The Highway Reciprocity Commission is authorized to negotiate reciprocal agreements with other states, territories, and foreign nations concerning commercial motor vehicle registration fees for the use of Missouri's highways. The commission is composed of the governor, attorney general, chairman of the Public Service Commission, director of the Revenue Department, superintendent of the State Highway Patrol, and chief engineer of the Highway and Transportation Department. The State Tax Commission is charged with administering the freight company excise tax, auditing reports, assessing the tax, and hearing appeals of property owners, merchants, and manufacturers from local boards of equalization. The commission includes three members appointed by the governor from the two major political parties with senatorial confirmation.

The revenues received by the state government for the fiscal year ending June 30, 1982 totalled $3,672,024,275: (1) $2,051,033,158 from the general revenue fund consisting mainly of sales, income, liquor, inheritance, corporation franchise taxes, county foreign insurance and general property taxes, etc. and (2) $1,620,991,117 from the non-general revenue sources such as federal grants, highway fund,

---

[21] Mo. Const. art. 4, sec. 22.

motor fuel tax fund etc. The state's expenditure for the
same fiscal year was $3,704,347,036.

Department of Social Services[22]

The Department of Social Services, one of the largest
and most diverse state departments, provides various services affecting the lives of all people throughout Missouri.
In order to promote social and economic well-being for all
Missourians, the department consolidates, coordinates, and
administers various programs, which cover health services,
public assistance, correctional rehabilitation, preventive
and protective services, and federal grants for welfare.
These programs are carried out through five divisions: Aging,
Family Services, Health, Manpower Planning, and Youth Services.

Among the five divisions the largest is the Division of
Youth Services, formerly the Board of Training Schools. The
division provides rehabilitation supervision to the juvenile
offenders, between ages 12 and 17, convicted by the state's
juvenile courts. Its other duties include aftercare supervision and prevention of delinquency as well as consultative
and information services to other youth agencies and technical assistance to local communities. There are four state
correctional institutions for juvenile delinquents,[23] 14
group homes and other facilities situated in communities
throughout the state, and five park campuses.

The Division of Family Services, formerly the Division
of Welfare, administers the federal and state public assistance programs of aid to dependent children, supplemen-
tal aid to the blind, medical assistance, nursing care,
child welfare services, general relief, and blind pension.
The Division of Aging, established in 1978, serves the
needs of our ever increasing number of aging citizens.

The Health Division plans, develops, and conducts
statewide public health activities with various services
such as medical care, disease control, laboratory, local
health, hospital and technical services. The Division of
Manpower Planning is responsible for all manpower programs
under the Comprehensive Employment and Training Act of 1978.

---

[22]Ibid., sec. 37.

[23]The Training School for Boys in Boonville, the W.E.
Sears Youth Center in Poplar Bluff, the Kansas City Treat-
ment Center, and the Hogan State Regional Youth Center in
St. Louis.

It offers a comprehensive range of manpower services and provides unemployed or underemployed or economically disadvantaged citizens in the state with the training needed to obtain unsubsidized employment.

SUMMARY

Among the thirteen departments, five are headed by bipartisan commissions or boards of from three to nine members appointed by the governor with Senate consent for staggered terms of from six to eight years. The boards or commissions appoint department directors or commissioners (and chief engineer of the Highway and Transportation Department) as the chief administrative officers, who in turn select and organize the staff subject to the approval of commissions or boards in some departments. These departments are Conservation, Elementary and Secondary Education, Higher Education, Highways and Transportation, and Labor and Industrial Relations. The directors of the other eight departments and the commissioner of Administration are directly appointed by the governor with senatorial confirmation. Governor Bond was the first Missouri governor who referred to his department directors as cabinet members. He held the so-called first cabinet meeting in the history of Missouri on July 6, 1974.

The departments and the Office of Administration are divided into divisions. The lines of responsibility run from each division head to the department director or commissioner or to him through a deputy director or commissioner. Within some departments there are also relatively autonomous boards or commissions, such as the State Milk Board in the Department of Agriculture; the Board of Accountancy in the Department of Consumer Affairs, Regulation and Licensing; and the State Tax Commission in the Department of Revenue. These boards or commissions either serve in an advisory capacity or perform specific duties. The members are also appointed by the governor with the consent of the Senate.

PUBLIC OFFICERS[24]

A public officer, military or civil, must be a U.S. citizen and a one-year state resident before his election or appointment, except for positions requiring technical or specialized skill or knowledge. No federal government officer can simultaneously hold any public office in Missouri except as militiamen or members of the reserve corps. All appoint-

---

[24]Mo. Const. art. 7.

ments must be made according to law. There shall be no discrimination in appointment of any officer, whether a board
member or a department director or a division head or even
an employee, because of race, color, creed, or national origin. No public officer is allowed to hire or appoint to
public office or employment any relative within the fourth
degree, by consanguinity or by affinity. Penalty for nepotism is to forfeit office or appointment. Women have an
equal right to hold office. But an honorably discharged
U.S. veteran who is a citizen of this state has preference
in examination and appointment as prescribed by law.[25] Before taking office, all civil and military officers are required to take an oath to support the U.S. and the Missouri
Constitutions. The salaries of elected officials shall not
be increased during their terms of office, nor shall their
terms be extended. All elective executive officers and
court judges are liable to impeachment for crime, incompetency, misconduct, wilful neglect of duty, corruption or
oppression in office, moral turpitude, or habitual drunkenness. Except the governor and the Supreme Court judges,
they are impeached by the House of Representatives, tried
by the Supreme Court, and convicted by five-sevenths thereof.
The only penalty after conviction is removal from office.
Impeached officials can be tried and punished by regular
courts of law for the same criminal acts for which they are
impeached. Those not subject to impeachment shall not be
removed except in the manner and for the causes provided by
law. Election contests for executive state officers are
heard by the Supreme Court, while election contests for all
other public officers are tried and determined by courts of
law or by one or more judges thereof.

MERIT SYSTEM[26]

---

[25]Ibid., art. 4, sec. 19.

[26]The merit system was first established in the federal
government by the Pendleton or Civil Service Act in 1883
after the assassination of President James A. Garfield on
July 21, 1881.

Late in 1883, the state of New York established a
civil service system and Massachusetts followed suit the
next year--the only two states adopted the system until the
turn of this century. Wisconsin and Illinois in 1905, Colorado in 1907, New Jersey in 1908, and Connecticut, California, Ohio, Kansas, and Maryland in 1920 adopted the merit
system, followed by five other states 17 years later. Today
more than half of the states have established this system.

In contrast with the old spoils system or the present-day patronage system, whereby appointments to office are made for political reasons, the merit system is the recruitment, appointment, and promotion of public officers on the basis of fitness and performance, and removal is subject only to incompetency or unethical conduct. Though interchangeably used with "civil service," the "merit system" stresses positive programs regarding in-service training, position classification, pay standardization, and retirement plans leading to the development of a career service, while the "civil service" merely negatively places restraints on favoritism, prejudice or discrimination.

The merit system was established in Missouri after the Merit System Law was enacted in 1946, pursuant to the Constitution. Article IV, Section 19 of the Constitution reads: "All employees in the state eleemosynary and penal institutions, and other state employees as provided by law, shall be selected on the basis of merit, ascertained as nearly as practical by competitive examinations." The law specifies that "every appointment or promotion to a position covered by this law shall be made on the basis of merit determined by such person's eligibility rating established by competitive examinations. No appointment, promotion, demotion or dismissal shall be made because of favoritism, prejudice or discrimination." By federal law, those who are on state jobs funded by federal grants must be hired through a merit system. As of August 1982, the following agencies are either completely or partially covered by the Missouri Merit System.[27]

Agency	Covered by the Merit System
Office of Administration	All employees
Department of Consumer Affairs, Regulation and Licensing	Division of Tourism Environmental Improvement Authority Housing Development Commission Office of Public Counsel
Department of Corrections & Human Resources	All employees
Department of Labor & Industrial Relations	Division of Employment Security

[27]Not an inclusive list of all state agencies. Source: State Agency and Personnel Office Guide published by the Personnel Division, Missouri Office of Administration, August 1982.

	Industrial Inspection Section
	Workmen's Compensation Statistical Unit
Department of Mental Health	All employees
Department of Natural Resources	All employees
Department of Public Safety	Disaster Planning & Operations Office
	Division of Water Supply
	Division of Veterans' Affairs
Department of Social Services	All employees

The Missouri Merit System covers about 25,257 of the
state's 70,000 employees,[28] more than one-third of the personnel in Missouri state government. The Personnel Division in the Office of Administration is in charge of the
state's merit system. Traditionally the elective offices
and the Department of Revenue make appointments more on a
patronage basis than most other departments. The state
elective officers appoint their own staffs, who serve at
their pleasure.

An employee under the merit system is prohibited from
participating in any political activity except to vote, to
express opinions, or to contribute up to a certain amount
of money to a political party or candidate as provided by
law. He cannot be a committee member of a political party,
national, state, or local, or an officer of a partisan political club, or a participant in any political campaign.
He must resign from his position or obtain a regularly
granted leave of absence before he becomes a candidate for
a public office.

_____

[28]Major agencies not covered by the merit system in
Missouri are: Department of Agriculture, Commission on Human Rights, Department of Conservation, Department of Elementary & Secondary Education, Highway & Transportation
Department, Highway Patrol, Division of Insurance, Division
of Liquor Control, Public Service Commission, Department of
Revenue.

CHAPTER XI THE JUDICIARY AND JUDICIAL PROCEDURES

THE JUDICIARY[1]

COURTS

The United States has a dual court system[2] based upon the principle of federalism. That is, in this country there exist two separate and distinct court systems: federal and state, and they each operate in different spheres of jurisdiction (the power to hear cases) independently of each other. Cases falling under state law are entirely within the jurisdiction of state courts. The federal courts do not have general authority to interfere with their proceedings and judgments. No case can be appealed from any state court to a federal court except those involving federal questions and appealed from the states' highest courts to the Federal Supreme Court. No case can be appealed directly from any state court to a lower federal court (Court of Appeals or District Court).[3]

Therefore, there is no federal general common law. Except in matters governed by the Federal Constitution or by congressional acts, the law to be applied in most cases is the law of the state.[4] In reviewing a state case or deciding the meaning of a state constitutional provision or statute, the U.S. Supreme Court accepts the states' highest courts' interpretations or local courts' decisions especially involving questions of local common law, unless they conflict with federal law. No state court is bound by the precedents established by a lower federal court in similar

---

[1] A collective term for courts and judges.

[2] Only the United States has this unique system.

[3] Though state prisoners may, by way of writ of habeas corpus, present their claims before federal courts (today, federal district courts) if their federal constitutional rights are denied in the state proceedings, they still first have to exhaust all state remedies before seeking federal relief unless such remedies are denied to them. Hazel B. Kerper, Introduction to the Criminal System, rev. Jerold H. Isreal, 2d ed. (St. Paul, MN: West Publishing Co., 1979), p.327. Nowadays the Federal Supreme Court restricts the federal proceedings available to state prisoners. However, the courts at all levels in Missouri, including the Supreme Court, issue original remedial writs.

[4] Erie Railroad Co. v. Tompkins 304 U.S. 64 (1938).

cases according to the rule of stare decisis. Further, even though a three-judge Federal District Court may declare a state statute unconstitutional as violating the U.S. Constitution, the state courts may not be bound by its ruling until the U.S. Supreme Court upholds its decisions.

The federal courts have jurisdiction over cases and controversies involving (1) federal questions and (2) certain parties to the suit. The federal questions refer to the Constitution, laws and treaties of the United States, and admiralty and maritime cases. The parties to the suit under the federal jurisdiction are foreign ambassadors, other public ministers, consuls, the United States, one of the fifty states, citizens of different states (diversity of citizenship), citizens of the same state claiming lands under grants of different states (obsolete today), and a state against citizens of another state or aliens, or a foreign country (with its consent). The federal courts have exclusive jurisdiction over the above mentioned foreign diplomatic personnel, the United States, one or more states, bankruptcy, patent, copyright, admiralty and federal criminal cases. But Congress has also granted the states exclusive jurisdiction over certain federal matters such as the diversity of citizenship case involving an amount below $10,000 or cases against states by individuals, citizens or aliens.

Figure 11.1 Dual Court System & Jurisdiction
in the United States

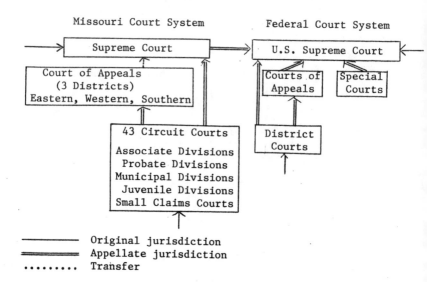

Missouri Court System   Federal Court System

─────── Original jurisdiction
═══════ Appellate jurisdiction
········ Transfer

Meanwhile, the federal courts and state courts have concurrent jurisdiction over the diversity of citizenship case
involving a sum above $10,000. Cases under concurrent juris-
diction may, upon the request of the defendant, be removed
(not appealed) from one court to another before actual trial
begins, usually from a state general trial court to a federal
district court.

More often than not, a single act may violate both a
state and a federal law. Crimes such as robbery of national
(federally insured) banks, narcotic violations, kidnapping,
prostitution, bootlegging, auto theft (across state lines),
and the like are both federal and state offenses because they
usually involve crossing state borders. Both federal and
state courts may try the same case separately without conflict
of jurisdiction or violation of the constitutional safeguard
against "double jeopardy."

Missouri is under the jurisdiction of the Eighth Circuit
of the U.S. Court of Appeals.[5] The three U.S. District Courts
in this state are: Eastern District in St. Louis, Western District in Kansas City, and Southern District in Springfield.

Missouri State Courts

Missouri has a three-level court system:[6] Supreme Court,
Court of Appeals, and 43 Circuit Courts. Their judicial
functions are (1) to settle disputes between individuals or
parties in civil cases, (2) to determine innocence or guilt
in criminal cases, (3) to interpret the federal and state
Constitutions and laws, and (4) to render declaratory judgments. A declaratory judgment is a court action based upon

---

[5]There are 12 Courts of Appeals in the United States.
The 8th Circuit of the U.S. Court of Appeals has jurisdiction
over Arkansas, Iowa, Minnesota, Missouri, Nebraska, North
Dakota, and South Dakota.

[6]The Constitutional Amendment establishing a new court
system in Missouri was adopted in an August 3, 1976 referendum and went into effect on January 2, 1979. Before 1979,
Missouri had a four-level court hierarchy: the Supreme Court,
the Court of Appeals, and the Circuit Courts with Magistrate
Courts, Probate Courts, and Municipal Courts generally com-
posing the fourth level. In addition, there were the St.
Louis Court of Criminal Correction and the Courts of Common
Pleas in Cape Girardeau and Hannibal, all on the same level
with the Circuit Courts. The Courts of Justice of the Peace
were replaced by the Magistrate Courts in 1945.

neither an actual nor a threatened wrong but merely to answer a legal question or to declare the rights of parties involved under a legal instrument, such as a statute, ordinance, will, deed, or contract, or other disputes before an actual lawsuit occurs.

In 1982 an Office of State Public Defender was created by the State Public Defender Act as an independent department of the judicial branch to administer the statewide public defender system in Missouri.[7] The whole system is supervised by a seven-member bipartisan non-salaried commission appointed by the govenor with senatorial consent for terms of six years. Four commissioners must be lawyers. The commission appoints a full-time state director, deputy directors, and public defenders for terms of four years, and the director must be an experienced defense lawyer in criminal proceedings. The Commission may also establish local and regional offices serving several counties and contract for services with private attorneys when neccessary. The public defenders appoint assistant and deputy defenders, investigators, and other personnel. All defenders must be state licensed lawyers. A complete budget for the system is approved by the governor and the General Assembly, not subject to diminution and alteration by the judicial branch.[8]

Supreme Court[9]

Article V of the Missouri Constitution vests judicial power in the Supreme Court with statewide jurisdiction. The court consists of seven judges with one elected (actually rotated) to serve as the chief justice for a term of two years. Sitting in Jefferson City, the court has both original (the case is tried for the first time) and appellate jurisdiction. Its original jurisdiction consists in (1) trying impeachment charges of high state officers except the governor and Supreme Court judges. (2) issuing and determining original remedial writs,[10] which can be filed directly

---

[7]§600.019, RSMo Supp. 1982.

[8]§600.040, RSMo Supp. 1982.

[9]The highest court is called the Supreme Court of Errors in Connecticut, the Supreme Judicial Court in Maine and Massachusetts, the Supreme Court of Appeals in Virginia, and the Court of Appeals in Kentucky, Maryland, and New York. The "Supreme Court" in New York is a lower court.

[10]Mo. Const. art. 5, sec. 4 (1). The remedies can be sought directly from the Supreme Court without following the usual procedure through the lower courts.

in the Supreme Court, such as habeas corpus, mandamus,[11] ouster,[12] and prohibition,[13] and (3) settling election contests for governor, lieutenant governor, and other executive state officials.[14] Its exclusive appellate jurisdiction covers four basic kinds of cases on appeal from the Circuit Courts. The four kinds of cases involve (1) the validity of a treaty or U.S. statute, or a statute or constitutional provision of Missouri, (2) the construction of the Missouri revenue laws, (3) the title to any state office, and (4) offenses punishable by a death sentence.[15] The Court of Appeals has jurisdiction over all other appeals from the Circuit Courts.

The Supreme Court holds three sessions each year in January, May, and September. It may sit in divisions, and each division must consist of at least three judges. A case may be transferred from a division to the court en banc (the entire court), (1) when the division is equally divided in opinion, (2) when the division so decides, (3) upon the request of a losing party when a judge dissents from the majority opinion, or (4) pursuant to Supreme Court rule.[16]

The Supreme Court is authorized to administer the entire state system including budgets from various courts. It therefore supervises all lower courts in the state, establishes rules as enforcible as law governing practice, procedures, and pleadings in all courts and administrative tribunals, and makes transfers of judicial personnel. It also licenses all lawyers practising law in the state and disciplines them for violations of the Legal Code of Professional Ethics. It appoints six judges of the state appellant courts to form a commission to apportion the Senate or the House of Representatives if the governor-appointed commission fails to file its report with the secretary of state in time.

---

[11] "Mandamus (in Latin: "We command")" directs a public official to perform an act required by law.

[12] "Ouster" seeks to remove a public official from office.

[13] A court order preventing a lower court from exceeding its jurisdiction, for example, to stop a judge from proceeding in a case or issuing an order.

[14] Mo. Const. art. 7, sec. 5.

[15] Ibid., art. 5, sec. 3.

[16] Ibid., sec. 9.

Court of Appeals

There is one Court of Appeals in three districts in Missouri, known as the Eastern, Western, and Southern Districts.

The Court of Appeals has general appellate jurisdiction in all cases from Circuit Courts within its respective districts except those over which the Supreme Court has exclusive jurisdiction. The cases not within the Supreme Court's exclusive jurisdiction may be transferred (not appealed) from the Court of Appeals to the Supreme Court, (1) when a dissenting judge in the Court of Appeals certifies that the majority opinion in the pending case is repugnant to any previous decision of the Supreme Court or of other districts of the Court of Appeals, (2) when a majority of judges of the participating district of the Court of Appeals so decides, (3) when the Supreme Court so orders because of the general interest or importance of the existing law, or (4) pursuant to Supreme Court rule.[17] The Court of Appeals also issues original remedial writs.

The Eastern District Court consists of 12 judges, the Western 10, and the Southern 7. Each district elects a chief judge to a term of two years. The Eastern Court sits in St. Louis the Tuesday after the second Monday in September, January, and April of each year. The Western Court sits in Kansas City on the first Monday in January, May, and September. The Southern Court sits at Springfield in January, March, June, and September, and at Poplar Bluff in April and November. The judges may sit in divisions. But each division must consist of no less than three judges. Each district court has general superintending control over all courts and administrative tribunals within its jurisdiction.

Circuit Courts

There are 43 Circuit Courts in Missouri, each having jurisdiction over up to five counties, except the 22nd circuit, which covers the entire city of St. Louis.[18]

---

[17]Mo. Const. art. 5, sec. 10. The Supreme Court may, at its own discretion, review the cases transferred from the Court of Appeals, similar to "certiorari".

[18]The Circuit Court in St. Louis City is the largest one in Missouri. It has an assignment division, 10 civil jury divisions, 2 domestic relation divisions, 2 equity divisions, 3 criminal divisions, and a clerk's office.

Each Circuit Court has at least one judge and several associate circuit judges, but there must be at least one resident associate circuit judge in each county. Under constitutional provisions which became effective on January 2, 1979, all original Magistrate, Probate, and Municipal Courts, the St. Louis Court of Criminal Correction, and the Courts of Common Pleas in Cape Girardeau and Hannibal became divisions of the Circuit Courts in their respective areas.[19] Probate judges in all first and second class counties of more than 65,000 population and in the City of St. Louis, and the judges of the two Common Pleas Courts and of the St. Louis Court of Criminal Correction became circuit court judges of their respective circuits. The magistrate and probate judges in counties with less than 65,000 inhabitants became associate circuit judges.[20]

The Circuit Court is the trial court, with general o-riginal jurisdiction over all criminal and civil cases. It issues and determines original remedial writs and reviews administrative decisions.[21] Circuit judges hear and deter-mine all cases and matters within the jurisdiction of the Circuit Courts, subject to certain restrictions.[22] They also hear, with some exceptions, de novo the cases previous-ly heard by associate circuit judges or by municipal judges within the circuit.[23]

Associate circuit judges have the power to hear and de-termine those matters formerly within the jurisdiction of magistrate and probate judges. Each associate circuit judge within the county and in St. Louis City therefore hears and determines, among other things, (1) all civil cases for the recovery of money resulting from tort or breach of contract, or for penalty or forfeiture when the sum demanded does not exceed $5,000; (2) criminal cases involving misdemeanor (in-cluding traffic) and infraction penalties as well as prelimi-nary hearings in felony cases; (3) municipal ordinance vio-lation cases in a municipality under 400,000 population and with no municipal judge provided; (4) small claims cases;

---

[19]Mo. Const. art. 5, sec. 27 (2: a-d). The Hannibal Court of Common Pleas became the second division of the Marion County Circuit Court.

[20]Ibid., sec. 27 (4-a).

[21]Ibid., sec. 27 (17); sec. 18.

[22]§478.220, RSMo 1978.

[23]Mo. Const. art. 5, sec. 27 (5).

and (5) juvenile proceedings.[24] The associate circuit judges of the St. Louis City Circuit also try all criminal cases formerly heard by the St. Louis Court of Criminal Correction.[25]

Meanwhile, associate circuit judges exercise probate jurisdiction within counties, except in St. Louis City and all first and second class counties with a population of more than 65,000 where the circuit judges in the probate divisions hear probate cases within their circuits and counties. In probate matters, the associate circuit judges have general equitable jurisdiction.[26] Further, associate circuit judges are subject to special assignments by the presiding judge of their circuit to hear de novo the cases previously heard by other associate circuit judges or municipal judges within the same circuit or additional cases or classes of cases.

Associate circuit judges hear and determine small claims cases and keep separate "small claims" dockets. When a judge is hearing small claims matters, the court is known as "small claims" court. While sitting as a small claims court, the judge has original jurisdiction over all civil cases, whether tort or contract, when the amount in dispute does not exceed $500 excluding interest and costs. The jurisdiction of small claims courts is limited to cases for the recovery of money rather than any form of equitable relief or other non-monetary remedies. The judgments of the small claims courts may never become liens on real property.

In a circuit covering a single county or city with more than one judge,[27] the court usually sits by individuals or in divisions. The court sits en banc only for rule-making or other procedural purposes, such as classification and assignment of business, having no power whatsoever to review the dicisions made by a division. The circuit and associate circuit judges in each circuit elect from among themselves a circuit judge to serve as presiding judge, who has general administration over the court.

---

[24] §478.063 & 478.225, RSMo 1978.

[25] Mo. Const. art. 5, sec. 27 (3).

[26] Ibid., sec. 17.

[27] Twenty-six judges (22nd circuit), 20 (21st), 19 (16th), 5 (31st), 4 (7th, 11th & 23rd), 3 (3rd & 5th), 2 (17th, 19th, 20th, 24th, 25th, 29th, 32nd and 42nd).

All former Municipal Courts, often called Police Courts, have become Minicipal Divisions of the Circuit Courts in the counties where cities are situated. The municipal judge hears and determines municipal ordinance violation cases such as traffic, peace-disturbing and other nuisance cases in the city and is not subject to special assignment procedures. In a municipality under 400,000 population with no municipal judge, or upon the request of the governing body of any municipality, the associate circuit judge performs judicial duties.[28] But a municipality having more than 400,000 population must have a municipal judge. A municipal judge may serve in more than one municipality.

The new judiciary is characterized chiefly by its unified system. Under the new system, all the sprawling lower courts have been integrated into the tightly-knit hierarchy headed by the Supreme Court, and the quasi-independent elected judges have been brought completely under its control. The state's highest court now has general supervisory authority over all courts and tribunals throughout Missouri. It thus has the power to make temporary transfers of judicial personnel from one court or district to another cr from a lower court to a higher court in order to facilitate the administration of justice. Meanwhile, the presiding judge in a lower court also has authority to assign judges additional duties within his jurisdiction to even workloads for fairness and efficiency. All judges, except municipal judges, are required to retire at age 70 so as to keep senile judges off the bench.

JUDGES

The judges in Missouri are chosen either by popular election or through the Non-partisan Selection of Judges Plan.

Judges and Commissions

Judges of the Supreme Court must be at least 30 years of age, American Citizens for 15 years, and qualified Missouri voters for 9 years preceding their selection. They are chosen through the Non-partisan Selection of Judges Plan (or non-partisan court plan) and retained for a 12-year term after serving one year in office following appointment by the governor. Before May 1982 there were commissioners assisting the court and drawing legislative districts in case the governor-appointed commissions failed to file their re-

---

[28]Mo. Const., art. 5, sec. 23.

ports with the secretary of state in time.[29]

The judges of the Court of Appeals possess the same qualifications, are chosen by the same non-partisan court plan, and serve for the same 12-year terms as the Supreme Court Judges. They must, however, be the residents of the district where they serve.

A circuit judge must be at least 30 years of age, an American citizen for 10 years, a qualified Missouri voter for three years preceding his selection and a one-year resident of his circuit. An associate circuit judge must be at least 25 years old, a qualified voter and resident of the county where he serves. All judges in Missouri must be state-licensed lawyers. All circuit and associate circuit judges, except those (circuit, associate circuit, and probate judges) in St. Louis City, St. Louis, Platte, Clay, and Jackson counties who are chosen through the non-partisan court plan, are elected by popular vote in the counties or circuits where they serve. Voters in any circuit may, by a majority vote at any general election, adopt the non-partisan court plan to choose judges. But the petition for the plan must be signed by 10 percent of the legal voters in each county of the circuit and filed with the secretary of state 90 days before the election. Kansas City selects municipal judges by this method. Circuit judges serve for terms of six years, while associate circuit judges serve for four-year terms. A municipal judge serves for a two-year term and may be a part-time judge.

Non-partisan Selection of Judges Plan[30]

The Non-partisan Selection of Judges Plan or the non-partisan court plan, also known as the "Missouri Plan" because it was first adopted in Missouri, includes the following steps:

---

[29] In 1911, the General Assembly authorized the Supreme Court to appoint four commissioners to assist the court. In 1927, the number was increased to six. The commissioners possessed the same qualifications as the Supreme Court judges, were appointed for four-year terms, received the same compensation as the judges. By the terms of the 1970 Constitutional Amendment Article V, the offices of the commissioners were gradually phased out. The last commissioner left the Supreme Court in April 1982.

[30] Mo. Const. art. 5, sec. 25 (a-d).

(1) In the event of a vacancy on the bench, the appropriate judicial commission nominates three persons to the governor, who appoints one of them to fill the vacancy. If the governor fails to do so within 60 days, the commission will make the judicial appointment.

(2) The new judge assumes his duties immediately. His term expires on December 31 following the regular November election after his full 12 months in office.

(3) If he wishes to continue in office upon the expiration of his appointive term, he must declare his candidacy with the secretary of state within 60 days before the general election.

(4) On a separate judicial ballot at the election, a question is asked: "Shall judge_____of the _____Court be retained in office?" If he receives a majority vote, he will serve for a full term beginning January first after the election.

The Appellate Judicial Commission, which makes nominations for the Supreme Court and the Court of Appeals, is composed of seven members: three lawyers each elected by state Bar members residing in each district of the Court of Appeals, three non-lawyers appointed by the governor, one from each district of the Court of Appeals, and a judge of the Supreme Court. The Circuit Judicial Commission for the nomination of circuit and associate circuit judges consists of five members: two lawyers elected by state Bar members residing in the judicial circuit, two non-lawyer residents in the circuit appointed by the governor, and the chief judge of the district of the Court of Appeals where the circuit or a major portion of its population lies. All commissioners serve for six-year staggered terms.

Political Activity and Law Business Prohibited

No judge appointed to or retained in office under the non-partisan court plan is allowed to participate in political activity by either making a contribution to, or holding office in, or campaigning for, any political parties. No judge, except municipal judges, is allowed to practice law or to conduct legal business.

Discipline, Impeachment, and Retirement

Upon the recommendation of the Commission on Retirement, Removal and Discipline of Judges, the Supreme Court en banc may discipline, reprimand, suspend, remove or retire from office any judge or judicial commissioner for misconduct, disability or moral turpitude, particularly after a felony conviction. The commission is composed of six members: two non-lawyer citizens appointed by the governor, two lawyers appointed by the state Bar, one Court of Appeals judge and one Circuit Court judge, both elected by their fellow judges. The commission investigates complaints of alleged misconduct or incompetence of judges and judicial commissioners. With at least four commissioners' concurrence, the commission makes a recommendation to the Supreme Court for action.[31] The commissioners serve for six-year terms.

All judges other than municipal judges are required to retire at age 70 with certain exceptions.[32] They may retire at an earlier age as provided by law. Any retired judge, associate circuit judge or commissioner may, with his consent, be appointed by the Supreme Court to serve as a senior judge or special commissioner with the same powers as an active judge.

Board of Law Examiners, Missouri Bar, and Missouri Bar Administration

Composed of five lawyers appointed by the Supreme Court for five-year terms, a State Board of Law Examiners is set up to conduct examinations for new lawyers twice a year in February and July. All lawyers practising law in Missouri and all Missouri judges are required to be members of the Missouri Bar, an official organization under the supervision of the Supreme Court. The Missouri Bar Administration was created by the Supreme Court to protect the public from persons unauthorized or unqualified to practise law in the state.

JUDICIAL PROCEDURES

The following are the important steps involved in criminal[33] and civil trials:

---

[31] In March 1980, the Missouri Supreme Court ousted Southeast Missouri Circuit Judge Lloyd Briggs from office upon the recommendation of the commission for his violation of judicial ethics by excessive involvement in Governor Joseph Teasdale's 1976 election campaign.

[32] Mo. Const. art. 5, sec. 26.

[33] see Chapter III.

CRIMINAL PROCEEDINGS

1. Arrest

Although constitutionally a warrant for search or
arrest is required to be issued upon probable cause, de-
scribed with particularity and supported by written oath
or affirmation, yet law enforcement or peace officers[34]
may make warrantless searches or arrests, particularly at
public places. They make searches or arrests without
warrants when they have probable cause to believe that
the facts and circumstances require immediate action or
while a crime is being committed in their presence. After
arrest, there occurs what is referred to as "booking"--
the formal registration of the name of the arrested person, the time and date of his arrest, and charge, together with the arresting officer's name. The arrested
person must be advised of his right to legal counsel.

2. Preliminary hearing or examination

The booked person may be released on a waiver or
discharge by the arresting agency if it finds no sufficient evidence to prove the charge against him. If
the charge cannot be dropped, he may be bailed out by
the posting of cash or security by himself or by some
one else on his behalf, or by bail bondsman, or on personal recognizance to guarantee his appearance in court.
In Missouri, no one can be held in jail for more than
20 hours without warrant; otherwise, he or some one else
acting on his behalf may petition the court having jurisdiction for a writ of habeas corpus. He may be brought
before an associate circuit judge for a preliminary hearing to determine the existence, validity, and sufficiency
of probable cause. Again, he may be freed, bailed out,
or detained pending a grand jury's or a prosecutor's
action after the hearing.

3. Formal accusation--indictment or presentment or information

If the charge cannot be dropped, a grand jury conducts
proceedings to decide if the evidence is sufficient to justify a trial. In Missouri, a grand jury includes 12 laymen
selected by lot at random from among the voters of the
county. A concurrence of nine jurors is required to return

---

[34]The principal local law enforcement officers are the
sheriff in the county, the constable in the township, the town
marshal, and city police.

an indictment, also known as a "true bill."[35] The grand
jury deliberates in secret on the evidence laid before
it by the prosecutor. With neither the accused nor his
attorney present, the proceeding is ex parte and excludes
the public, even the judge. But the jury may call in the
accused without an attorney with him, though he may retire from time to time to consult his attorney in the
hallway. The jury may investigate, summon witnesses, subpoena records, and compel testimonies under oath. After
investigation, the grand jury presents a formal written
accusation of crime based upon its findings, known as
"presentment." However, the prosecutor may file an "information" in lieu of an indictment or presentment after
the findings by the judge during the preliminary hearing
that the accused be bound over for a trial. Missouri
makes the information an alternative to the indictment
for the charging of all crimes.[36] When the formal charge
is filed,[37] the accused is either bailed out or detained
in custody. The bail may be rejected by the court or the
amount be raised if the offense is exceedingly grave, such
as a capital crime. The bail will be forfeited, and a
bench warrant[38] will be issued if the accused fails to appear in court.

---

[35]A "true bill" means that the bill of evidence presented
to the grand jury by the prosecutor is true. Therefore, when
the grand jury cannot find the evidence sufficient to justify
a trial, it issues what is known as "no bill."

[36]Mo. Const. art. 1, sec. 17; Scurlock, p. 163. Under
the common law, an information was used in misdemeanor cases,
while all felony prosecutions were commenced by indictment.
Now in 22 states including Missouri, felonies may be prose-
cuted by either indictment or information at the prosecutor's
option. However, indictment is still generally used for
major offenses and information for all lesser crimes in the
majority of states.

[37]Prosecution is commenced by either indictment or information. In Missouri, a prosecution for murder or any Class A
felony may be commenced at any time; a prosecution for any
other felony must be commenced within three years; for any
misdemeanor one year; and for any infraction six months.
§556.036, RSMo 1978.

[38]An order issued directly by a judge to the police or
other peace officers to arrest a person to compel his attendance in the court in order to answer a charge of contempt
or for his failure to respond to the subpoena served on him.

4. Arraignment and Plea Bargaining

In Missouri, a person accused of a felony is guaranteed by law the right to arraignment proceedings within ten days after the filing of information or indictment.[39] The arraignment takes place in the court where the case will be tried. The purpose is to advise the accused of the charges made against him and to take his plea: guilty, not guilty, nolo contendre ("I don't wish to contend") or insanity. But he may file a demurrer[40] to quash or dismiss the accusation or plead abatement. If he pleads quilty, the judge can pass sentence immediately; otherwise, a date is set for his actual trial. The court will assign him a public defender or an attorney for his defense if he is indigent and cannot afford one. Subject to certain exceptions, he must be brought to trial within 180 days of arraignment.

5. Trial

In a criminal case, a petit or trial jury is normally used; but the accused, now called the defendant, may waive a jury trial. Under the original common law,[41] the jury consisted of 12 jurors, who decided the facts and reached verdicts by unanimous concurrence, with the judge passing sentence. Now in Missouri, a jury of less than 12 jurors (but not less than six) is permissible[42] in court not of record, but unanimous verdicts are still required in trials of all crimes including misdemeanors. The petit jurors are also selected by lot from voters or from taxpayers of the community. Veniremen, potential jurors, are subject to voir dire ("to speak the truth") examinations.

At trial, the prosecutor opens the case by speaking

---

[39] §545.780, RSMo 1978.

[40] A legal pleading that the accusation is defective.

[41] In Thompson V. Utah, 170 U.S. 343 (1898), the U.S. Supreme Court strengthened the common law tradition by requiring 12-man jury trials.

[42] On June 22, 1970, the U.S. Supreme Court, breaking from a 72-year tradition, ruled in William v. Florida (299 U.S. 78) that juries in criminal trials may consist of less than 12 jurors. Two years later, the Court upheld a state non-unanimous vote in Apadaca v. Oregon (406 U.S. 404) and Johnson v. Louisiana (406 U.S. 356).

first and offering testimony and evidence. The prosecutor represents the state as the plaintiff in criminal
cases. The victim of the crime can only be a prosecuting
or complaining witness. After the prosecutor's opening
statement, the defense counsel may follow with his opening statement. Then witnesses are called to give evidence and to be cross-examined.

Under the constitutional protection of "non-self-
incrimination," the defendant may choose not to testify
in his own behalf on the witness stand. But if he chooses
to appear as a witness, he has to waive immunity and to
subject himself to cross-examination by the prosecutor.
Every witness must speak the truth or he will be found
guilty of perjury, which is punishable by imprisonment in
the penitentiary. Both the prosecutor and the defense
counsel make summing-up addresses or closing arguments to
review and analyze the evidence. In order to guide the
jurors to reach a true and just verdict, the judge gives
them "charges" or "instructions" concerning the legal
principles applicable to the facts of the case. Then the
jurors retire to the jury room for secret deliberations.

6. Verdict by the Jury

Upon return, the foreman announces the verdict in
open court, simply "guilty" or "not guilty."[43] If the

_____

[43]Criminal Proceeding Involving Mental Illness Law (§552.
020-050, 080 RSMo 1978). Shortly after John W. Hinckley, Jr.
was acquitted, after a 42-day trial, by reason of insanity
on June 21, 1982 of his assassination attempt on President
Ronald Reagan, a bill to change Missouri's current insanity
defense to "guilty but insane" was rushed into the Senate
for consideration. Hinckley shot and wounded President
Reagan and three other officers on March 30, 1981. Delaware,
Georgia, Illinois, Michigan and New Mexico already have similar laws. Under such laws those convicted could be treated
in mental institutions until they recover and then transferred to prisons to serve out their terms. Montana abolished the insanity plea in 1979 and Idaho followed suit on
July 1, 1982.

The doctrine of legal insanity, which may be traced
back to the M'Naghten Rule in 1843, holds that persons who
could not distinguish between right and wrong while committing a crime, could not be held criminally liable.

On June 22, 1982, Governor Bond signed a bill into law

jury is unable to reach a unanimous decision—commonly known as "hung jury," a retrial before a new jury may be ordered by the court. The defendant is immediately released, imprisoned, bailed out, or moves for a new trial if he believes there is a reversible error committed in the course of his trial. Sentence is usually announced by the judge within 20 days of the verdict.

In Missouri, the judge may, before the jurors retire to the jury room, instruct them about the range of punishment as part of its verdict unless the defendant requests the judge to fix sentence.[44] Therefore, the jury may, besides deciding facts, determine law, fix sentence or reduce a charge. But a Missouri judge may reduce the punishment assessed by the jury and enter a judgment of acquittal if he finds the evidence is not sufficient to sustain a guilty verdict.[45]

CIVIL PROCEEDINGS

When an individual or group, known as "plaintiff" or "petitioner," files a formal written "complaint" with a court against the party being sued, a civil case begins. The complaint describes the injury the petitioner has suffered and claims damages. The defendant or respondent,[46] the party who is being sued, may then respond by filing a formal written answer to the charges. Both the complaint and answer are known as pleadings. Sometimes the court issues a writ of summons requiring the defendant to appear in court to answer the complaint made against him or issues a subpoena to compel his attendance. At this stage,

---

toughening the procedure for releasing insane criminals from state mental institutions who may be likely to commit further crimes. §632.475, RSMo Supp. 1982.

On August 3, 1981, a Crime Compensation Law was enacted by the Missouri legislature requiring criminals to compensate victims of violent crimes for their medical bills and lost income. The maximum payment to a crime victim is $10,000. Meanwhile, "Crime Victims' Compensation Fund" is established in the state treasury. §595.030, RSMo Supp. 1981.

[44]§557.036, RSMo 1978.

[45]Scurlock, pp. 316, 319.

[46]In an appellate case, the party who appeals is the appellant or petitioner; the other party is the respondent or appellee.

the lawyers of both parties may settle the dispute privately, and the defendant may file a motion to dismiss the complaint known as a "demurrer." Sometimes a pretrial conference may be held with the judge to solve the controversy.

If the plaintiff rejects all compromises, the case is docketed on the calendar of the court and a day set for trial. In trial of a civil case, a petit jury may be used unless waived by the two parties in mutual consent. A jury may consist of less than 12 jurors in courts not of record and a two-thirds majority of such number concurring may render a verdict. In courts of record, three-fourths of the jurors concurring may render a verdict.[47] In suits and prosecutions for libel, the jury, under the direction of the court, determines the facts and the law.[48] The procedure in civil suits is almost the same as in criminal cases—oral testimonies, debates, cross-examinations, concluding statements by lawyers, instructions, verdict, judgment, appellate review (if any), and enforcement. The losing party will pay the costs of trial and damages (to the plaintiff) or "counter damages" (to the defendant if such claims are made and granted by the court), depending upon which party has lost the case. In civil cases, but generally not in criminal suits, a judge may reverse the jury's verdict.

---

[47]Mo. Const. art. 1, sec. 22 (a).

[48]Ibid., sec. 8.

CHAPTER XII   LOCAL GOVERNMENT

UNITS OF LOCAL GOVERNMENT

The local governmental units in Missouri may be classified according to legal status, purpose of government, and
functions.

Figure 12.1   Local Governmental Units[1]
(ca. 2908 as of 1981)

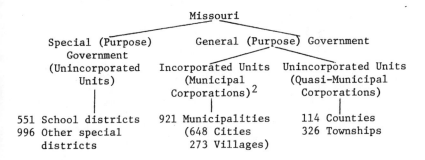

Missouri

Special (Purpose)   General (Purpose) Government
Government
(Unincorporated   Incorporated Units   Unincorporated Units
Units)   (Municipal   (Quasi-Municipal
                      Corporations)[2]   Corporations)

551 School districts   921 Municipalities   114 Counties
996 Other special   (648 Cities   326 Townships
    districts   273 Villages)

---

[1]The figures are by no means accurate, particularly the
figures of special districts. It is impossible to make an
accurate listing of local governmental units in Missouri because there is no central reporting agency. The figures
from various sources are highly contradictory and the numbers
are very elusive. The writer has contacted many agencies,
public and private, and made every effort possible for cor-
rect figures, but in vain. Most of the above figures were
obtained from the Missouri Legislative Library at the State
Capitol in Jefferson City, Missouri.

[2]A corporation is an artificial body, created by law under a charter or act of incorporation, is treated as a natural person in many aspects. Thus as an artificial person, a
corporation may own property, make contracts, incur debts,
sue and be sued in a court of law. A municipal corporation
is a corporation created to administer a political subdivision of a state and has a large measure of self-government.
A quasi-municipal corporation or quasi-corporation is unincorporated administrative subdivision of a state and is not
given general corporate powers. The distinction between
these two corporations is gradually disappearing in many states.

Both counties and municipalities are political subdivisions of the state. By law, municipalities (cities and villages)[3] are municipal corporations, while counties, townships, and special districts (including school districts) are quasi-municipal corporations. Municipal corporations are created at the request, or at least with the acquiescence, of the local inhabitants of the area. Quasi-municipal corporations are created for the convenience of the state to serve as an arm or agent of the state government without substantial popular consent, approval, or solicitation. Therefore, municipalities primarily provide local services and secondarily administer state functions, while counties primarily administer state functions and secondarily provide local services, though this situation is changing. All local governmental units provide general public services except special and school districts, which perform a single specific function.

The Missouri Constitution prohibits local governments from owning corporate stock, lending their credit and granting public money to any private individual, association, or corporation, except for pensions for their officers and employees, benefits upon retirement, disability, or death to those employed or to their beneficiaries or for educational services as authorized by law.[4] By a two-thirds majority vote of the qualified voters, any local government may become indebted in a specified limited amount.[5] By the same majority vote, any local government may incur limited debt to acquire and furnish industrial plants, but any city may incur limited additional indebtedness to cover such costs as construction of city-owned utility plants.[6] By a majority vote, any city or village may issue revenue bonds for utility, industrial, and airport purposes with some restrictions.[7] But before incurring indebtedness, every local government must collect an annual tax sufficient to retire the obligations within twenty years.[8]

In an effort to give recognition to various local needs

---

[3] Loosely referred to as "town" in the Missouri Official Manual, 1981-1982, pp. 1187-1196.

[4] Mo. Const. art. 6, secs. 23 & 25.

[5] Ibid., sec. 26 (b).

[6] Ibid., secs. 23 (a) & 26 (d,e). A city may incur additional limited indebtedness for public improvements, water and light plants and so on.

[7] Ibid., sec. 27.   [8] Ibid., sec. 26 (f).

the Missouri state legislature, under the authorization of the State Constitution,[9] has classified counties and cities into four categories and defined the organization and powers of each class of government. The Constitution also allows counties and cities to determine their own forms of government and to control matters of local concern under home rule charters[10] with some freedom from state interference.

Counties[11]

A county is the largest subdivision of local government in the United States. There are 115 counties in Missouri including the City of St. Louis, which has county status but no organized county government. Traditionally counties serve as administrative units for state services in rural areas, and their functions include health, welfare, education, conduct of elections, some judicial administration,[12] and maintenance of roads. But later due to rapid growth in suburn areas around many cities or urbanization of counties, the so-called "urban counties," as distinguished from the traditional "rural counties," furnish certain municipal services as well, such as sewage disposal, water supply, fire protection, planning and zoning,[13] library and hospital services, and parks and recreation facilities.

---

[9]Ibid., secs. 8 & 18.

[10]Ibid., secs. 18 (a) & 19.

[11]In Missouri, Worth County is the smallest county, both in population (3359) and in area (267 square miles), while Texas County is the largest one in area (1183 square miles) and St. Louis County is the largest in population (951,671). In the United States, the counties vary in size from 26 square miles in Arlington, Virginia to 20117 in San Bernardino, California. In population they vary from 164 in Loving County, Texas to 7 million in Los Angeles, California. There are 3042 counties in the United States ranging from three in Delaware to 254 in Texas including the "parishes" of Louisiana and the "boroughs" of Alaska, which are politically and legally comparable with counties. Organized county government exist in every state except Connecticut and Rhode Island, where "counties" have no governments.

[12]Much of judicial administration has been taken over by the state after the judiciary reorganization in 1979.

[13]Planning is the preparation of projects for the future social, economic, and physical development of a county or city. Zoning is the division of a county or city into areas where only specified buildings and uses of the land are permitted.

Counties may be consolidated or divided by a majority vote of the qualified voters in each county affected, but no county can be dissolved without approval of two-thirds of the qualified voters. As many as ten contiguous counties may, by a majority vote of electors in each county involved, join in performing common functions or services.[14]

Townships[15]

A township is a unit of rural government, usually a subdivision of a county. There are 326 townships in 23 counties in Missouri. Their major functions are tax collection and road construction, besides some minor law enforcement and election service. In urban areas, townships have taken on some urban services such as police and fire protection, public works, and school administration.

Municipalities[16]

Whereas counties are primarily for rural government, municipalities are principally governmental units for urban areas. Missouri has 921 municipalities including about 648 cities and 273 villages. Cities are divided into three categories: special, classified, and home rule. Major municipal functions include police protection, fire protection, water supply, health service, sewage disposal, park and recreational facilities, utilities, transportation services, welfare services, and planning and zoning, depending upon the size of cities. A village is small municipality with simpler governmental organization and less authority than cities. A local government may contract and cooperate with other local governments, other states, or even the federal government, for planning, development, construction, and the like, or for a common service.[17]

---

[14] Mo. Const. art. 6, sec. 14.

[15] The subdivisions of a county are called "townships" in 16 states in the Midwest including Missouri but known as "towns" in the New England states. These civil townships are different from congressional or survey townships, which are established by federal law merely for the purpose of surveying the land.

[16] Certain small municipalities are called "boroughs" in Connecticut, New Jersey, and Pennsylvania.

[17] Mo. Const. art. 6, sec. 16.

Special Districts[18]

Special districts are designed to provide a single specific service transcending local governmental boundaries or even crossing state border lines. The major reason for creating such a special unit is to meet modern needs, because many present-day problems concern areas not conterminous with one single traditional governmental unit. Moreover, high costs may be shared and taxation and debt ceilings evaded. Since state law imposes stringent restrictions upon the power of local governments to incur debt, the only avenue to raise additional funds for a new service may be to create a new unit of government. Special districts enjoy considerable autonomy, both fiscal and administrative. They have their own taxing power. They have their own authority to borrow money, issue bonds, and levy assessments. The governing body is either popularly elected or appointed by officials of other governments.

Cities are normally located within counties, legally and geographically; but there are five counties situated in New York City, and partions of three counties located within Kansas City. The City of St. Louis is legally separated from St. Louis County,[19] which borders the city on the west, south and north. An inhabitant of the United States may live under at least five or six layers of government: national, state, county, city, township, and at least one special district. Sometimes several special districts are superimposed.

COUNTIES

The state law has classified counties into four categories according to the assessed valuation of the property (changed in 1979) in each county as follows:

---

[18]Special districts other than school districts in Missouri include: drainage, fire protection, health, hospital, levee, library, nursing home, parks and recreation, road, sewer, water supply districts, Housing and Community Development Authorities, Greater Kansas City Port District and Authority, Jackson County Sports Complex Authority, Kansas City Area Transportation Authority, Bi-State Metropolitan Development District, and the Missouri-Kansas Development District and Agency. Four American states having no special districts are: Hawaii, Maryland, North Carolina, and Virginia.

[19]Similar situations exist with 33 "independent" cities in Virginia and with Baltimore in Maryland.

Figure 12.2   Four Classes of Counties

Class I ($400 million & up)	Class II ($125 million-&400 million)	Class III ($10 million-$125 million)	Class IV (Below $10 million)
Clay	Boone	All remaining counties	Carter
Greene	Buchanan		
Jackson	Callaway		
(home rule)	Cape Girardeau		
Jefferson	Cass		
St. Charles	Cole		
St. Louis County	Franklin		
(home rule)	Jasper		
	Johnson		
	Lafeyette		
	Pettis		
	Platte		
	St. Francois		
	Saline		

COUNTY GOVERNMENT

County Court[20]

The county court, the governing body of the county, consists of three (administrative) judges--one presiding judge elected by the whole county for a four-year term and two other judges, each from two different districts for two-year terms. Despite its name, the court actually has few judicial functions. It has legislative and administrative duties, its foremost legislative power being control over county finance. Under the authority conferred by the state and subject to some limitations, it levies taxes, makes appropriations, and incurs debts. It also enacts zoning ordinances for suburban and rural areas and regulates amusement resorts and businesses outside municipal boundaries. Meanwhile, it enforces state law in the county, controls county property, supervises roads and highways, appoints officers, holds elections, and lays out election precincts. The following officers are found in most counties of Missouri:

---

[20] The official title varies from state to state. The most common titles are "board of commissioners," "board of supervisors," and "county court," but particularly the "county board."

Figure 12.3 Organization of the County Government

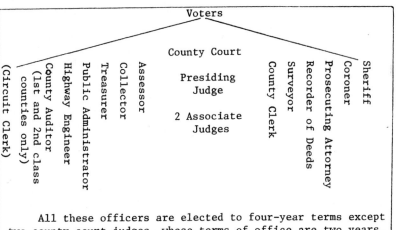

Voters

County Court

Presiding Judge

2 Associate Judges

(Circuit Clerk)
County Auditor (1st and 2nd class counties only)
Highway Engineer
Public Administrator
Treasurer
Collector
Assessor
County Clerk
Surveyor
Recorder of Deeds
Prosecuting Attorney
Coroner
Sheriff

All these officers are elected to four-year terms except two county court judges, whose terms of office are two years.

County Clerk

The county clerk serves as secretary to the county court. This official conducts elections (except in the counties where elections are conducted by boards of election commissioners), keeps birth, marriage, and death records, issues business certificates and licenses, and prepares the county budgets in Class III and Class IV counties.

Sheriff[21]

The most time-honored county officer is the sheriff, who is generally elected by popular vote. He performs three basic duties: (1) to maintain law and order and to make arrests outside municipalities as a law enforcement officer; (2) to enforce court orders such as serving summonses, subpoenas, and warrants, to execute court decisions in criminal cases, and to sell property to satisfy judgements in civil cases as a court officer; and (3) to hold the accused pending trial as a jail keeper. In addition, he collects delinquent taxes and provides patrol services on the county highways and in the

---

[21]Sheriff is an elective position in all states except Rhode Island, where the officer is appointed by the governor. In Hawaii, the sheriff is a state office filled by the attorney general.

rural fringes of the urbanized counties.

Prosecuting Attorney[22]

The prosecuting attorney gives legal advice to county officers and represents the county in lawsuits. In criminal cases, he investigates, collects evidence, conducts formal proceedings before grand juries or brings charges himself in the form of an information, and represents the state at trials.

Coroner

The primary function of the county coroner is to hold inquests (judicial inquiry) to determine the cause of deaths occurring by violence or under suspicious circumstances. At an inquest, he may summon a jury (frequently of six laymen), subpoena witnesses, secure evidence and render an official report on the testimony and findings. The office requires extensive knowledge of medicine and of criminal investigation and judicial proceedings, but the coroner is often a layman. The trend is therefore toward replacing the coroner with a physician as medical examiner and having the prosecutor in holding inquests. Some counties in Missouri such as St. Louis, Jackson and Cole presently use medical examiners.

Recorder of Deeds

Known as a register of deeds in some states, the county recorder is responsible for recording and keeping legal documents regarding real estate ownership and transfers, mortgages, deeds of trust, and articles of incorporation for the purpose of protecting property owners against flaws in title.

County Surveyor

The county surveyor is charged with surveying the land in the county. But he may also survey land for individuals and charge a fee for service rendered.

Assessor

The basic duty of the assessor is to determine the value of the property in the county for the purpose of taxation. The assessed valuations (one-third of the actual value of the

---

[22] In some states, this officer is called the county attorney, county prosecutor, or solicitor.

property) are submitted to the county clerk, who then compiles tax books and turns them over to the county collector of revenue. Any complaints against the valuation placed upon one's property may be brought before the county Board of Equalization. The property tax is the major source of revenue to local government.

Collector of Revenue

The collector of revenue collects property taxes in the county according to the tax books compiled by the county clerk. All taxes collected are turned over to the county treasurer.

Treasurer

The county treasurer (1) receives county revenues, (2) keeps custody of all county funds, and (3) disburses them upon authorization of the county court (county governing body).

Other County Officers

Besides the above-mentioned officers, many others are found in a number of counties across the state. About 100 counties have public administrators, who, functioning through the probate divisions of the circuit courts, administer the estates of physically and mentally incompetent persons until these estates are legally disposed of, such as the property of those who die without wills or the property of guardianless orphans. Approximately 24 counties have appointive highway engineers (or supervisors, commissioners, or road supervisors), who advise on the construction and maintenance of roads and bridges in the county. Only Class I and Class II counties have auditors, who prepare budgets and audit the expenditure of appropriated funds.[23] Only Class I counties have counsels, who serve as legal advisers to the county courts (governing bodies) and represent the counties in civil lawsuits. About five counties have superintendents of public schools.

Boards and Commissions

Each county has various boards or commissions, such as the Board of Equalization, which hears complaints against the assessed valuation on property. Many counties have Planning and Zoning Commissions to plan for the development

---

[23]By law, the state auditor audits the accounts of Class III and Class IV counties.

of the unincorporated places of the county and to recommend
regulations to the county courts.

HOME RULE COUNTIES[24]

In Missouri, any county having over 85,000 population
according to the U.S. census, or at least 80,000 inhabitants
according to the 1970 U.S. census, may adopt a special (home
rule) charter for its own government.[25] To apply for a home
rule charter, a petition to establish a charter commission
must be signed by 20 percent of the legal voters in the county
and filed with the county court. The court then notifies the
county circuit and probate judges of the valid application.
Within 60 days the judge appoints a bipartisan non-salaried
commission of 14 freeholders to write a charter. If approved
by a majority of the qualified voters of the county at a
special election, the charter will take effect on the day
specified in the charter and supersede any existing one. St.
Louis County adopted a home rule charter on March 28, 1965
and Jackson County followed suit on January 1, 1973.

RECENT TRENDS

Unlike the state, which has the General Assembly and the
governor, and the city, which has the council and the mayor,
the county generally has neither a central legislative body
nor a central executive officer. Moreover, because so many
executives are elected by popular vote in the county, they
are independent and not readily subject to the supervision
and coordination of any governing body. The weakness of
county government is therefore lack of any effective central
agency and integration. Currently some 20 percent of all
counties in the United States have an administrator appointed
by the county governing body or have an independently elected
executive like the county executive in Jackson County and
the county supervisor in St. Louis County in Missouri. Some
5 percent of counties have an appointed county manager with
fewer elective officers. Recent years have seen counties
steadily growing in importance. Due to the rapid development
of urban fringe areas and more responsibilities and functions
assigned to them, counties indeed play a vital role in our
system of government today.

---

[24]California was the first state to grant home rule to
counties in 1911. So far 13 states have conferred home rule
charters upon counties.

[25]Mo. Const. art. 6, sec. 18 (a), amended August 8,
1978.

TOWNSHIP

There are altogether 326 townships in 23 counties in Missouri, ranging from 7 in Stoddard to 24 in Bates. The township government includes a three-member board, a collector, and a clerk-assessor. They are all elective officers. The board may have both chief legislative and administrative authority, similar to the commission form of city government. Since modern communications have made county governments easily accessible, township government has declined in importance.

MUNICIPALITIES

KINDS OF MUNICIPALITIES

There are four kinds of municipalities in Missouri: (1) classified cities, (2) constitutional home rule charter cities, (3) special (legislative) charter cities, and (4) villages.

Figure 12.4   Classification of Municipalities and Forms of Government

Kinds	Population Requirement When Incorporated	Total Number	Form of Government Permitted
Village	Less than 500	ca.260	Board of Trustees
Class IV	500 - 2,999	ca.500	Mayor - Board of Aldermen
C i			City Administrator
t i	Class III	3,000 - 29,999	ca.58	Any form of government
e s	Constitutional (home rule)	Over 5,000	22	To be decided by people
	Special (legislative) charter	No requirement	7	Provided in each charter

Classified Municipalities

The Missouri statutes classify municipalities according to population at the time of incorporation and limit the forms of government available in each category. Only Class III and Class IV cities exist in Missouri. A community may incorpo-

209

rate (organize) as a village or a city of either class on the basis of population at the time of incorporation. Once incorporated, it cannot automatically change classification because of a shift in population. The new status must be approved by a majority vote of the inhabitants.

Constitutional (Home Rule) Charter Cities

In 1875, Missouri became the first state to grant constitutional home rule to cities. Now any city in Missouri with a population of more than 5,000, or any other incorporated city if provided by law, may adopt any form of government the people approve in the charter. To apply for a home rule charter, a petition to establish a charter commission must be signed by at least 10 percent of those who voted at the last general city election. The commission includes 13 members elected without party affiliation and frames a charter. The charter becomes effective when approved by the voters of the city.

A home rule city has all powers conferred by law in addition to home rule powers. It is also entitled to all powers granted by the General Assembly to any city and not denied nor limited by the State Constitution, statutes and its own charter. Twenty-two cities[26] have adopted home rule charters and selected a wide variety of governmental structure, mostly the council-manager form.

Special Legislative Charter Cities

The General Assembly granted special charters to specific cities until the new Constitution in 1875 forbade further issuance of such charters in order to avoid favoritism. Today there are seven cities[27] under special charters granted before 1875. If these cities later decide to relinquish their special charters, they will be classified into one of the two categories. All the seven special cities have some form of the mayor-council government.

---

[26]Berkeley, Bridgeton, Clayton, Columbia, Creve Coeur, Ferguson, Florissant, Hannibal, Hazelwood, Independence, Joplin, Kansas City, Maplewood, Neosho, Normandy, Olivette, St. John, St. Joseph, St. Louis, Springfield, University City, and Webster Groves.

[27]Carrollton, Chillicothe, LaGrange, Liberty, Miami, Palmyra, and Pleasant Hill.

FORMS OF CITY GOVERNMENT

There are four forms of municipal government in Missouri: Mayor-Council, Commission, Council-Manager, and Administrator.

Figure 12.5   Forms of City Government in Missouri

Mayor-Council	ca.760*
City Administrator	74
Council-Manager	36
Commission	4

*Includes villages which have a chairman and board of trustees.

The Mayor-Council Form

The mayor-council form is the most popular form of city government in Missouri as well as in most other states. Under this form of government, the people elect a city council as the legislative body to make laws called "ordinances" and a mayor as the chief executive to enforce the law. There are two types of mayor-council government: the strong-mayor type and the weak-mayor type. The strong mayor has extensive powers to appoint and remove city officials, to veto ordinances, and to control the budget, therefore able to exercise political and policy-making leadership to coordinate and direct the city business. The weak mayor has limited executive powers and administrative authority. With the city council controlling not only legislative but also administrative matters and most city officials popularly elected and accountable to the electorate, the mayor is the chief executive in name only. In Missouri, as the state law requires the election of numerous city officials, the municipalities with the

Figure 12.6   Mayor-Council (Board of Aldermen)
Form of Government

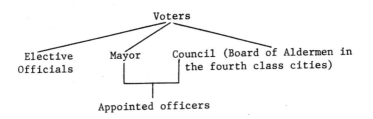

mayor-council government, except some home-rule cities, have therefore the weak mayor-council variety.

Mayor-Council Form in Class III and Class IV Cities

In Class III cities the city council consists of at least eight councilmen elected from four wards, while in Class IV cities the council, known as the board of aldermen, includes at least four aldermen elected from two wards. The elective officials in the third class cities, besides the mayor and councilmen, are the municipal judge (optional), city attorney, assessor, collector, treasurer, and marshal (except in cities where the police department is under the merit system). In fourth class cities, the elective officers are, besides mayor and aldermen, collector and marshal. These two offices may become appointive, if authorized by an ordinance approved by popular vote. The assessor, attorney, clerk, and street commissioner are among the appointive officers, but they may be elected if the board of aldermen provides for their election.

The important duties and powers of the mayor in both class cities include: to enforce state laws and city ordinances, to manage and control the city and its finances along with the council or board, to appoint, subject to council or board confirmation, city officers authorized by ordinances, to recommend measures to the council or board, and to sign or veto all bills passed by it.

In Class III cities, the mayor may remove for cause any elective and appointive officer with council approval. But the city council may also, with the mayor's consent, remove any elective officer by a two-thirds vote. In Class IV cities, the mayor may remove any appointive officer at will or an elective officer for cause with the consent of an absolute majority of the board. However, the board may also remove them by a two-thirds absolute majority vote without the mayor's consent or recommendation. Both the city council and the board of aldermen enact ordinances and may override the mayor's vetoes. The council can override the mayor's veto of an ordinance by a two-thirds vote and his veto of a resolution or order by a three-fourths vote of the elected councilmen. The board of aldermen can override the mayor's veto of bills by a two-thirds absolute majority vote.

Commission Form[28]

The commission form of government is actually a city

council, referred to as a commission, with each member heading an administrative department as a commissioner. Collectively the commissioners serve as a legislative body to formulate policy and make ordinances; individually they each run a department as an executive. This system features the concentration of legislative, executive, and administrative powers in a single body and is therefore characterized by a fusion rather than separation of powers.

Figure 12.7   Commission Form of Government

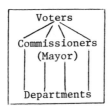

In Missouri, in order to adopt the commission form, a petition must be signed by qualified voters equal in number to 25 percent of those who voted in the last election for mayor. If the voters accept the proposition, they elect a mayor and commissioners--four commissioners in cities of 20,000-30,000 population, three in cities of 12,000-20,000, and two in cities of 3,000-12,000. The mayor, who is elected by the people, presides at all commission meetings, may vote, but has no veto power. By state law, the mayor must be superintendent of the Department of Public Affairs. In cities under 20,000 population, a commissioner may be assigned to head more than one department. There are four municipalities with the commission form in Missouri: Kirkwood, Monett, Richmond Heights, and West Plains. Because of the lack of coordination and supervision over department activities, the tendency is toward a continuing decrease in the number of cities with this form of government.[29]

The Council-Manager Form[30]

---

[28]Galveston, Texas, first adopted the commission form in 1900.

[29]Four municipalities have abandoned the commission form during recent decades: Cape Girardeau, Aurora, Maplewood, and Kirksville.

[30]In 1908, Staunton, Virginia, created the office of gen-

Under the council-manager form, the city council appoints a manager to run the government at its pleasure with the mayor serving as a political and ceremonial head. This system features a division of authority and responsibility with the city council maintaining full authority to make policy and to supervise the city manager, who is completely responsible for administration. In Missouri, Excelsior Springs was the first city to adopt this form of government in 1922, and Kansas City followed suit four years later. Though four municipalities[31] have abandoned the manager form of government during recent decades, it continues to grow. At present, 35 cities are operating under this form

Figure 12.8   Council-Manager Form of Government

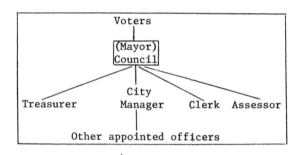

The council-manager cities have a city council of five councilmen elected at large to staggered three-year terms. The council elects from among themselves a mayor and a chairman pro tem for a term of one year. The mayor presides over council meetings, may vote, but has no administrative or veto power. The council appoints a city manager, who in turn appoints and discharges other city officers under the direction and supervision of the council.

Application for the manager form of government requires a petition signed by voters equal in number to 25 percent of the votes cast for all candidates for mayor at the last election. A special election must be called by the mayor within 60 days after the submission of the petition. If the issue

_____

eral manager. In 1912, Sumter, South Carolina, was the first city to adopt the council-manager form of government.

[31]Lebanon in 1946, Hannibal in 1947, and Marshall in 1948. Brookfield adopted this form of government in 1945, abandoned it the following year, but restored it in 1972.

fails to receive a majority vote, it may not be voted on again for at least one year. No municipality may abandon this form within six years of its adoption.

The City Administrator Form

In order to provide municipalities with professional management, the Missouri General Assembly, in 1969, passed legislation permitting third and fourth class cities to adopt the administrator form of government. Under this form, the mayor and council appoint a trained full-time city administrator, known as a "city supervisor," or "city superintendent" in some cities, who serves at the pleasure of both the mayor and council. In 1950, Centralia, then a fourth class city, created the office of city administrator but could not formally adopt the administrator system until 1969, after the law was enacted. This system actually brings an experienced full-time administrative expert into the mayor-council form of government. At present there are 74 cities under this form.

Figure 12.9 City Administrator Form of Government

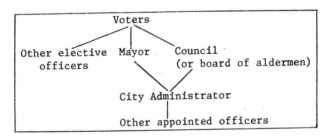

Seven major differences between the city manager form and the city administrator system:

Administrator Form	Manager Form
1. Established by ordinance of the governing body;	After a petition and a popular vote;
2. In either Class III or Class IV cities;	Only in Class III or home rule cities;
3. Administrator as chief administrative assistant under the mayor's direction and supervision;	Manager under the direction and supervision of the council;

215

4. The powers to hire and fire other appointive officers either exercised by the administrator subject to the city rules or retained by the mayor;	The manager's exclusive power;
5. The powers of the administrator derived from the city ordinances may be altered at any time;	The manager's powers specified in either state law or the city charter;
6. The mayor elected directly by the people;	Chosen from among the councilmen;
7. The mayor has all powers and authority conferred by statute.	No greater power and authority than any councilman.

VILLAGE

The only governing body permitted by the Missouri law to villages is a board of trustees, which consists of five members in villages under 2,500 population and nine in villages over 2,500. They are elected by the people for two-year terms. The board members then elect from among themselves a chairman and a clerk. The board has the power to make ordinances in over 40 specific areas. It may also appoint and remove from office such officers as assessor, collector, marshal, treasurer, and others. It may provide by ordinance for either the election or appointment of a municipal judge. The board chairman presides over board meetings, may vote, and publishes a semi-annual financial report.

Figure 12.10   Organization of Village Government

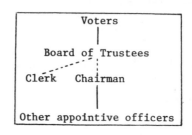

BIBLIOGRAPHY

Books & Pamphlets

Abraham, Henry J. The Judicial Process. 3d ed. New York:
    Oxford University Press, 1975.

Books of the States, 1980-1981. Lexington, Kentucky: Council
    of State Governments.

Burns, James M.; Peltason J.W.; and Cronin, Thomas E. State
    and Local Politics. 2d ed. Englewood Cliffs, New Jersey:
    Prentice Hall, Inc., 1980.

Christenson, Reo M.; Engel, Alan S.; Jacobs, Dan N.; Rejai,
    Mostafa; and Waltzer, Herbert. Ideologies and Modern
    Politics. 2d ed. New York: Harper & Row Publishers,
    Inc., 1981.

Congressional Quarter Service. Representation and Apportion-
    ment. Washington, D.C.: Congressional Quarterly, Inc.,
    1966.

Duchacek, Ivo P. Comparative Federalism. New York: Holt,
    Rinehart & Winston, 1970.

Dvorn, Eugene P. and Misner, Arthur J. Governments Within the
    States. Reading, Massachusetts: Addison-Wesley Publish-
    ing Company, 1971.

Dye, Thomas R.; Greene, Lee S.; and Parthemos, George S.
    Governing the American Democracy. New York: St. Martin's
    Press, 1980.

Forms of Government for Missouri Municipalities. Jefferson
    City, Missouri: Missouri Municipal League, September,
    1980.

German, A.C.; Day, Frank D.; and Gallati, Robert, R.J. Intro-
    duction to Law Enforcement and Criminal Justice.
    Springfield, Illinois: Charles C. Thomas Publisher, 1970.

Grant, Daniel R. & Nixon, H.C. State and Local Government in
    America. Boston: Allyn & Bacon, Inc., 1975.

Gunther, Gerald. Individual Rights in Constitutional Law.
    3d ed. Mineola, N.Y.: The Foundation Press, 1981.

217

Inbau, Fred E.; Thompson, James R,; and Zabel, James B. *Criminal Law and Administration*. 2d ed. Mineola, New York: The Foundation Press, Inc., 1974.

Jacob, Herbert; and Vines, Kenneth, eds. *Political Parties in the American States*. 3d ed. Boston: Little, Brown and Company, 1976.

Karsch, Robert. *The Government of Missouri*. 14th ed. Columbia, Missouri: Lucas Brothers Publishers, 1978.

Kempin, Frederick G., Jr. *Historical Introduction to Anglo-American Law in a Nutshell*. 2d ed. St. Paul, Minnesota: West Publishing Company, 1973.

Kerper, Hazel B. *Introduction to the Criminal Justice System*. Revised by Isreal, M. Jerold. 2d ed. St. Paul, Minnesota: West Publishing Company, 1979.

Macridis, Roy C. *Contemporary Political Ideologies*. Cambridge, Massachusetts: Winthrop Publishers, Inc., 1980.

Maddox, Russell W., and Fuquay, Robert F. *State and Local Government*. 4th ed. New York: D. Van Nostrand Company, 1981.

Missouri Counties in Transition. Jefferson City, Missouri: Missouri Association of Counties, 1979.

Missouri, Office of Administration. Personnel Division. *Missouri Merit System Facts*, 1979.

Saffell, David C. *State and Local Government*. 2d ed. Reading, Massachusetts: Addison-Wesley Publishing Company, 1982.

Sargent, Lyman Tower. *Contemporary Political Ideologies*. 3d ed. Homewood, Illinois: The Dorsey Press, 1975.

Saye, Albert B. *American Constitutional Law, Cases and Test*. 2d ed. St. Paul, Minnesota: West Publishing Company, 1979.

Sigler, Jay A. *An Introduction to the Legal System*. Homewood, Illinois: The Dorsey Press, 1968.

Snider, Clyde F. *American State and Local Government*. New York: Appleton-Century-Crofts, Inc., 1965.

Volkomer, Walter E. American Government. New York: Appleton-
    Century-Crofts, 1972.

Weisberg, Robert, Understanding American Government. New
    York: Holt, Rinehart & Winston, 1980.

Weston, Paul B.; and Wells, Kenneth M. The Administration
    of Justice. Englewood Cliffs: Prentice-Hall, Inc., 1967.

Winter, William O. State and Local Government in a De-
    centralized Republic. New York: Macmillan Publishing
    co., Inc., 1981.

Wright, Deil S. Understanding Intergovernmental Relations.
    Belmount, California: Wadsworth, Inc., 1982.

Journals

Congressional Quarterly Service. Congressional Quarterly
    Guide. (Fall 1969). Washington, D.C.: Congressional
    Quarterly Inc.

Missouri Municipal Review (1980, 1981, 1982). Jefferson City,
    Missouri: Missouri Municipal League.

Scurlock, John. "Basic Principles of the Administration of
    Criminal Justice with Particular Reference to Missouri
    Law." UMKC Law Review 38 (Winter 1970): 172-339; 44
    (Winter 1975): 153-387. Kansas City, Missouri: Univer-
    sity of Missouri.

Public Documents

Missouri. Constitution (1945, revised 1982).

_____. Democratic Party. Constitution & By-laws (1975,
    amended 1978). Democratic State Committee of Missouri.

_____. _____. Affirmative Action & Delegate
    Selection Plan for the 1980 Democratic National Con-
    vention. Democratic State Committee of Missouri.

_____. Department of Revenue & State Treasurer. Annual
    Combined Report, 1981-1982.

_____. General Assembly. House of Representatives. Hand-
    book, 81st G.A., 1981-1982.

Missouri. General Assembly. House of Representatives. <u>Rules</u>, 81st G.A., 1981–1982.

_____. _____. Senate. <u>Handbook</u>, 80th G.A., 1981–1982.

_____. _____. _____. <u>Rules</u>, 81st G.A., 1981–1982.

_____. Office of Administration. Personnel Division. <u>Missouri Laws Relating to the State Merit System</u>, 1980.

_____. Secretary of State. <u>Election Laws</u>, 1978.

_____. _____. <u>Official Manual</u>, 1981–1982.

_____. <u>Revised Statutes</u> (1978).

United States. <u>Constitution</u>.

INDEX

ABOUT THE AUTHOR

Dr. Stephen C.S. Chen is currently professor of Political Science at Lincoln University of Missouri. Educated in China in his early years, he received his M.A. in 1959 and his Ph.D. in 1963, both in Political Science at Southern Illinois University, Carbondale, Illinois. Following graduation from SIU, he taught two years at Texas College, Tyler, Texas, as assistant professor. In 1965, he went to England to pursue his post-doctoral study at Oxford University. While in London, he spent much time in parliament observing the pompous ceremonies of its dissolution and opening of a new session, but particularly the legislative procedures in both Houses. He also observed trials at the Old Bailey.

From London Dr. Chen returned to Hongkong in the fall of 1966 and taught at Hongkong Baptist College for one year. He then came back to the United States and taught at Hardin-Simmons University, Abilene, Texas, as associate professor and later professor.

Dr. Chen joined the faculty of Lincoln University in Missouri in 1970. He established the Department of Political Science in 1975 and served as acting head until 1977 when it was merged into the Social Sciences Department because of the University's retrenchment. He was vice president of the Missouri Political Science Association, 1977-1978, and a panel chairman at the MPSA annual meeting in 1978.

With Robert Payne, a prolific British writer, Dr. Chen co-authored Sun Yat-sen, A Portrait, published by the John Day Book Company in New York in the mid-1950's.